SILENT WITNESSES

SILENT WITNESSES

*Lessons on Theology, Life, and the Church
from Christians of the Past*

Garry J. Williams

THE BANNER OF TRUTH TRUST

THE BANNER OF TRUTH TRUST

3 Murrayfield Road, Edinburgh EH12 6EL, UK
P.O. Box 621, Carlisle, PA 17013, USA

*

© Garry J. Williams 2013

*

ISBN:
Print: 978 1 84871 217 1
Kindle: 978 1 84871 218 8
EPUB: 978 1 84871 219 5

*

Typeset in 10/13 pt Bembo at
The Banner of Truth Trust, Edinburgh
Printed in the USA by
Versa Press, Inc.,
East Peoria, IL

*

To my parents
David and Dorothy Wiliams,
with
gratitude, love, and affection.

CONTENTS

ACKNOWLEDGEMENTS

Most of this book was written during time set aside for study as part of my role as Director of the John Owen Centre at London Theological Seminary. It is a privilege to serve in a seminary that has the foresight to guard such time for its staff. The chapters originate in talks that I have given over the last thirteen years at various conferences around the United Kingdom. I am grateful to the organizers of those conferences who invited me to speak and propelled me to study the material reflected here, namely: the Banner of Truth Trust, the Evangelical Fellowship of Congregational Churches, the Evangelical Movement of Wales, New Word Alive, the Proclamation Trust, the Protestant Truth Society, and the Westminster Conference. Chapter 7 was given at the John Owen Centre Conference in 2011. The positive response to the addresses at these conferences and elsewhere encouraged me to think that publishing a fully reworked, expanded, and interwoven version of them might bring glory to Christ and good to his people, which is my prayer for this book. It is dedicated to my parents, and it could not have been written without the loving support of my wife Fiona and our children, Emily, Ben, Alice, and Jonathan.

TO THE READER

Mention of 'history' evokes different responses from different people. For the older generation it may recall lessons spent learning rather uninspiring lists of dates and facts. For those educated more recently it may bring to mind very little specific information, just vague memories of exercises in empathy ('How did it *feel* to be there?'), or the study of photographic sources. Either way, the memory is not exactly gripping, and for many history is something that they happily leave behind in more than one sense. The extent to which history is widely equated with irrelevance is highlighted by Mark Steyn:

> The past is history. That's to say, it's history in the sense of that robust and revealing American formulation: 'Bob Dole? Aw, he's history!'—as in fuhgeddabout him, he's through, he's washed up, he don't mean diddlysquat, he won't trouble us no more, we need pay him no further heed. He's history.[1]

Preachers sometimes point out that it is dangerous to neglect the ultimate future that we all face. It is true that the world lives without regard to the coming day of judgement. In one sense, however, we live in a culture that is very preoccupied with the future rather than the past; it is preoccupied with the immediate future. Steyn points out that this is a feature of the way in which technology so readily offers something new in the very next moment:

> A modern, electronic culture exists in a state of perpetual anticipation: even as the credits of your favourite sitcom start to roll, the screen consigns them to a tiny corner and a trailer commends the delights of the next, even funnier sitcom.[2]

---

[1] *The Future of the European Past*, ed. by Hilton Kramer and Roger Kimball (Chicago: Ivan R. Dee, 1997), p. 157.
[2] *Future*, p. 160.

In the midst of this orientation to the short-term future, some do still think more positively about history. Indeed, measured by the amount of historical drama on British television, we might think that history in Britain is enjoying a mini-revival. There is some truth in this, but there is a big difference between the immediate gratification of watching television and the slower labour of reading and studying books. Television history is often convenience-history, much like convenience-food: easy to prepare but not always the most nourishing.

Some conservative philosophers and cultural commentators do maintain a serious enthusiasm for the past, but they know they are in the minority. At the end of a celebrated Dutch television series on consolation and beauty, the philosopher Roger Scruton expresses his concern for the loss of the past:

> I think one of the saddest things about the modern world, partly a result of television, is that people live in a tiny time slice of the present moment, which they carry forward with them, but nothing remains and there's nothing in their experience which reverberates down the centuries, because the centuries to them are completely dark, just un-illuminated corridors from which they stagger into the single little sliver of light.[3]

Why bother with history?

If you are a Christian, then reading a book like this is a little like finding out about your ancestors. In fact, it is more like finding out about your ancestors than finding out about your biological ancestors would be. You are spiritually united to dead Christians, the silent witnesses with whom we are concerned. They are closer to you as a Christian than your own deceased non-Christian biological ancestors. The bond that we have in Christ is stronger than the bond of flesh and blood. It is said that blood is thicker than water, but the bond created by the Holy Spirit is thicker than both.

Imagine, then, how intrigued you would be if you found out that you had a famous relative, perhaps a relative who did something singularly brave or who endured extraordinary suffering. Genealogy is fascinating

---

[3] The documentary was made in 2000 by Wim Kayzer and is entitled *Van de Schoonheid en de Troost* ('Of Beauty and Consolation'). The words are spoken over the closing credits.

to many people, at least in part because they hope they might find some such relative with a fascinating story or a degree of historical significance that might leave its after-glow on their own lives. Sometimes genealogists strike gold. A chance find in a library led my father-in-law to discover that my wife's family can be traced back to the Emperor Charlemagne the Great and three of the wives of Henry VIII (a fact that he reminds us of only very occasionally!). That may be an unusually lucky strike, but all Christians have such an array of significant relatives in Christ Jesus.

The good, the bad, and the ugly?

I am concerned that unequivocally positive portrayals of Christians from the past may leave us with highly unrealistic expectations for our own lives. If our spiritual ancestors seem never to have sinned, then why do we sin? Is there something wrong with us alone? Are important details being left out of Christian biographies? Did Charles Spurgeon really only ever sin by smoking tobacco? We can be left with an acute and destructive sense of inadequacy by relentlessly positive Christian biography. To avoid these kinds of effects, I do not wish to white-wash the sins of our Christian ancestors. Every Christian is a sinner. In principle there can be no objection to the claim that any Christian hero sinned. For example, one recent biography of John Calvin tells us that he 'was the greatest Protestant reformer of the sixteenth century, brilliant, visionary and iconic. The superior force of his mind was evident in all that he did. He was also ruthless, and an outstanding hater.'[4] To a contemporary Calvinist these may be shocking words. We may be so used to thinking of Calvin as a hero that the very statement jars. Yet Calvin was a sinner like all the other children of Adam, and the statement that he sinned is one that we not only can but must believe. How ironic if Calvinists, who believe in the total depravity of human beings, refused to admit the sinfulness of Calvin! We do the Saviour no favours by diminishing the sins of the people he came to save and the burden that he therefore bore for them. Christians of the past were new creations who lived with the sinful nature at war with the Spirit. As such, their lives exhibit a mix of the fruit of the Spirit and the fruit of the flesh. It would be as wrong to pretend that they had no sin as it would be to pretend that they had no holiness. To adapt the words of 1 John 1:8, if we say they had no sin, we

[4] Bruce Gordon, *Calvin* (New Haven: Yale University Press, 2009), p. vii.

deceive ourselves and the truth is not in us. This does not of course mean that we must automatically approve any *particular* negative verdict on a Christian's conduct, but it would be unbiblical to maintain a principled aversion to *any* claim that he sinned.

It is interesting to ask what kind of historical writing about the Lord's people the Bible itself both models and enjoins. In terms of modelling, we find frank descriptions of the sins of Israel and her kings. It is important to note why it describes their sin. It does so not for the sake of a journalistic exposé, but to highlight the patience, justice, and forgiveness of God. There is no mandate in Samuel and Kings, for example, for any attempt to slur the character of a great Christian leader. But the sins even of the greatest kings, such as David and Solomon, are plainly set forth. As they are framed in the biblical narrative, they serve to vindicate God's justice in punishing his people (for example, in the collapse of David's kingdom), or to magnify his mercy in forgiving them (for example, in its restoration). Who has not been warned by reading about how even the great King David fell into sin? And who has not been encouraged by reading of the Lord's mercy to him? If we did not know about his sin, we would have neither the warning nor the encouragement.

On the other hand, when the biblical writers seek the edification of their readers, the emphasis seems to fall on paying attention to the holiness of our Christian ancestors. Scripture itself focuses on the work of Christ in individuals when it provides examples for us to imitate. This is clear, for example, in Luke's account of the Apostle Paul in Acts. Indeed, Paul himself commands his readers to imitate what is good in him: 'Be imitators of me, as I am of Christ' (*1 Cor.* 11:1; cf. 4:16; *Phil.* 3:17). If we are to incline in any direction in writing for the edification of Christians, it should be toward focusing on the work of the Spirit, not the flesh. Where the sins of our ancestors are described, it should be within the positive framework of God's redemptive grace, for our warning and encouragement, not to satiate our prurience. This suggests that in the context of a book about historical figures written to help Christians the emphasis should be on the good example of our spiritual ancestors. When their sins are described, it should be in order to warn and to encourage and not to ogle.

The balance and indeed the aims would be different in an academic historical work. It is important for Christian scholars to produce such books, but that is not my aim here. In fact it is often difficult for the writer of any kind of book to find out much about the sins of a famous Christian. The intention of eye-witness writers, such as Theodore Beza in his sketch of John Calvin's life, was to describe the ways in which their subject was a good example, not a bad one. Beza mentions Calvin's own apologies for his failures of duty, his vehemence, and his peevishness, but we do not see much more of his sin than that.[5] On the other hand, where there are negative accounts of Christian heroes, they are often written by those who were further away from the subject, both relationally and theologically. Their criticisms are often more theological than personal, and sometimes the former fuels the latter, producing unreliable results. The other factor that obscures our knowledge of the sins of our ancestors is the often private nature of sin. Most Christians live lives that appear to be more holy than they are, not necessarily because they are deliberate hypocrites, but because many of their sins are committed in the mind and will and affections, but do not come to fruition in visible actions. It is no surprise that the heroes of the past appear more holy than they were, or that we cannot document most of their sins. The same is true of each of us. This is one reason why Augustine's *Confessions* is such an unusual work: it describes Augustine's sins from his own perspective, and it is written by the only person who had direct access to that perspective. Not many famous figures provide such a window into their inner lives. And even in Augustine's case, we will see that there are writers who point out how carefully he controls his self-presentation in the *Confessions*.

You are you

As a reader of this book, you need to avoid thinking that you are called to *be* any of these people. You are not to long to reproduce their lives or their ministries in your own. God has called you to be who you are, where you are. Let me put this more strongly: it would be a sin for any Christian to expect himself to be, for example, John Calvin. Calvin was there and then with the gifts and responsibilities that God gave him. We are here and now with a quite different set of gifts and responsibilities. As we study history it is a distracting and dangerous fantasy to dream of being someone else, the kind of fantasy that we can use to

---

[5] *The Life of Calvin*, ed. and trans. by Henry Beveridge, in *John Calvin: Tracts and Letters*, ed. by Henry Beveridge and Jules Bonnet, 7 vols (Edinburgh: Calvin Translation Society, 1851; repr. Edinburgh: Banner of Truth, 2009), 1: lxxxvii, xc, xciv.

evade the urgent call to obey the Lord Jesus Christ in our own skin. Just as we are called to obey the Lord today and not to be preoccupied with fantastical plans for a future that will probably never happen, so we are to hear the Lord's voice addressing *us*, not to avoid his call by pretending we are someone else. This means that learning from any other Christian's example requires careful thought. I should not read about Calvin and then think 'So let's have a Genevan Reformation here and now'. A moment's thought tells us how different Geneva was from today's London or New York, let alone from rural Somerset or Montana. Certainly we can learn lessons from Calvin in Geneva, but they must be carefully filtered and adapted to today's context.

Sources and selection

Before we plunge in, a word is necessary about my use of sources and the selection and arrangement of the chapters. I make no claim to originality for the narrative sections of this book: they are entirely derivative. In most cases, they draw extensively from a single secondary source, such as a reliable biography, referenced near the start of the chapter. In academic writing it is presumed that material is original unless otherwise stated: please presume the opposite for the narratives here. Further references in footnotes are therefore usually given only for quotations. If there are any original elements in the book, they are to be found in the direct interaction with primary sources and in the applications made from the material.

The selection of topics is unrepresentative in a number of ways: there are more men than women, there are more pastors and theologians than lay people, and the coverage of different periods of church history is uneven. How then have the individuals and topics been chosen? The figures included are among the silent witnesses with whom I have spent time over the last twenty years, those I have studied formally, and those about whom I have been asked to speak. They have been chosen to fulfil the aim of the book: to provide a primer in theology, life, and the church from Christians of the past for Christians of the present. They are arranged not chronologically, but to reflect those three areas. The first part covers some of the essentials of theology: the Bible, the incarnation, the cross, grace, and justification. The second looks at issues in the Christian life: loving God with the heart, suffering, identity, loss, and work. The third section is addressed primarily to pastors and elders and concerns priorities for the church, preaching, and the Lord's supper. By the time you reach the Epilogue I hope that you will already be persuaded by the preceding chapters of its argument for a distinctively Christian account of history.

ON THE ESSENTIALS

1

PRIZING THE BIBLE:
WILLIAM TYNDALE (1494-1536)

Thomas More on William Tyndale

Let me introduce you to a man. He was 'a hell-hound in the kennel of the devil', 'a drowsy drudge drinking deep in the devil's dregs', 'a new Judas', 'worse than Sodom and Gomorrah', 'an idolater and devil worshipper', 'discharging a filthy foam of blasphemies out of his brutish beastly mouth'. This was William Tyndale: William Tyndale, that is, according to Sir Thomas More.[1] Perhaps you know More from *A Man For All Seasons*? Perhaps you see him as a principled, refined man? He certainly had a noble side, but the historical More was also a man who wrote lurid invective in the language of the barrackroom, invective that I would hesitate to reproduce here even in our own loose-lipped times. One of his biographers notes in More's writing 'a monotonous scatology as wearing as the talk of small boys in school washrooms'.[2] Serious writers in the sixteenth century were generally more vehement than their counterparts today, but Tyndale's biographer David Daniell observes that More 'digs far below others'.[3] As one commentator puts it regarding

---

[1] The descriptions are cited in David Daniell, *William Tyndale: A Biography* (New Haven: Yale University Press, 1994), p. 277. Daniell's biography is the main source used in this chapter for the narrative of Tyndale's life.

[2] R. Marius, cited in *Biography*, p. 258.

[3] *Biography*, p. 258.

some of his writing, he had 'a wit and malice hyper-satanic'.[4] It was this Thomas More who hated William Tyndale.

Hated for the Bible

Why was Tyndale so hated? Quite simply, because he wanted to reform the church, to restore the gospel, and especially to give the people of England the Bible. This description implies that the church was in need of reform, that the gospel was at least obscured, and that the Bible was not available to the people. To see how this was so we will take a brief glimpse at the state of the church in the late mediaeval period, just before the times of William Tyndale and the Reformation of the sixteenth century.

The Bible was not officially available in English. In 1408 the Constitutions of Oxford banned translation of any part of the Bible; anyone doing so would be punished as a heretic. Not just the Bible but also the church's liturgy was in Latin, and only a small proportion of even the clergy knew the language. There are horrifying statistics on ignorance of Scripture among the late mediaeval English clergy. For example, in 1551 among unsatisfactory ministers in Gloucestershire, nine did not know how many commandments were given to Moses, thirty-three did not know where they could be found in the Bible, and 168 could not recite them. Thirty-nine did not know where the Lord's Prayer could be found, thirty-four could not say who authored it, and ten could not repeat it. England was actually unusual in having no approved vernacular Bible (albeit the translations other countries had were for a long time from the Latin Vulgate). The German Bible was published in 1466, the first Italian Bible was printed in 1471, the first French New Testament in 1474, a whole Catalan Bible in 1478, a New Testament in Czech in 1475, and a whole Dutch Bible in 1477. In some respects the church in England was not as bad as it was on the continent, but in this respect it was worse.

Even in England, and even as described by a sympathetic modern Roman Catholic writer like Eamon Duffy, the popular religion looks highly superstitious. As Duffy describes it, few often took communion. The Mass, the central act of the church's life, was mostly *watched* by the people, often from a distance and through elevation squints cut

[4] Charles Lamb, cited in *Biography*, p. 182.

in the screen that separated them from the priest. In the doctrine of transubstantiation, Rome taught that the substance of the bread and wine changed into the actual body and blood of Jesus. Such was the supposed power of the transubstantiated elements that even seeing them from afar was meant to bring spiritual and physical benefit. People would leave their bed linen to the church so that it could be used on the altar and might, by its proximity to the substance of the body and blood of Christ, bring them good fortune. Stories of astonishing events involving the Mass abounded, telling, for example, of cows gathering in a field to kneel down before a consecrated wafer dropped by a priest.

Tyndale's significance

What was Tyndale's significance in this context? Quite simply, he gave the church the Bible. His translation was not from the Latin Vulgate preferred by the church and used for many other vernacular translations, but directly from the Hebrew and Greek. This was deeply significant, for the Vulgate's mistranslations of the Greek of the New Testament were used to defend various doctrines maintained by the Roman Catholic Church but not found in the original text of Scripture. For example, the Vulgate translation of Luke 1:28 described Mary as being 'full of grace' (*gratia plena*), suggesting a reservoir from which she might dispense grace to those who asked her. The Greek simply says that she found favour with God. The Vulgate translated the command to repent in Matthew 4:17 as 'do penance' (*poenitentiam agite*), justifying the extensive works of satisfaction required by the church. The Greek speaks simply of a profound change of mind and direction. Tyndale's translation was the first ever from Hebrew to English. Indeed, few could have attempted it, since in 1529-30 Hebrew was known to, at most, a tiny handful of scholars in England.

Tyndale also gave us a translation that has lasted. Nine-tenths of Tyndale's original renderings in such parts of the Bible as he did translate were retained in the Authorised (King James) Version, and have entered our common parlance: the salt of the earth, let there be light, the spirit is willing, the signs of the times, fight the good fight, the fat of the land, even newly coined words such as 'scapegoat'. These are the words of eternal life and it was Tyndale who rendered them this way for us.

His life, work, and death

Tyndale was born into a successful family in Gloucestershire. His brother John was a cloth producer and seller. This is an important detail, since the Bible and evangelical writings spread widely in Europe in sacks carried by merchants. Tyndale learned seven languages. He went up to Oxford in 1506 where he would have studied grammar, rhetoric, and logic (known as the *trivium*), and then arithmatic, music, geometry, and astronomy (the *quadrivium*). Tyndale formed a pretty low view of his Oxford education, especially of the way that it was preoccupied with the study of obscure scholastic terms and debates instead of with the Bible. He pressed his criticism to the point of satire, a satire that can be appreciated even if one does not know the technical terms he piles up in an increasing frenzy of Latin:

> Ye drive them from God's word and will let no man come thereto, until ye have been two years masters of arts. First they nosel [nurture] them in sophistry and in benefundatum. And there corrupt they their judgements with apparent arguments, and with alleging unto them texts of logic, of natural philautia, of metaphysic, and moral philosophy, and of all manner books of Aristotle, and of all manner doctors which they never yet saw. Moreover, one holdeth this, another that. One is a real, another a nominal. What wonderful dreams they have of their predicaments, universals, second intentions, quiddities, hecceities and relatives. And whether species fundata in chimera be vera species. And whether this proposition be true non ens est aliquid. Whether ens be equivocum or univocum. Ens is a voice only say some. Ens is univocum saith another and descendeth into ens creatum and into ens increatum per modos intrensecos. When they have thiswise brawled eight or twelve more years and after that their judgements are utterly corrupt: then they begin their divinity.
>
> Not at the scripture: but every man taketh a sundry doctor, which doctors are as sundry and as divers, the one contrary unto the other, as there are divers fashions and monstrous shapes, none like another, among our sects of religion.[5]

Tyndale here criticizes the way in which the education system kept the

[5] Cited in *Biography*, p. 230.

student away from the Scriptures. When he did eventually make it past the philosophical debates to theology, it was not the theology of the Bible but of the warring schools of thought in the mediaeval church. It was this lack of attention to and distortion of the Bible that really troubled Tyndale:

> And in the universities they have ordained that no man shall look in the Scripture until he be noselled [nursed] in heathen learning eight or nine years and armed with false principles with which he is clean shut out of the understanding of scripture.[6]

For Tyndale, the theological education of his day seemed to be designed to immunize students against the word of God.

It was not long before Tyndale addressed himself to this problem. After Oxford he spent time in Cambridge and as a tutor in Gloucestershire. Then, in the summer of 1523, he made an approach to Cuthbert Tunstall, the Bishop of London, asking him to support his effort to translate the Bible. This approach made sense, since Tunstall was himself a learned man. Nonetheless, the bishop replied that his house was full and advised Tyndale to seek support elsewhere in London. Tyndale soon realized 'not only that there was no room in my lord of London's palace to translate the new Testament, but also that there was no place to do it in all England'.[7] So he left England, probably in April 1524, to pursue his translation work on the continent. At some point he settled in Cologne where he worked on translating the New Testament, though it was not long before he was being pursued by the authorities and had to flee from Cologne to Worms. The New Testament translation was finished probably by early 1526, and either 3,000 or 6,000 copies were printed. At the time a book would often have an initial print run of around 700, so this was a large number. The translation was an immediate success and was soon pirated. Including both official and pirate copies there were around 20,000 of Tyndale's New Testament in circulation before the second edition came out in 1534. This represents an extensive influx of the word of God to England prior to Henry VIII's official break with Rome.

We might hope that the church would have rejoiced at the Bible being in the hands of the people, but it did not. The church feared losing

---

[6] Cited in *Biography*, p. 37.

[7] 'Preface to the Five Books of Moses', in *The Works of William Tyndale*, ed. by Henry Walter, 2 vols (Cambridge: Cambridge University Press, 1848; repr. Edinburgh: The Banner of Truth, 2010), 1:396.

control of the people if they were to read the Scriptures for themselves. The Archbishop of Canterbury William Warham hatched a scheme to buy and burn them to remove them from circulation (evidencing little understanding of how markets work!). Bishop Nix of Norwich wrote to congratulate him for 'a gracious and a blessed deed'.[8] Tunstall too ordered the gathering and burning of the New Testaments. Tyndale was stunned. He put the point plainly in these words: 'he burnt the new Testament, calling it *Doctrinam peregrinam*, "strange learning."'.[9]

It was not, however, enough to burn the book. Now other enemies went after Tyndale himself. By this stage the translator was in Antwerp, a centre of scholarship and printing. There he met and became friends with a man called Henry Phillips. Tyndale invited Phillips to the house where he was living, that of Thomas Poyntz. The martyrologist John Foxe tells us what happened:

> Then said Philips, 'Master Tyndale! you shall be my guest here this day.' 'No,' said Master Tyndale, 'I go forth this day to dinner, and you shall go with me, and be my guest, where you shall be welcome.' So when it was dinner-time, Master Tyndale went forth with Philips, and at the going forth of Pointz's house, was a long narrow entry, so that two could not go in a front. Master Tyndale would have put Philips before him, but Philips would in no wise, but put Master Tyndale before, for that he pretended to show great humanity. So Master Tyndale, being a man of no great stature, went before, and Philips, a tall comely person, followed behind him; who had set officers on either side of the door upon two seats, who, being there, might see who came in the entry: and coming through the same entry, Philips pointed with his finger over Master Tyndale's head down to him, that the officers who sat at the door might see that it was he whom they should take, as the officers that took Master Tyndale afterwards told Pointz, and said to Pointz, when they had laid him in prison, that they pitied to see his simplicity when they took him. Then they took him, and brought him to the emperor's attorney, or procurer-general, where he dined. Then came the procurer-general to the house of Pointz, and sent away all that was there of Master Tyndale's, as well

---

[8] Cited in *Biography*, p. 175.
[9] *The Practice of Prelates*, in *Works*, 2:337.

his books as other things: and from thence Tyndale was had to the castle of Filford, eighteen English miles from Antwerp, and there he remained until he was put to death.[10]

It seems certain that Henry Phillips was not paid by the English government to pursue Tyndale, since Phillips was himself a traitor and detested the King. He was working with agents of the Holy Roman Emperor, and he was probably funded by Stokesley, the Bishop of London. In fact, the English government almost successfully intervened in Tyndale's favour, so that Thomas Poyntz was told that Tyndale would be released. At that point Phillips denounced Poyntz too, who, unlike Tyndale, was fortunate enough to escape.

In early August 1536, after he had been in prison for 450 days, William Tyndale was condemned as a heretic and degraded. This means that the signs of his ordination were undone: anointing oil was scraped from his hands, the bread and wine of the Lord's supper were placed into his hands and then removed, and his clerical vestments were stripped from him. In October 1536, probably on the 6th, he was executed. Here is Foxe's description:

> Although he deserved no death, he was condemned by virtue of the emperor's decree . . . and, upon the same, brought forth to the place of execution, was there tied to the stake, and then strangled first by the hangman, and afterwards with fire consumed.[11]

Tyndale's dying words were: 'Lord! Open the king of England's eyes.' The Lord did, and quickly. In 1537 Matthew's Bible, much of which was Tyndale's translation, was licensed for use by the king. In 1539 a royal injunction *required* a copy of the English Bible to be held in every church. The spread of the word of God was rapid: Daniell estimates that there were 100,000 copies of the Bible in English in print by 1547.

Tyndale's convictions

What convictions carried Tyndale all the way to death for the sake of translating the Bible? His passionate longing was for people to have the word of God in a language they could understand. To a scholar who said

---

[10] Cited in *Biography*, p. 364. The variant spellings of Poyntz and Phillips reflect Daniell's usage here.

[11] Cited in *Biography*, pp. 382-3.

that we would be better off without God's law than without the Pope's, he said these now famous words: 'If God spare my life ere many years, I will cause a boy that driveth the plough, shall know more of the scripture than thou dost'.[12] For Tyndale it was obvious why this mattered:

> I do marvel greatly, dearly beloved in Christ, that ever any man should repugn or speak against the scripture to be had in every language, and that of every man. For I thought that no man had been so blind to ask why light should be shewed to them that walk in darkness, where they cannot but stumble, and where to stumble is the danger of eternal damnation.[13]

Tyndale marvelled that anyone could ask why his work mattered. Obviously, if people without the word of God are trapped in the darkness of sin, then they need the word of God in an accessible form so that they can be saved. Tyndale at one point stated to Thomas Cromwell's emissary that he was prepared to return to England to face the consequences of his actions if the king would just support the distribution of a translation of the Bible:

> If it would stand with the king's most gracious pleasure to grant only a bare text of the scripture to be out forth among his people, like as is putting forth among the subjects of the emperor in these parts, and of other Christian princes, be it of the translation of what person soever shall please his majesty, I shall immediately make faithful promise never to write more, not abide two days in these parts after the same: but immediately to repair unto his realm, and there most humbly submit myself at the feet of his royal majesty, offering my body to suffer what pain or torture, yea, what death his grace will, so this be obtained.[14]

To the end of his life Tyndale remained dedicated to this cause. Even as he languished in prison his focus remained on the work, though he never finished his translation of the Old Testament. His biographer Mozley translates a letter that Tyndale wrote in Latin to someone responsible for supervising his imprisonment, probably the Marquis of Bergen-op-Zoom:

---

[12] Cited in *Biography*, p. 79.
[13] *A Pathway into the Holy Scripture*, in *Works*, 1:7.
[14] Cited in *Biography*, p. 216.

I believe, right worshipful, that you are not unaware of what may have been determined concerning me. Wherefore I beg your lordship, and that by the Lord Jesus, that if I am to remain here through the winter, you will request the commissary to have the kindness to send me, from the goods of mine which he has, a warmer cap; for I suffer greatly from cold in the head, and am afflicted by a perpetual catarrh, which is much increased in this cell; a warmer coat also, for this which I have is very thin; a piece of cloth too to patch my leggings. My overcoat is worn out; my shirts are also worn out. He has a woollen shirt, if he will be good enough to send it. I have also with him leggings of thicker cloth to put on above; he also has warmer night-caps. And I ask to be allowed to have a lamp in the evening; it is indeed wearisome sitting alone in the dark. But most of all I beg and beseech your clemency to be urgent with the commissary, that he will kindly permit me to have the Hebrew bible, Hebrew grammar, and Hebrew dictionary, that I may pass the time in that study. In return may you obtain what you most desire, so only that it be for the salvation of your soul. But if any other decision has been taken concerning me, to be carried out before winter, I will be patient, abiding the will of God, to the glory of the grace of my Lord Jesus Christ: whose Spirit (I pray) may ever direct your heart. Amen W. Tindalus[15]

Tyndale wanted warmer clothes, but 'most of all' he wanted to continue with his work. Tyndale's determination to produce an English translation invites us to ask about his view of the Bible. When he was in a bitterly cold prison without adequate clothing or light, why was he more concerned about having his Hebrew materials than something warmer to wear? What did he believe about the Bible that made translating it matter so much to him?

Tyndale was driven by the conviction that we need *all* of the Bible. To understand why this is so we need to consider who determines the interpretation of the Bible, who shows us what it means. There have been many candidates for this role, be they the Pope, the bishops of a denomination, the elders in a congregation, or a prophetic individual. The Bible's own answer to this question is that the Bible, as the living and

---

[15] Cited in *Biography*, p. 379.

active word of God, is self-interpreting. The Holy Spirit who breathed the words through human authors now uses his words to interpret his words. There is no authority above God himself, and so he is his own authoritative interpreter. Indeed, he must be his own interpreter. Here is how Tyndale explained the importance of context, and of Scripture interpreting Scripture:

> One scripture will help to declare another. And the circum-
> stances, that is to say, the places that go before and after, will give
> light unto the middle text. And the open and manifest scriptures
> will ever improve the false and wrong exposition of the darker
> sentences.

For Tyndale it was, therefore, not enough to have snatches of the Bible in mediaeval services; the people needed the whole text in order to grasp the truth of the gospel:

> I had perceived by experience, how that it was impossible to
> establish the lay-people in any truth, except the scripture were
> plainly laid before their eyes in their mother-tongue, that they
> might see the process, order, and meaning of the text.

Tyndale believed that the church had quenched the word of truth by 'juggling with the text', making it impossible for the people to grasp its message.[16]

Second, Tyndale knew that the Bible is an intimate book. It is God's word to us as individuals, addressing us in our own lives. This is not to say that he was an individualist who believed that the Bible is a hotline from God directly to me without regard for the original contexts in which the words were spoken long ago. Nor did he believe that it speaks to me in isolation from the rest of the Lord's people today. Tyndale knew that the Bible is a series of books given at different stages of God's dealings with his people, and he knew that it is the church's book, the book of the whole church gathered together to read it. But he also knew that when read properly it does address us as individuals. In his prologue to the Pentateuch, addressing the practical use of Scripture, he gave this simple but profound advice to the reader: 'As thou readest, therefore, think that every syllable pertaineth to thine own self, and suck out the pith of the

---

[16] 'Preface to the Five Books of Moses', in *Works*, 1:394.

scripture, and arm thyself against all assaults'.[17] Think: it pertains to me. He made the same point in the opening words of the first prologue to the 1534 edition of the New Testament: 'Here thou hast (most dear reader) the new testament or covenant made with us of God in Christ's blood'.[18] In his prologue to Jonah, Tyndale explained that when the enemies of the truth read Scripture they deliberately do the opposite, distancing themselves from it: 'The lives, stories, and gests [doings] of men, which are contained in the bible, they read as things no more pertaining unto them than a tale of Robin Hood'.[19]

Tyndale's teaching on Scripture as God's personal address to the believer is an example of the emphasis he placed on God's covenants with his people. He viewed the Bible as God's intimate address to us because he understood it as God's covenant book. It sets out the terms of God's covenantal relationship with his people, and it is itself the means by which he begins and continues that relationship. For Tyndale, every promise of God is a covenant: 'where thou findest a promise, and no covenant expressed therewith, there must thou understand a covenant'.[20] It is, therefore, the covenant that we are to look for above all else in Scripture:

> Seek therefore in the scripture, as thou readest it, chiefly and above all, the covenants made between God and us; that is to say, the law and commandments which God commandeth us to do; and then the mercy promised unto all them that submit themselves unto the law. For all the promises throughout the whole scripture do include a covenant.[21]

During the next 150 years Reformed theologians would come to explain the unity of the Bible in terms of God's covenants, and we see in Tyndale an early example of this approach. Ralph Werrell rightly comments in his work on Tyndale's theology: 'The doctrine of the covenant runs through the whole of Tyndale's theology and binds it into a coherent whole.'[22]

---

[17] 'Prologue to the Book of Genesis', in *Works*, p. 400.
[18] *William Tyndale's New Testament* (Ware: Wordsworth Editions, 2002), p. 3.
[19] 'The Prologue to the Prophet Jonas', in *Works*, 1:450.
[20] 'Prologue upon the Gospel of St Matthew', in *Works*, 1:471.
[21] 'Prologue to the Book of Genesis', in *Works*, 1:403.
[22] *The Theology of William Tyndale* (Cambridge: James Clarke, 2006), p. 24.

Tyndale's challenge

These two far-reaching convictions held by Tyndale provide us with points for reflection in our own lives today. We need to be convinced like Tyndale that we should read the whole Bible. At times of course it is right to read and meditate on just a verse, even a single word. At times it is right to pick out an isolated proverb. Such narrow meditation must, however, take place in the context of a wider pattern of reading that embraces the whole sweep of the Bible. If we are to understand the truth of Scripture, we cannot settle for just the 'Greatest Hits' of John or Paul. For most Christians the challenge will be to read the Old Testament with understanding, since much of it may seem alien to us, and the New Testament with freshness, since much of it is familiar. Tyndale's commitment to providing the whole word of God should prompt us to reflect on what practical steps we can take to widen and refresh our acquaintance with the whole of Scripture. Should we alter the pattern of our personal Bible reading? Are there books which can help us with the parts of Scripture with which we struggle? If these are new approaches for you, then you might wish to seek advice from others, especially your pastor. Even experienced students of the Bible will benefit if their church has a culture of sharing good ideas for methods of Bible reading and books that will help.

Second, Tyndale encourages us to be careful always to read Scripture as a word to us: 'It pertaineth to thine own self'. We need to read Scripture as address, as God's voice to us. Now obviously this does not mean cutting out individual words or sentences and trying to take them as words to us. Consider Paul's words in 1 Corinthians 12:3: 'Jesus is accursed'. Taking these words in isolation we would struggle to find any way in which they are addressed to us. We must hold this second application together with the first: the words of Scripture are to be read in context. Taken that way, we can certainly learn something from Paul's warning that 'no one speaking in the Spirit of God ever says "Jesus is cursed"'.

The public preaching of the word of God is also to be viewed as God's direct address to his people. A sermon is not a 'talk'. A preacher does not just 'explain the Bible' to us. These are phrases that should be expunged from church services. Least of all does a preacher lecture. He *preaches*. A faithful sermon is the moment in which God is speaking to us. Even in a poor sermon God can address us. This means that we should gather around the preached word on the Lord's Day with great expectations. God is about to speak! As the Second Helvetic Confession puts it, 'The Preaching of the Word of God Is the Word of God'.[23] Our gatherings are not to be stuffy, but they are to be serious and not flippant, since we gather to hear the word of the living God. There is a particular challenge here in teaching children: how can we make studying the Bible in the home and the church engaging without losing the seriousness of it as God's address to us?

In all this, we need to hold the second application together with the first: our broad study of the Bible is not just to fill our heads with encyclopaedic knowledge. We seek to widen our acquaintance with Scripture, but not just for the sake of information. We study Scripture to meet with our God, to be comforted and challenged by him. It was the emphasis on covenant in the theology of Tyndale that protected this relational and practical aspect of the Bible in the life of church. Viewing the Bible as God's covenant book reminds us of its true function and prevents us treating it as an object 'out there' that we analyse coldly like a laboratory specimen. This is, however, an emphasis that has been lost to many Christians today, at the same time as many of us have struggled with dryness in our approach to Scripture. Perhaps we might pause to ask if there is a connection between the two: a weakened emphasis on the Bible as God's covenant book and a cerebral coldness in how we treat it.

Lastly, we may draw a lesson from Tyndale's life, or rather, from his death. What will a man die for? A sane man will only die for what he prizes. Tyndale's sacrifice shows us that he was a man who trembled at the word of God. Let us too prize it. Let us wonder at the ease with which we have it, its availability, the fruit of his labour. Let us delight in having it. William Tyndale died to give us this word. We cannot, however, stop with Tyndale. He points us beyond himself. He died to give us the testament or covenant of God in its written form, the Old and New Testaments. But who really died to give us God's covenant? The Lord Jesus Christ, in whose blood the covenant is sealed. And so Tyndale's death for the covenant points us to Christ, and to the true blood of the covenant shed on the cross. We may wonder at William Tyndale and his sacrifice, but he points us to the immeasurably greater sacrifice of his Master.

---

[23] *Reformed Confessions of the 16th Century*, ed. by Arthur C. Cochrane (London: SCM Press, 1966), p. 225.

2

WHO IS JESUS?
THE COUNCIL OF CHALCEDON (451)

Understanding the Incarnation

My aim in this chapter is to set out the orthodox doctrine of the incarnation, the belief that the one Lord Jesus Christ was and is fully man and fully God. This is obviously a distinctive of orthodox Christianity that is denied by many cults and sects, such as the Jehovah's Witnesses. Most Christians know that they are meant to believe in the divinity and the humanity of Christ, that he is fully God and fully man, but very few understand the biblical and classical Christian account of what that actually means. Having taught the classical doctrine to seminary students for many years, I know that even those who have been called to train for Christian ministry, and who have probably read and thought more about doctrine than the average church member, usually embrace what would have been regarded as heresy by the great theologians of the early church. To explain the orthodox understanding of the person of Christ (or 'christology') we will look at the controversy that occasioned the Council of Chalcedon in the year 451 A.D. Chalcedon was an attempt to resolve a great conflict that had arisen between the preachers of Antioch and those of Alexandria, so we will delve behind the Council into those two different schools of thought. Chalcedon is one of the great ecumenical councils accepted by Protestants, but its authority is derivative: its teaching binds us in so far as it is faithful to Scripture. As such, it will be important to revisit the biblical foundations of the Council's conclusions. The theologians of the early church, themselves exegetes before they were anything else, would expect nothing less.

The aim here is to honour Christ by being precise in how we think and speak of him. The aim is not to be exhaustive, since we must be humble before the mystery of the incarnation, aware of the limits of our knowledge. Precision involves speaking carefully as God has spoken. It is important to note that speaking as God has spoken does not mean just repeating biblical statements word for word. It means realizing the *implications* of the plain biblical statements and their *inter-relationship*. These matter as much as the plain statements of Scripture themselves. The importance of the logical implications of biblical statements is described well in the Westminster Confession of Faith (1648): 'The whole counsel of God concerning all things necessary for His own glory, man's salvation, faith and life, is either expressly set down in Scripture, or by good and necessary consequence may be deduced from Scripture'.[1] In defence of this claim we should note that many of Paul's arguments in his letters presume the basic laws of logic. Take, for example, Galatians 2:21: 'if justification were through the law, then Christ died for no purpose'. This statement is only true if the idea of logical contradiction holds. If two statements may both be true at the same time in the same regard even though they are contradictory, then we might simply assert that we are justified both through the law and through Christ's death.

The importance of the inter-relationship of biblical texts is stated in the Thirty-Nine Articles of the Church of England (1571): 'it is not lawful for the Church to ordain anything that is contrary to God's word written, neither may it so expound one place of Scripture that it be repugnant to another'.[2] The church thus has a responsibility to see and articulate the coherence of Scripture. We may not posit flat contradictions between texts. This does not mean that every apparent contradiction is fully explicable. There may occasionally be examples where we have to assert coherence without being able to demonstrate it. But there is a difference between an as-yet-unresolved tension and a definite flat contradiction. The former can co-exist with belief in an inerrant Bible, while the latter cannot. In sum, we will be looking at biblical christology, taking 'biblical' to mean the plain

---

[1] *Westminster Confession of Faith* (Edinburgh: Banner of Truth, 2012), 1. vi p. 21.
[2] *Documents of the English Reformation*, ed. by Gerald Bray (Cambridge: James Clarke, 1994), Article 20, pp. 296-7.

statements *and* their implications and coherence as far as they are presently knowable to us.

The start of the controversy: Mary as Theotokos

The controversy that ultimately led to the Council of Chalcedon began in 428 when Nestorius, the new Bishop of Constantinople, preached against the description of Mary as the *Theotokos*, or 'mother of God' (more properly, the 'God-bearer').[3] In his writings Nestorius fears that teaching that Mary was the mother of God implies that God himself was born and had a mother. For this to be the case, the incarnation would have involved the divine and human natures of Jesus being mixed up into one. Only then could Mary have given birth to God as well as man. Nestorius agrees that Mary was the mother of Christ as man, but thinks that viewing her as the mother of God would collapse his two natures into one. This would leave both of the natures compromised, with neither intact following their union. In other words, Nestorius fears that if Mary were the mother of God, then Christ would be neither properly God nor properly man, because his two natures must have been confused, leaving neither whole. The Christ born of Mary as *Theotokos* was, Nestorius shudders to think, a third thing: 'he is not God truly or God by nature, nor yet man truly or man by nature'.[4] Thus he denied the title and preached against it.

We can see that the intention of Nestorius here is in large part good. He wants to emphasise the reality and integrity of both natures in Christ, the divine and the human. He defends the vital truths that Jesus is God and man. He rightly tries to avoid various heresies that deny either nature. He is concerned to refute in particular two errors from the previous century: the Arian denial of the divinity of the Son, and the Apollinarian denial of his full humanity (specifically of his human soul). These were healthy concerns. The problem is not that Nestorius wants to protect the integrity of both natures; it is that in so doing he jeopardises the unity of

---

[3] My main secondary sources in this chapter are John A. McGuckin, *St. Cyril of Alexandria and the Christological Controversy: Its History, Theology, and Texts* (Crestwood, NY: St Vladimir's Seminary Press, 2004), and Thomas G. Weinandy, *Does God Change? The Word's Becoming in the Incarnation*, Studies in Historical Theology, 4 (Still River, MA: St. Bede's Publications, 1985). The McGuckin volume contains an extensive selection of primary texts as well as a full introduction.

[4] *The Bazaar of Heracleides*, ed. and trans. by G. R. Driver and Leonard Hodgson (Oxford: Clarendon Press, 1925), p. 16.

Christ the single person. This problem is even clearer in some of the other theologians from the school of Antioch. They so emphasise that the two natures remained intact in the incarnate Christ that they end up talking about there being 'two Sons' of God, one human and one divine. Diodore of Tarsus does this explicitly, and even the more careful Theodore of Mopsuestia writes of 'the man Jesus' speaking to God the Son in the second or third person as a 'you' or 'he'.[5] The Antiochene Christologies, varied as they are, are controversial because they teach, or at least imply, that there was not one Lord Jesus Christ.

It is worth pausing to look at how Nestorius and his Antiochene predecessors arrive at their position. They hold a particular philosophical conviction that drives their view of Jesus. They believe, like the Greek philosopher Aristotle, that human nature is not something general shared by different people. Instead, humanness only exists in a specific concrete entity, an individual person complete in him- or herself. Thomas Weinandy explains that for the Antiochene Theodore of Mopsuestia, human nature 'is not just a general abstract term specifying what is common to all men, but is an individual concrete human being'.[6] In effect this is a denial of any idea of universal human nature. It involves insisting that wherever we truly find human nature we must find a full human person. So too with the divine nature: wherever it is found we must find a full, concrete divine person. Now imagine applying this view of natures to Jesus. It is a small step to the conclusion that because Jesus had two natures therefore he must have been made up of two concrete, complete realities, two persons.

When Nestorius denied that Mary was the mother of God, it seemed to many of his contemporaries that he too held this view. If Mary did not give birth to God, then she must have given birth only to the human Jesus. The divinity and humanity must therefore have been entirely separate. His opponents concluded that he too believed in 'two Sons'. In his writings Nestorius denies that he thinks this. He rejects Diodore's formulation, but the problem is that he never manages to explain convincingly why his teaching does not logically imply it. It is not that he formally states that there were two sons, but that he fails to show why, given his views, there were not. The weakness was in his positive account of the unity of Christ. When he tries to express the unity of the natures he does so in terms of their united appearance. They had a single outward presentation

[5] For references see Weinandy, *Does God Change?*, p. 35 n. 5.
[6] *Does God Change?*, p. 35.

or manifestation (the Greek term is *prosōpon*, used of an actor's mask in a play). But that is all. When you probe behind the united presentation you find that there is no depth of being to the Nestorian Christ. There is instead just a combined appearance of the natures, or as Weinandy puts it more technically, a 'mere phenomenal representation of the interplay between the two natures'.[7] So we only see one reality when we see Jesus, but behind it there are two persons. Nestorius is clear that we can never bypass the single manifestation. But behind it there is no personal union of the two natures. As Nestorius himself states, the two manifestations of the natures are united, but the natures are not: 'the *prosōpa* [manifestations] take and give one another but not the *ousias* [natures]'.[8] Nestorius is right to deny the mixing of the two natures, since the fullness of both must be preserved. The problem is that he fails to give a sufficient account of the unity. The natures were not mixed, but they must be united in more than their appearance.

Cyril of Alexandria

The arch-opponent of Nestorius was Cyril, the Patriarch of Alexandria in Egypt. Cyril was a master tactician and a cunning politician, but he was also driven by a burning zeal for the truth about the Lord Jesus Christ. In his works he insists on maintaining that Mary was the mother of God to protect the divinity and unity of Christ. The heart of his reasoning can be stated quite simply: if Christ was divine and Mary gave birth to him, then she was the mother of God. He asks: 'if our Lord Jesus Christ is God, then how is the holy virgin who bore him not the Mother of God?'[9] He rejects the Antiochene claim that the divinity was so separate from the humanity that Mary could be the mother of just the human Christ. To Cyril's mind, this involves dividing Jesus in two. It means that the human nature could exist on its own, acting independently of the Son of God. If Mary only bore Christ as man, then the man Christ seems to have been born apart from the Son of God. Cyril thinks that Nestorius could only consistently say 'The man Jesus was born' and 'God the Son was not born', leaving him with two Sons living separate lives.

Against this, Cyril insists that the humanity of Christ was God the Son's very own humanity, in which *he* lived and acted. Cyril explains that

---

[7] *Does God Change?*, p. 44.
[8] *Bazaar*, ii. 1, p. 252.
[9] 'Letter to the Monks of Egypt', §4, in *Christological Controversy*, p. 247.

the Word 'became flesh, that is became man, appropriating a human body to himself in such an indissoluble union that it has to be considered as his very own body and no one else's'.[10] He repeats this kind of language again and again: the humanity of Christ belongs to the Son, only to the Son, and always to the Son. The humanity of Christ has no existence apart from God the Son who possesses it as his humanity. Cyril stresses that Christ is a single acting subject, one person. This is why he affirms that Mary is the mother of God: it is because Christ is one person that Mary gave birth to God. John McGuckin explains: 'The phrase "Mother of God" for Cyril was a quintessential synopsis of his doctrine that the divine Word was the direct and sole personal subject of all the incarnate acts (including that of his own birth in the flesh).'[11] In other words, all that Jesus Christ did, as God or man, the eternal Son did. If Jesus Christ was born, then the eternal Son was born. Consequently, if Mary gave birth to the human Christ she gave birth to God the Son. She must, therefore, be the mother of God. Cyril's view of the single subjectivity of Christ means that everything that Christ did was an act of God the Son, and that everything that happened to him happened to God the Son. This is true even of his suffering on the cross: 'even the suffering might be said to be his because it was his own body which suffered and no one else's'.[12]

This does not mean that God was literally born as God, or suffered as God. It is obvious to Cyril that Mary did not give birth to the Word as such, literally as God. He knows full well that God could not be born. But she did give birth to God the Son in his humanity, the humanity which he had united to himself as his very own. In the same way, Cyril knows that God cannot suffer and die, but God the Son did suffer and die in the humanity which he made his very own. As he puts it: 'In the crucified body he impassibly appropriated the suffering of his own flesh'.[13] In other words, God did not suffer as God (he remained 'impassible'), but he made the suffering of his flesh his very own. He could not suffer as God, and yet *he* suffered as man:

> For he was the Word in his own body born from a woman, and he gave it to death in due season, but he suffered nothing at all in

[10] *On the Unity of Christ*, ed. and trans. by John Anthony McGuckin (Crestwood, NY: St Vladimir's Seminary Press, 1995), p. 63.
[11] *Christological Controversy*, p. 154.
[12] *Unity*, p. 118.
[13] 'Third Letter to Nestorius', §6, in *Christological Controversy*, p. 270.

his own nature for as such he is life and life-giver. Nonetheless he made the things of the flesh his own so that the suffering could be said to be his.[14]

In all this, Cyril does not collapse the two natures of Christ into one: 'That which indwells, that is the divine nature in the manhood, does not suffer any mixing, or confusion, or change into something that formerly it was not.'[15] In the incarnation God the Son did not change into human nature, but he did, in a unique and mysterious personal (or 'hypostatic') union, take a human nature to himself:

> We do not say that the nature of the Word was changed and became flesh, nor that he was transformed into a perfect man of soul and body. We say, rather, that the Word, in an ineffable and incomprehensible manner, ineffably united to himself flesh animated with a rational soul, and thus became man and was called the Son of Man.[16]

The Council of Chalcedon

The controversy between Nestorius and Cyril raged through various events and took on new dimensions until it was finally settled, after Cyril's death, at the Council of Chalcedon. By then it had engulfed much of the church and the Empire in a long, convoluted, and highly politicized conflict. The controversy involved stacked synods and counter-synods, attempts to exert influence via members of the imperial family, and even the use of military power. It affected all levels of society, from the emperor to the mob. The denial that Mary was the mother of God was particularly provocative to the increasing number devoted to her cult. In many places the widespread pagan worship of the goddess Isis had transmuted into devotion to Mary, as we can see from the similarity between images of Isis suckling her infant son Horus and Mary nursing the baby Jesus. This devotion worked against Nestorius, for example at a key synod at Ephesus in 431 that condemned him.

We will pass over the often troubling details of the conduct of the controversy. I do not want to whitewash them: both sides clearly acted

---

[14] 'Letter to the Monks', §24, in *Christological Controversy*, p. 260.
[15] 'Scholia on the Incarnation', §25, in *Christological Controversy*, p. 319.
[16] 'Second Letter to Nestorius', §3, in *Christological Controversy*, p. 263.

in sinful ways and used shockingly worldly means to achieve their ends. But the narrative is incredibly complex, and our concern here is more for the doctrine than the events.[17] The Council of Chalcedon was essentially a victory for Cyril's christology, but its doctrinal definition also manages genuinely to protect the central concern of the Antiochenes for the preservation of the two natures. The genius of the Council is that it does this not by obscuring the disagreement or leaving two contradictory positions standing alongside each other, but by finding a genuine way to maintain the right concerns of both sides. Here is the Council's definition:

> Following the holy Fathers we teach with one voice that the Son of God and our Lord Jesus Christ is to be confessed as one and the same Person, that he is perfect in Godhead and perfect in manhood, very God and very man, of a reasonable soul and human body consisting, consubstantial with the Father as touching his Godhead, and consubstantial with us as touching his manhood; made in all things like unto us, sin only excepted; begotten of his Father before the worlds according to his Godhead; but in these last days for us men and for our salvation born into the world of the Virgin Mary, the Mother of God according to his manhood. This one and the same Jesus Christ, the only-begotten Son of God must be confessed to be in two natures, unconfusedly, immutably, indivisibly, inseparably united, and that without the distinction of natures being taken away by such union, but rather the peculiar property of each nature being preserved and being united in one Person and subsistence, not separated or divided into two persons, but one and the same Son and only-begotten, God the Word, our Lord Jesus Christ, as the Prophets of old time have spoken concerning him, and as the Lord Jesus Christ hath taught us, and as the Creed of the Fathers hath delivered to us.[18]

The first point established in this definition is the unity of Christ: 'the Son of God and our Lord Jesus Christ is to be confessed as *one and the same* person'; 'the peculiar property of each nature being preserved and being united *in one Person and subsistence*, not separated or divided into two

---

[17] McGuckin offers a full account of the complex and sorry details in *Christological Controversy*.

[18] *The Seven Ecumenical Councils*, ed. by Henry R. Percival, *Nicene and Post-Nicene Fathers: Second Series, 14* (New York: Charles Scribner's Sons, 1900; repr. Peabody, MA: Hendrickson, 1994), pp. 264-5.

persons, but *one and the same* Son and only-begotten, God the Word, our Lord Jesus Christ'. This is a clear stand against the Antiochene teaching, or implication, of two Sons. Chalcedon affirms the unity of Christ as one person. At this point it stands closer to Cyril than Nestorius.

Nonetheless, the Council also affirms what Nestorius wants to protect, the fullness of the two natures: 'perfect in Godhead and perfect in manhood, very God and very man'; 'the peculiar property of each nature being preserved'. Chalcedon here guards against the extreme Alexandrian position of another figure, Eutyches. He had taken the concern for the unity of Christ too far by maintaining that there is just one new nature formed from the two after the union. This position is known as a Monophysite or 'one nature' christology.[19] The problem with it is that it denies the full humanity of Christ. He is no longer truly human, because his humanity is collapsed into his divinity. If he is no longer truly human, then he can no longer save humanity. The fathers of Chalcedon are careful to teach that Christ had full possession, after the union, of both natures perfectly intact.

The fathers of the Council thus manage brilliantly to maintain the concern of both Antioch (the full possession of two natures) and Alexandria (the unity of Christ). How do they do this? How do they fit together these two concerns that had torn the church apart in a lengthy theological and political battle? Implicit in their definition is a rejection of the philosophy that drove the Antiochene position. Remember that the Antiochenes thought that human nature could only exist as a specific concrete entity, an individual complete in itself. As Diodore teaches, a Christ with two natures must therefore be two concrete individuals, two Sons. Against this, Chalcedon holds that Christ had two complete, perfect natures, without therefore being two persons. Implicit here is the view that a nature can be a proper nature without being its own complete person. A distinction can be made between persons and natures, so that the one person can have two natures without becoming two persons. It was this understanding of the single person in two natures that led Chalcedon to side with Cyril on the crucial question that had originally sparked the controversy. Chalcedon affirms that Mary is indeed the 'mother of God'.

---

[19] Cyril himself had spoken of one nature after the union, but it is clear that he did not mean a third nature mixed together from the divine and human, a nature that ended up being neither. Rather, when he spoke of one nature he meant in effect what Chalcedon meant by the single personhood of Christ.

This must follow since the human nature of Christ is the humanity of the single person, the eternal Son. When Mary bore Jesus she bore the eternal Son of God in his humanity.

Two later technical terms make this clearer (yes clearer—bear with me and try not to be put off by the words!): 'anhypostatic' and 'enhypostatic'. Christ's human nature is said to be anhypostatic, which means that it never has its personal existence from itself. Christ has a full human nature, but that nature is not therefore a concrete entity, a person in and of itself. This denies the Antiochene idea that a nature must be a concrete individual. To say that Christ's humanity is anhypostatic is not to suggest that it ever actually does exist without personhood. It does not, because it is always also enhypostatic. This means that it always has its personhood by being the human nature of God the Son. It is always personalized in its union with the eternal Son. The human nature is not a person, an acting subject, apart from the eternal Son, but it always finds personhood in its union with the eternal Son. Thus there could be one acting subject, one Son, existing in his two natures.

For Chalcedon, we must note, the two natures are not directly united to each other, and so are not mixed. They are united 'unconfusedly' and 'immutably' as the two natures of the one person. They are bound indissolubly, but by being the two natures of the same one person, not by being blended into one another. We need to bear this in mind when we find theologians speaking of the properties of one nature as the properties of the other. For example, when we say that 'God was born' or 'God died' we ascribe the property of one nature to the other. In these examples, human experiences such as birth or death are attributed to God. But these properties are not communicated by the two natures being mixed together in a direct union. In the incarnation the properties of both natures become common to the one person. They are really shared, but as the properties of the one person, not directly between the natures. Francis Turretin, one of John Calvin's successors at the Genevan Academy, put it like this:

> The communication is not only verbal, but is rightly called 'real'; not indeed with respect to the natures (as if the properties of the one nature were really communicated to the other), but with respect to the person.[20]

---

[20] *Institutes of Elenctic Theology*, ed. by James T. Dennison, trans. by George Musgrave Giger, 3 vols (Phillipsburg, NJ: P&R Publishing, 1992-97), XIII. viii. 4, 2:322.

This is important because the idea that the properties are directly shared from one nature to the other undermines the reality of both natures. If the human nature literally possesses in itself the properties of the divine, then it is no longer human, and vice versa. A literal, direct communication of properties would undermine both natures. Hence Chalcedon affirms that the 'peculiar property' of both natures is preserved.

Theologically, I believe that the Council of Chalcedon resolved the Christological controversy. But there are two qualifications. It did not do so on the ground, since both Monophysite and Nestorian Christologies survived and often flourished. Coptic-speaking Egypt, Syria, Ethiopia, and Armenia were Monophysite. Missions to the east in the fifth century and later, some of which reached as far as Central Asia and China, were Nestorian. Second, the Council left some significant theological questions unanswered and raised several new issues that would provoke further controversy, for example over whether Christ had one or two wills.

Is Chalcedon biblical?

Did the Council of Chalcedon reach a biblical position? Does its definition accurately reflect the portrayal of Christ in Scripture? Despite the technicalities that I have outlined, the Council's definition makes or implies four key and relatively simple claims:

1. That Jesus Christ is fully God.
2. That he is fully man.
3. That there is one person Jesus Christ.
4. That there is a communication of properties in the one person Jesus, such that Mary is the mother of God.

Each of these claims is biblical. This is not the place to rehearse all of the evidence, but we may recall some of the main lines of argument. It would be useful for us to have these at our fingertips when we try to engage with others who deny the divinity of Christ.

There are in Scripture direct descriptions of Jesus as God (for example *John* 20:28, *Rom.* 9:5, and *Heb.* 1:8). There are Old Testament titles for Yahweh used of Jesus (*Isa.* 9:6). Roles ascribed to Yahweh in the Old Testament, including roles uniquely his, are given to Jesus in the New Testament (among others, the work of creation in *Heb.* 1:10-12, quoting *Psa.* 102:25-27). Perhaps most striking of all in the light of the command to worship

Yahweh alone is the command to worship Jesus (*Heb.* 1:6, quoting *Deut.* 32:43).

The humanity of Christ is less commonly denied today than his divinity. It is shown by his bodily actions and experiences as described in the Gospels (growing in *Luke* 2:40, 52, weeping in *John* 11:35), and by the suffering of his human soul (*Matt.* 26:38). A different but equally important strand of evidence is found in the explicit biblical assertions of the necessity of Christ's humanity for his saving work (for example *Heb.* 2:14).

The unity of Christ is shown first of all by the absence of language suggesting any kind of dual personhood. It is particularly striking that passages that do express the duality of the two natures of Christ do not express a duality of persons. For example, Philippians 2:5-11 speaks of Christ in the form of God and the form of a servant, but there is no hint here that two persons are involved. Throughout the passage it is the same subject, the same 'he', who is both. Similarly, it is the same Word who 'was God' in John 1:1 who 'became flesh and dwelt among us' in verse 14. Later in the same Gospel, the incarnate Jesus speaks of his own pre-existence before his incarnation: 'before Abraham was, I am' (8:58).

We find examples of the communication of the properties of the natures in Scripture. The most convincing translation of Acts 20:28 speaks of 'the church of God, which he obtained with his own blood'. Here we have blood ascribed to God. Similarly, Paul speaks in 1 Corinthians 2:8 of how the rulers of this age 'crucified the Lord of glory', referring to the crucifixion of Jesus using the divine title 'Lord'. Similarly, in Romans 9:5 (NIV) Paul speaks of the 'human ancestry of Christ, who is God over all', thus identifying the humanly descended Jesus as God. While we do not find the term *Theotokos* used in Scripture, we do come very close to it in Luke when Elizabeth asks 'And why is this granted to me that the mother of my Lord should come to me?' (1:43). Here Mary is described as the mother of the 'Lord'. The Greek term used here (*kurios*) can simply be a title of respect, like the English 'Sir', but it can also be a divine title since it was used in the Greek translation of the Old Testament to translate the name of God himself. Luke himself uses it that way (*Luke* 1:15). Which is it here? Even conservative commentators such as Darrell Bock think it unlikely that Elizabeth intended more than a title of 'messianic respect' here. But Bock also notes how the title *kurios* 'will take on significant proportions in the latter part of the Gospel' (see, for example, 24:3).[21] To my

---

[21] *Luke*, 2 vols (Grand Rapids, MI: Baker Books, 1994; repr. 2002), 1:137.

mind it is hardly likely that Luke, himself writing in retrospect, wanted his readers to avoid seeing the overtones of divinity in the words of Elizabeth. If this is so, then in its wider context the title implies the identification of Mary as 'the mother of God', even if this goes beyond what Elizabeth herself meant. Apart from these exegetical arguments, the use of the title *Theotokos* follows from the same logic that we find in assertions that Scripture does make, such as speaking of the blood of God. If God could have blood, then he was born and had a mother.

At this point if you are a Protestant reader you may be feeling a little queasy. You may be very wary of the Roman Catholic view of Mary. Mariolatry, let me be clear, is unbiblical. There is, however, nothing un-Protestant about accepting the term *Theotokos*. It is hard to think of a more Protestant figure than Turretin, Calvin's successor at Geneva, who wrote: 'Mary is rightly called the Mother of God (*theotokos*) in the concrete and specifically because she brought forth him who is also God'.[22] He was careful to point out that this is not 'in respect of the deity', and that the title 'was perverted by superstitious men into an occasion of idolatry', but he still affirmed it.[23] It may feel to some Protestants that they have a duty to reject on principle as much as possible of what Rome says, but that is actually a dangerous way to operate. The reformers did not reject something just because Rome believed it; they rejected it because it was unbiblical. Protestants test a doctrine by asking 'Does the Bible deny it?' not 'Does the Roman Catholic Church teach it?'

Following the wisdom of Chalcedon

We have had a number of visits to our home from Jehovah's Witnesses, both in the United Kingdom and while staying in the United States. In our discussions over an open Bible, I find it helpful to bear in mind the theological position of Chalcedon, and especially what the church fathers were doing in their theological endeavours. While our visitors always profess their belief in the Bible alone, it becomes clear that their theology is in fact a kind of rationalism. They deny the doctrine of the incarnation because they cannot accept, in their own minds, the different elements of the biblical christology. They have got hold of one aspect of biblical teaching and they use it to counter the others. For example, they assert texts showing the humanity of Christ as an argument for denying his

[22] *Institutes*, XIII. vii. 11, 2:320.
[23] *Institutes*, XIII. v. 18, 2:310; XIII. vii. 12, 3:320.

divinity. As well as urging them to reread particular passages of Scripture, I also try to describe the kind of approach that we have seen with Chalcedon. The genius of the Council is the way in which it does not use one element of the biblical teaching to squeeze out another. It affirms both that Christ is fully divine and that he is fully human; both that he is one person and that he has two natures; both that his two natures are united and that their properties are preserved. Our calling is to follow the example of Chalcedon in submitting to the authority of Scripture, not to try to prescribe what Scripture can and cannot teach about him. In witness to the divinity of Jesus we should thus urge on its opponents a glad acceptance of all the elements of the biblical christology.

In submitting to Scripture we should worry less about whether what it teaches is possible in our eyes and more about making sure that we grasp what it does actually teach. Please do not take this as a mandate for intellectual laziness: take it as an encouragement to accept that even after all of the close theological work is done there remain mysteries at the heart of biblical doctrines. The incarnation is mysterious to us because it describes something utterly unique and miraculous. There is no other example of a single person having two natures, and God does not become man by a process that occurs routinely in nature. Amid all the complexities of Chalcedon we can find helpful ways of articulating the biblical doctrine (using terms like 'person' and 'nature'), but we cannot find anything that will serve to lay out the metaphysical realities of the incarnation like an engineer's drawing. We are called to work hard to understand the biblical teaching, and then to rest content with it; better, to rest in it with wonder and delight at the good news of great joy for all people: 'For unto you is born this day in the city of David a Saviour, who is Christ the Lord' (*Luke* 2:11).

3

THE CROSS AND ITS CARICATURES:
JOHN OWEN (1616-83)

John Owen and his work

John Owen is in the first rank of Reformed theologians from all nations and times. By the time of his birth in 1616, Tyndale's emphasis on Scripture was the established teaching of the Church of England. And yet in 1637 Owen would find himself ejected from the University of Oxford because of his unwillingness to accept the innovations of its Chancellor, Archbishop William Laud. Laud was engaged in a programme of changes to the church that attempted to reintroduce some of the ceremonies of Roman Catholicism, and that downplayed the Augustinian emphasis on God's sovereign grace. Eventually these religious innovations, combined with the autocratic style of King Charles I's government, provoked the Civil War, and led to the execution of the king in 1649. During the Interregnum that followed, Owen served as Oliver Cromwell's chaplain, was made Dean of Christ Church, Oxford in 1651, and Vice-Chancellor of the University the next year. He was the main reviser of the Westminster Confession into the congregational form of the Savoy Declaration (1658). After the Restoration of the monarchy, when nonconformists were excluded from ecclesiastical and civic office, he preached and wrote in London until his death in 1683.

I am convinced (with many others) that Owen has a claim to be the greatest English theologian. His work is a wonderful blend of scholastic precision, deep spiritual insight, and obvious love for the glory of Christ.

He can move in a single breath from intricate theological distinctions based on the smallest detail of Hebrew to extolling the attributes of God and the excellencies of Christ. It is this blend of theology and spirituality which makes his work so important. He explains it like this in the preface to one of his most technical and difficult works:

> I hold myself bound, in conscience and in honour, not even to imagine that I have attained a proper knowledge of any one article of truth, much less to publish it, unless through the Holy Spirit I have had such a taste of it, in its spiritual sense, as that I may be able from the heart to say with the psalmist, 'I have believed, and therefore have I spoken'.[1]

Despite its obvious spirituality, Owen's writing can be hard to read. But the length and complexity is often a strength, for it usually indicates thorough treatment of a subject. As his biographer Andrew Thompson wrote, Owen 'more than any other writer makes you feel, when he has reached the end of his subject, that he has also exhausted it'—and us, we might add, but that can be a virtue.[2]

In this chapter we will consider specifically Owen's understanding of the atonement. Famous among his many works which address this subject is *The Death of Death in the Death of Christ* (1647). I write 'famous', but I might have written 'infamous'. Today the work is known primarily as a defence of 'effectual' or 'limited' atonement, the teaching that Jesus died intending to save only his chosen people (I will comment on the terminology later). For many this is enough to discourage them from reading it. I will end this chapter with some comments on effectual atonement, but there is much more to Owen's doctrine of the atonement than his position on its extent, and it is on this wider teaching that my attention will focus here. In fact, Owen himself believed that his view of the extent of the atonement derived from, among other things, his view of its nature. In that sense, it is the right sequence to give prior attention to what Owen says more generally about the nature of the atonement.

We find in Owen's writing a rich theological resource for our understanding of the death of the Lord Jesus Christ. This richness arises in part

---

[1] *A Dissertation on Divine Justice*, in *The Works of John Owen*, ed. by William H. Goold, 16 vols (Edinburgh: Banner of Truth, 1965-68; repr. 1993), 10:488, quoting Psalm 116:10 in 2 Corinthians 4:13.

[2] Life of Dr Owen, in *Works* 1:xxxviii.

because he articulates the biblical teaching on the cross so carefully and accurately. There is in Owen's work a great deal of interaction with the details of biblical Hebrew and Greek, with the patterns of Old Testament sacrifice, and with their interpretation in the epistle to the Hebrews. But more than that, he explains this teaching systematically, showing how it coheres and how it fits with other biblical doctrines. Owen needed to provide this rich resource of detailed teaching because of the controversies by which he was surrounded. These controversies drove him to the text and propelled his systematic reflections. In this sense his writings are a good example of the way in which the Lord can use false teaching as a foil for the truth.

Caricatures of penal substitutionary atonement

Owen found that foil in the writings of the Arminians, followers of Jacobus Arminius (1560–1609), a Dutch theologian who deviated from the Reformed emphasis on the sovereignty of God, and especially the Socinians, followers of the heretic Faustus Socinus (1539–1604). In addressing them he deals with arguments which are still used today against the biblical teaching, with the result that he can help us in our own controversies. Given this, I begin not in the seventeenth century but in our own time, with some examples of the way in which the classical evangelical doctrine of the cross is represented among those who oppose it. With that in mind we will then turn back to Owen's teaching to see if we can find there an answer to these contemporary challenges.

Critics of the evangelical doctrine of the atonement such as feminist theologians and radical Anabaptists seem to think that it views the Father as being angry with us and no more. He has, of himself, no will to save. His will toward sinful men and women is only hostile, he seeks only their destruction. In fact, his anger is not even a settled implacable opposition to evil; it is a nasty, capricious, volatile, seething kind of senseless personal resentment. Second, they find the Son detached from the Father. The Son appears seemingly from nowhere with a will to rescue us from an angry Father. He is the one with the will to save, who somehow manages to persuade the Father to stop being angry. In the end the erratic Father gives in and agrees to be merciful. Third, the Son is thus depicted in his death as the Father's victim, like an abused child, caught up in the violence of his Father. The Father vents his wrath on this unfortunate, vulnerable child. The Son's plan is to surrender himself as an innocent victim to the capricious will of his Father, to allow himself to be the victim of the Father's senseless anger. Atonement in this depiction involves the unjust, unjustifiable punishment of an innocent man in the place of guilty men and women. The substitution portrayed is obviously an immoral miscarriage of justice.

The will of the Father

We turn now to Owen to test this picture, starting with the assertion that in the doctrine of penal substitutionary atonement the Father needs to be moved to love us by the Son. This is certainly not what we find in Owen's account. In *The Death of Death*, Owen begins as far as could be from the picture of the unwilling Father and the willing Son. He strongly emphasises the united will of the Holy Trinity to save. His treatment of the atonement is arranged under three headings: the agent (the one who does it), the means (how he does it), and the end (his goal in doing it). Our interest here is in the agent: who is it that saves? In particular, is it the Son and not the Father, or the Father only reluctantly after being persuaded by the Son? Here are Owen's words:

> The agent in, and chief author of, this great work of our redemption is the whole blessed Trinity; for all the works which outwardly are of the Deity are undivided and belong equally to each person, their distinct manner of subsistence and order being observed.[3]

This is very significant. It is clear that for Owen each Person of the Trinity is involved in willing the atonement. The Holy Trinity wills to save. The cross is the purpose of the triune God. Owen is not innovating here; he speaks out of an ancient tradition of trinitarian theology, his words being an echo of Augustine and his famous principle that the external works of the Trinity are undivided. What the Father does, the Son does. What the Father does, the Holy Spirit does. What the Son does, the Holy Spirit does. Each person wills each work of God with the one divine will. For Owen and for the tradition of catholic theology, this is a vital and indispensable insight.

If we *were* to say that the persons of the Trinity are divided in their external work, it would have devastating theological consequences. Why? Because who God *is* determines the way in which he does what he does. God's *actions* arise from his *being*. We can, therefore, infer from his actions

[3] *The Death of Death in the Death of Christ*, in *Works* i. 3, 10:163.

back to his being. If God were disunited in his activity, he would by implication be disunited in his being. To put it plainly: if the Father and the Son willed different things, they would be different gods.

We have seen that the unity of God requires the united activity of the three persons of the Trinity: they work together because they are one. At the end of the sentence quoted above Owen states the unity of the persons: 'all the works outwardly of the Deity are undivided'. Yet it is also true that the persons preserve their distinctions within their united work: 'their distinct manner of subsistence and order being observed'. This emphasis on distinction alongside unity is vital. As we assert that God is one, so we assert that he is three. Here is the mystery of the Holy Trinity, in oneness and threeness. Owen's conception of God's work as the one united work of three distinct persons results from his understanding of the triune life of God.

How does this work out in practice? What does the oneness and threeness look like in any particular activity of God? Here we are thinking about the role of the Father in the death of Christ. Owen explains that the Father and the Son covenant together for our redemption. The Father sends the Son, laying the office of mediator on him. The Father promises to the Son that he will strengthen him in his work and that he will reward him with glory and the gift of a people. It is this promise which sustains Jesus in his sufferings. Owen writes:

> Hence arose that confidence of our Saviour in his greatest and utmost trials, being assured, by virtue of his Father's engagement in this covenant, upon a treaty with him about the redemption of man, that he would never leave him nor forsake him.[4]

In this description of the Father sending the Son and providing for him we see as plainly as can be that the Father wills the work of the Son. He covenants with him, he lays the office on him, he provides him with the gifts needed to fulfil it.

We might expand Owen's case at this point. In John's Gospel, we read repeatedly that the Son wills what he wills and does what he does, following the will and action of the Father. For example, we read in John 5:19 that 'the Son can do nothing of his own accord, but only what he sees the Father doing'. It is evident here that the Father is the initiator of the sending of the Son and his incarnate work. There is therefore within

---

[4] *Death of Death*, i. 3, 10:169.

the history of the evangelical understanding of the atonement no room for the idea that the Son turns the will of an unwilling Father. Rather, it is the willing Father who initiates the work of the Son by sending him. The love of God precedes the sending of the Son, it does not result from it: 'For God so loved the world that he gave …' (*John* 3:16). The Son does not make the Father love. The Son comes because the Father loves.

Given that the Father is already willing to save, it is worth pausing to ask in what sense the Son turns aside the wrath of the Father. The Bible teaches that the Son propitiates the Father (*Rom.* 3:25), which means that he removes the wrath of the Father against our sin. What can that mean if the Father already wills to save? The answer is that apart from the work of Christ, the Father is both loving *and* wrathful toward sinners. Following the work of Christ, his wrath has been removed, leaving only his love. It is not a contradiction to say that God is both loving and wrathful before the cross. It would be a contradiction if we maintained that the Father *acts out* his love and his wrath toward the same person in the same moment. That is impossible to conceive, since they would be contradictory actions. One cannot save in love and condemn in wrath the same individual at the same time. But we can imagine simultaneously regarding someone with both love and righteous anger, for example a disobedient child. This is what it means to say that God is loving and wrathful toward sinners. He regards them with both love and wrath; then, because of his love, he sends his Son to bear his wrath, leaving only his love. The full punishment is borne by the Son, and then the sentence is spent, so that there is only love left. In this way we can see how Owen can maintain that the Father is at once wrathful and yet also willing to save.

The will of the Son

When Owen talks about the Father sending the Son, he does not mean that the Son is the unfortunate victim of the Father, dragged into dying against his will. This is the importance of seeing the covenant of redemption as a mutual agreement between the Father and the Son. What the Father wills, the Son wills willingly. Just as the unity of the Trinity shows that the Father wills to save, so too it shows that the Son wills to be the Saviour. Owen here speaks of the 'voluntary susception' of the Son.[5] The Son wills to become incarnate, he wills to lay down his life under the

---

[5] *Death of Death*, i. 4, 10:174. 'Susception' comes from the Latin *suscipere*, 'to take up' or 'undertake'.

punishment for sin, and he wills to intercede for his people. There is for Owen no sense in which the Son is forced to be our Saviour. As Jesus himself puts it:

> For this reason the Father loves me, because I lay down my life that I may take it up again. No one takes it from me, but I lay it down of my own accord. I have authority to lay it down, and I have authority to take it up again (*John* 10:17-18).

If we were trying to give a rounded theological account of the cross we would now go on to consider the work of the Holy Spirit. All that has been said of the united purpose and personal distinction of the Father and Son is true also of the Spirit. Indeed, when he died the Son offered himself 'through the eternal Spirit' (*Heb*. 9:14), and in his resurrection he was 'vindicated by the Spirit' (*1 Tim*. 3:16). We have not considered his role here only because the caricatures of the cross tend to focus on the Father and the Son.

At this point we may fruitfully pause to consider the wonderful benefits of the united purpose of the Holy Trinity. We have seen that the sacrifice of the cross is intended by the Father and the Son. It is planned by them from before the foundation of the world. But they do not just decide to do it in a divine decree. Rather, they bind themselves together in a covenant to accomplish the work of redemption. This is a great assurance to us when our consciences remind us of our sins. The Father and the Son planned before the foundation of the world to redeem us. What greater assurance can we look for than this certain, eternal plan of the Holy Trinity, fixed in place before God even said 'Let there be light'?

We see here too the beautiful harmony of the Holy Trinity. The Father, the Son, and the Holy Spirit eternally will the same salvation. They work together in each act of redemption. Everything one does, the other does, appropriately to their distinct personhood and relationship. It is a glorious redemption, accomplished in a glorious manner by this perfect, harmonious, united co-working of the three persons of the Godhead.

Unjust punishment?

We turn now to consider the objection that the Son was innocent, and so was unjustly punished on the cross for sins that he had not committed. This is one of the oldest criticisms of penal substitutionary atonement. It is found, for example, in the theology of Socinus, and was very much on

Owen's mind because of the work of the English Socinian John Biddle (1615–1662). We may feel the force of the criticism. Perhaps in persuading people of their need for Christ we explain that sin must be punished because of the demands of God's justice. Yet the more we press the necessity of justice the more we may be troubled by the apparent injustice of the cross. Can it be that a doctrine which so insists on the demands of justice also teaches that God punished the wrong man?

The answer is that penal substitutionary atonement does not teach this. We must recall here the Reformed emphasis on union with Christ. Like Owen's trinitarian theology, union with Christ is an ancient theme in the church. Indeed, some writers in the early church, such as Eusebius of Caesarea, appeal to our union with Christ when explaining a penal substitutionary view of the atonement.[6] It is when we connect penal substitutionary atonement with an emphasis on union with Christ that we see why the charge of injustice against the doctrine is invalid. In the charge the picture is of the innocent Jesus wholly isolated from the guilty sinner and having nothing to do with him. They are two utterly separate, unrelated individuals, and one was punished instead of the other.

This is not the Bible's picture of the atonement, as Owen explains in his *Dissertation on Divine Justice*. In this work he argues that the holiness of God makes the punishment of every sin necessary. He considers the objection that God would then have to punish everyone and could never save anyone. In a bold move, he meets this objection by arguing that in effect God *does* punish everyone, even his chosen people. How so? Because the elect, spared the experience of punishment in their own bodies, are punished 'in Christ'. He explains that God could punish his people in two ways:

> He might punish the elect either in their own persons, or in their surety standing in their room and stead; and when he is punished, they also are punished: for in this point of view the federal head and those represented by him are not considered as distinct, but as one; for although they are not one in respect of personal unity, they are, however, one,—that is, one body in mystical union, yea, *one mystical Christ;*—namely, the surety is the head, those represented by him the members; and when the head is punished, the members also are punished.[7]

[6] See Eusebius, *The Proof of the Gospel*, ed. and trans. by W. J. Ferrar, 2 vols (London: SPCK; New York: Macmillan, 1920), x. 1, 2:195-96.

[7] *Dissertation*, ii. 15, 10:598.

Rather than seeing Jesus and the sinner as isolated from one another, Owen finds the sinner in Christ. These words are very important, and they are biblical. Paul writes:

> For the love of Christ controls us, because we have concluded this: that one has died for all, therefore all have died; and he died for all, that those who live might no longer live for themselves but for him who for their sake died and was raised (*2 Cor.* 5:14, 15).

Note here how Paul explains that those for whom Christ died have died with Christ. It is not only that Christ has died *for* them, but also that they have died *with* him. In Romans 5 and 1 Corinthians 15, Paul explains union with Christ in terms of representative headship. Jesus Christ is the representative of the new humanity as Adam was representative of the old. He is the one in whom his people are included. Therefore when Christ dies we die with him. Owen thus follows Paul. He is clear that this does not mean that we become literally one person with Christ; rather, we are mystically united with him, we are together 'one mystical Christ'. Owen uses the language of the body that we find recurring in Paul (for example in *Eph.* 1:22, 23; *Col.* 1:18). We are together the body of which Christ is the head. On the basis of this representative headship and mystical union, Owen can declare that 'when the head is punished, the members also are punished'. Here is the conclusive proof that penal substitutionary atonement does not entail God punishing an innocent man who has nothing to do with sinners. It involves Christ bearing the punishment for those who are his very own body.

This is a glorious thought: we are reminded of the most intimate bond which ties the head to his body, which holds together every believer with his Saviour, which allows him to take our sins from us. Consider the strength of the union, the relation between Christ and his people. It has its inviolable basis in eternity. Paul praises God the Father because 'he chose us in him before the foundation of the world' (*Eph.* 1:4). Jesus even prays to the Father that we would share their eternal union:

> I do not ask for these only, but also for those who will believe in me through their word, that they may all be one, just as you, Father, are in me, and I in you, that they also may be in us, so that the world may believe that you have sent me (*John* 17:20, 21).

Effectual atonement

We come lastly and briefly to the most controversial aspect of John Owen's teaching on the cross, namely the doctrine of effectual atonement. This doctrine holds that Christ died intending to effect the salvation of God's chosen people, the elect, and no one else. For Owen this is a major issue. My choice of heading explains why. The doctrine is more commonly known as 'limited atonement', but it is more accurately described by the title 'effectual atonement'. Calling it 'limited atonement' makes it sound as if Owen has a reduced, constrained, shrunken view of the cross. It sounds as if he is essentially being negative. Calling it 'effectual atonement' has the opposite connotation. It makes clear that whatever we may think of his position, Owen has no intention of limiting the cross. Rather, he seeks to exalt the work of Christ by emphasising that it is powerful and effective. Owen maintains that the doctrine of effectual atonement is vital for grasping the greatness of the sacrifice of the cross. He explains how he is exalting the work of Christ and not limiting it:

> That which the Father and the Son intended to accomplish in and towards all those for whom Christ died, by his death that is most certainly effected . . . but the Father and his Son intended by the death of Christ to redeem, purge, sanctify, purify, deliver from death, Satan, the curse of the law, to quit of all sin, to make righteousness in Christ, to bring nigh unto God, all those for whom he died, as was above proved: therefore, Christ died for all and only those in and towards whom all these things recounted are effected.[8]

Here Owen summarizes his investigation into the purposes of the cross. He argues that if God is powerful and sovereign, then the cross must achieve its purposes. If the blood of Christ is effective, then Christ must achieve his ends in shedding it. If Christ died intending to save someone, then that person must be cleansed, purged, and sanctified. The atonement, if it is not to fail, must be effectual for all for whom Christ died. This leaves a choice. Either we hold that Christ intended to save everyone and everyone will be saved, or we hold that he intended to save a particular people and they will be saved. Given that Scripture contradicts universal salvation, we must conclude that Christ had a particular intention for the cross.

Owen seeks to exalt the cross by teaching that it is actually effective. If Christ died for someone, then he saves them. His blood is powerful

---

[8] *Death of Death*, ii. 3, 10:211.

to save and is never spilt in vain. Ironically, it is by believing that Christ died intending to save every individual without exception (the Arminian position) that we limit the power of the atonement. As Loraine Boettner puts it: 'The Arminian limits the atonement as certainly as does the Calvinist.'[9] On the Arminian view, Christ died intending to save millions who are never saved. Boettner has a striking way of putting this:

> The Calvinist limits it quantitatively, but not qualitatively; the Arminian limits it qualitatively, but not quantitatively. For the Calvinist it is like a narrow bridge which goes all the way across the stream; for the Arminian it is like a great wide bridge which goes only half-way across. As a matter of fact, the Arminian places more severe limitations on the work of Christ than does the Calvinist.[10]

The doctrine of effectual atonement is a glorious, Christ-exalting doctrine. Nothing about the cross fails. It achieves exactly what the Lord intended by it. Christ carries those for whom he died all the way across the river, safe home to the other side. Owen likewise judges that he is exalting the cross by affirming its efficacy. He is concerned to magnify the Saviour, not to 'limit' him. Here is how he states it:

> I can truly say that I desire to know nothing but Christ and him crucified; and I shall labour to make the honour, glory, exaltation, and triumph of the cross of Christ, the whole of my aim and business in this world. May I be convinced of speaking, uttering, writing any one word to the derogation of the honour, efficacy, power of the death and merits of our dear Lord Jesus, I shall quickly lay my mouth in the dust, and give myself to be trampled on by the feet of men; which perhaps on other accounts I am only meet for. It is only that Christ may have the pre-eminence in all things that I will voluntarily contend with any living. That as a king, and priest, and prophet, he may be only and all in his church, is the design of my contesting.[11]

[9] *The Reformed Doctrine of Predestination* (Phillipsburg, New Jersey: Presbyterian and Reformed, 1932), p. 153.

[10] *Predestination*, p. 153. Boettner elsewhere argues for the postmillennial view that the great majority of the human race will be saved. Given such a view of the end-times we can see that the quantitative limiting of the atonement need not mean that that there will be a small number saved.

[11] *Of the Death of Christ, and of Justification*, in *Works*, 12:605.

Is that not a sentiment that we long to make our own? May he be 'only and all' in our churches, only and all in our families, only and all in our own lives, only and all in our hearts.

4

THE INFINITE LOVE OF THE DYING CHRIST: JONATHAN EDWARDS (1703-58)

Jonathan Edwards

Jonathan Edwards was a minister in Northampton, Massachusetts during the time of the Great Awakening of the eighteenth century. This was the North American manifestation of a movement of the Holy Spirit that occurred, often independently, in different countries, reaching its height in the 1740s. Northampton saw a heightened spiritual interest among the people with around 300 converted. Despite leading his congregation through such an experience, Edwards was removed from office in 1750 when he attempted to raise the requirements for admission to the Lord's supper. Edwards then moved to the obscure and sometimes dangerous frontier town of Stockbridge, where his ministry extended to the white settlers and Native Americans. It was in Stockbridge that he wrote most of his major theological works, including his classic works on free will, true virtue, and original sin. In these volumes Edwards showed himself to be a classical Reformed theologian well-versed in the writings of the Puritans and the Reformed scholastics of the previous century. But he also evidenced a profound originality and showed himself capable of devastating polemic directed against the 'enlightened' theologies of his own day. In 1757 he was invited to lead the College of New Jersey (which would develop into what is today Princeton University). He resisted the invitation, but in the end agreed to submit the decision to a council of ministers. He was amazed and moved to tears when they rejected his arguments against the move, and duly assumed the office of President in 1758. It was there that he received a smallpox vaccination that led to his death on 22 March. His wife Sarah, herself a remarkable Christian, wrote to her daughter words that express some of the deepest convictions she shared with her husband:

> What shall I say? A holy and good God has covered us with a dark cloud. O that we may kiss the rod, and lay our hands on our mouths! The Lord has done it. He has made me adore his goodness, that we had him so long. But my God lives; and he has my heart. O what a legacy my husband, and your father, has left us! We are all given to God; and there I am, and love to be.[1]

The hated and loved Jonathan Edwards

Like William Tyndale, Edwards provoked a remarkable range of reactions during and after his lifetime. They span the utmost extremes: from the damnation of his memory to exuberant praise. After reading one of his books, Mark Twain spoke of him as 'a resplendent intellect gone mad'.[2] But Twain is comparatively mild. Here are some comments from Charles Angoff: 'There is no more devastating argument against Calvinism and all it means than the life and deeds of Jonathan Edwards'; 'Edwards was the most bitter hater of man the American pulpit ever had . . . There was no love in him for the human race'. He was, Angoff tells us, 'a pathetic, sickly, angry, Puritan'.[3] By contrast, George Whitefield describes Edwards as 'a solid, excellent Christian'. He comments: 'I think I have not seen his fellow in all New England'.[4] Benjamin Warfield writes of Edwards as 'the one figure of real greatness in the intellectual life of colonial America'.[5] Something of the stature of Edwards is captured by John De Witt, who observes that he was 'inexpressibly great in his intellectual endowment, in his theological achievement, in his continuing influence. He was greatest

[1] Cited in Iain H. Murray, *Jonathan Edwards: A New Biography* (Edinburgh: Banner of Truth, 1987; repr. 1988), p. 442.

[2] *Mark Twain's Letters*, ed. by Albert Bigelow Paine, 2 vols (New York: Harper & Brothers, 1917), 2:719.

[3] Cited in Clyde A. Holbrook, 'Jonathan Edwards and His Detractors', *Theology Today*, 10 (1953), p. 387.

[4] Cited in *A New Biography*, p. xv.

[5] Cited in *A New Biography*, p. xvii.

in his attribute of regnant, permeating, irradiating spirituality'. De Witt maintains a special place for Edwards: 'we still in our heart of hearts reserve the highest honor for the great American who lived and moved and had his being in the Universe which is unseen and eternal'.[6] Samuel Hopkins, who knew Edwards personally, likewise records that he 'seemed to enjoy an uncommon degree of the presence of God'.[7] The physician who attended Edwards on his death-bed describes his complacency in God: 'never did any mortal man, more fully and clearly evidence the sincerity of all his professions, by one continued, universal, calm, cheerful resignation, and patient submission to the divine will, through every stage of his disease, than he'.[8]

How are we to understand this polarity of verdicts on Edwards? As we saw with Tyndale, the extremity of reactions to Edwards should be understood as a reflection of the extremity of reactions to his God and his gospel. Iain Murray explains: 'depending on where we stand in relation to Christ, we shall join ourselves to one side or the other in interpreting this man who was, first of all, a Christian'.[9] Many Christians are hated by the world, but there was and is so much hatred for Edwards because he so powerfully stood for controversial aspects of the truth in his writings. His works are pervaded by a resolve to speak as the Scriptures speak, to speak of God as he has spoken of himself, no matter where it leads.

My aim here is to set out Edwards's understanding of the atoning work of Christ to supplement what we have learned from John Owen. Although he was a later writer than Owen, Edwards is rightly also understood as a Puritan. His teaching typically followed the standard Puritan pattern of 'doctrine' and then 'use' or application. I will employ that method here, drawing material (selectively) from *The History of the Work of Redemption*, a series of sermons that Edwards intended to form the basis of his magnum opus, had he lived.

Doctrine: God's infinity and the necessity of the incarnation

Theology was never just theoretical for Edwards: he was deeply affected by what he knew of God. He was a man captivated by a sense of the living

---

[6] Cited in *A New Biography*, p. xvii.

[7] Cited in George M. Marsden, *Jonathan Edwards: A Life* (New Haven: Yale University Press, 2003), p. 491.

[8] Cited in *A Life*, p. 494.

[9] *A New Biography*, p. xxvii.

God. He was gripped by what he frequently described as the infinity and excellency of God and Christ. These two descriptions recur often in his works, and are applied in many different ways. In his 'Personal Narrative', he records this experience of God in his studies:

> God in the communications of his Holy Spirit, has appeared as an infinite fountain of divine glory and sweetness; being full and sufficient to fill and satisfy the soul: pouring forth itself in sweet communications, like the sun in its glory, sweetly and pleasantly diffusing light and life.[10]

When he read the Bible, Edwards found the living word that Tyndale so prized, and he described it using these favourite terms: 'I have sometimes had an affecting sense of the excellency of the word of God, as a word of life; as the light of life; a sweet, excellent, life-giving word'.[11]

Given how pervasive these themes are in the writings of Edwards, it is no surprise to find him employing them to explain the work of Christ in his *History of the Work of Redemption*. In showing why God needed to become man in order to atone for sin, Edwards argues that in one sense God as God is too infinite to make atonement. While the blood of bulls and goats cannot take away sins because they are less than human (*Heb.* 10:4), God as God could not atone for sin because he is so much greater than a man. The substitute for sinners needs to be a man like those for whom he is substituted. This does not mean that there is some deficiency on God's part. Rather, it is the infinity of the eternal Son of God which means that he could not make atonement as God. It is, therefore, the exceeding greatness of God that necessitates the lowliness of the incarnation:

> Though Christ as God was infinitely sufficient for the work, yet viewed as to his being in an immediate capacity for it, it was needful that he should not only be God but man. If Christ had remained only in the divine nature, he would not have been in a capacity to have purchased our salvation, not from any imperfection of the divine nature, but by reason of its absolute and infinite perfection.[12]

---

[10] Jonathan Edwards, *Letters and Personal Writings*, ed. by George S. Claghorn, in *The Works of Jonathan Edwards* (New Haven: Yale University Press, 1998), 16:801.

[11] *Letters*, 16:801.

[12] *A History of the Work of Redemption*, ed. by John F. Wilson, in *The Works of Jonathan Edwards* (New Haven: Yale University Press, 1989), 9:295 (Hickman ed.

Christ was too perfect to be our substitute. He was, as God, too perfect to suffer: 'The divine nature is not capable of suffering, for it is impassable and infinitely above all suffering'.[13] Because of this infinite perfection, the excess of his divine nature, 'it was needful that he should not only be God but man'.[14] The necessity of the incarnation arose from the infinity of the Son of God.

Doctrine: the infinite humiliation of Christ

Edwards sets out a traditional Reformed understanding of the work of Christ consisting of two stages, his humiliation and exaltation. The time of his humiliation was the supreme period of human history, 'the most remarkable article of time that ever was or ever will be'. It was the high-point of God's redeeming activity: 'more was done in it than had been done from the beginning of the world to that time'.[15] The eternal Son of God, infinite as he was as God, stooped down in becoming a man. He was humiliated. This does not mean that the eternal Son left behind the fullness of his divinity in the incarnation. That is not what Edwards means by humiliation. To use the technical term, his is no 'kenotic' christology, no christology where Christ empties himself of divinity. That view, Edwards would have said, is a heresy because a Christ who has emptied himself of Godhead is no longer fully God. It is a denial of the divinity of Christ. For Edwards, as for Chalcedon, the Son cannot lose any of his divine attributes and still be God.

What then does Edwards mean by humiliation? He means that the eternal Son of God, while remaining fully God, assumed another nature in which his glory was concealed. In that sense, he was humbled, brought low. Here is the point at which the emphasis on the infinity of Christ becomes profound and gripping. How high was Christ before his incarnation? How lofty was he? How great was the display of his glory? He was infinitely high, he was infinitely lofty, he was infinitely glorious. In coming as a man he stooped down from an infinite height. He was willing to be brought low. In one of his *Miscellanies*, Edwards contrasts Lucifer and Christ in this regard. Lucifer was meant to serve Christ and his people, but he was

---

[Edinburgh: Banner of Truth, 1974], 1:572).

   [13] *History*, 9:295-96 (Hickman, 1:572). 'Impassable' is used by Edwards here where we would put 'impassible'.

   [14] *History*, 9:295 (Hickman, 1:572).

   [15] *History*, 9:294 (Hickman, 1:572).

not prepared to do so. He was proud and clung to his height. This pride, Edwards thinks, explains the fall of the angels. When the obedient angels look at Lucifer and look at Christ, they see the total contrast between grasping and humility: 'Lucifer thought what God required of him too great an abasement for so high and worthy a creature as he. But in Christ Jesus, they see one infinitely higher than he descending vastly lower than was required of him.'[16]

The picture that Edwards paints is a powerful one. We can only wonder when we consider how exalted Christ was, and how far down he came. Here is a purple passage on the unequalled humility of Christ, worth quoting at length:

> Yea, he was the most humble of all creatures. No angels nor men ever equaled him in humility though he was the highest of all creatures in dignity and honorableness. Christ would have been under the greatest temptations to pride if it had been possible that anything could have been a temptation to him. The temptation of the angels that fell was the dignity of their nature and the honorableness of their circumstances, but Christ was infinitely more honorable than they. The human nature of Christ was so honored as to be in the same person with the eternal Son of God, that was equal with God, and yet that human nature was not at all lifted up with pride. Nor was the man, Christ Jesus, at all lifted up with pride with all those wonderful works [such as] raising the dead. And though he knew that God had appointed him to be the king over heaven and earth, angels and men, as he says, Matt. 11:27, 'All things are delivered unto me [of my Father],' though he knew he was such an infinitely honorable person, and 'thought it not robbery [to be equal with God],' and though he knew he was the heir of God the Father's kingdom, yet such was his humility that he did not disdain to be abased and depressed down into lower and viler circumstances and sufferings than ever any other elect creature was; so that he became least of all and lowest of all. The proper trial and evidence of humility is stooping or complying with those acts or circumstances when called to it that are very low and contain great abasement. But none ever stooped

---

[16] *The "Miscellanies": 833-1152*, ed. by Amy Plantinga Pauw, in *The Works of Jonathan Edwards* (New Haven and London: Yale University Press, 2002), No. 941, 20:199 (Hickman ed. [Edinburgh: Banner of Truth, 1974], 2:606-7).

so low as Christ, if we consider either the infinite height that he stooped from, or the great depth to which he stooped. Such was his humility, that though he knew his infinite worthiness of honor, and of being honored ten thousand times as much as the highest prince on earth, or angel in heaven, yet he did not think it too much when called to it to be bound as a cursed malefactor, and to be the laughingstock and spitting stock of the vilest of men, and to be crowned with thorns and a mock robe and crucified like a slave and malefactor and one of the meanest and worst of vagabonds and miscreants, and a cursed enemy of God and men that was not fit to live on the earth, and that not for himself but for some of the meanest and vilest of creatures, some of those cursed wretches that crucified [him]. Was not this a wonderful manifestation of humility when he cheerfully and most freely complied with this abasement?[17]

When do we see this unparalleled humiliation? Here we come to a major theme for Edwards in the *History of the Work of Redemption*. He argues that the time of Christ's humiliation was not just the cross, but the whole of his incarnation up to the moment of his resurrection. There are some very striking and moving thoughts here. Edwards holds that Jesus was humiliated even before he could act responsibly. While an infant, he could not act intentionally with his human will, yet he was humiliated by the circumstances of his birth. By being laid in a manger he suffered as if he 'had been of the rank of the brute creatures'.[18] Edwards even suggests that there was a particular kind of humiliation for Jesus in living a private life for his first thirty years:

> Let us consider how great a degree of humiliation the glorious Son of God, the creator of heaven and earth, was subject to in this: that for about thirty years together he should live a private, obscure life among laboring men, and all this while to be overlooked, and not taken notice of in the world, as more than other common laborers. Christ's humiliation in some respects was greater in his private life than in the time of his public ministry.[19]

This is an expansive vision of the humiliation of Jesus. He bore humiliation

[17] *History*, 9:321-2 (Hickman, 1:577-8).
[18] *History*, 9:324 (Hickman, 1:578, but text missing in Hickman ed.).
[19] *History*, 9:325 (Hickman, 1:578).

for us not only at the end of his life, but at every stage of his existence as a man. It makes perfect sense when we begin where Edwards begins, with the infinite dignity of the eternal Son: even existing as a man without the glory of his resurrection was a humiliation for the Son of God.

First use: the paucity of our own love

What then is the 'use' or application of this understanding of the infinite love of Christ in his humiliation for us? The first use concerns our own love. Put simply, the more clearly we see the infinities of Christ, the more clearly we shall see what love we ought to have for him. A being who is infinitely glorious, who stooped down an infinite distance to redeem us, who loves God and his people with an infinite love, should be loved by us with an infinite love. Edwards speaks of this in his treatise on original sin. His aim there is to show how we cannot even live for a moment without falling short of what is required of us. Perhaps like me you find that the blinding effects of sin can be so great that you sometimes struggle to feel the gravity of the sins you commit. You sit down to confess and there may not be marked sins that stand out about which you feel a particularly strong conviction. Sometimes we wrongly think that we are not sinning, or at least we significantly underestimate the seriousness of our sins. Presumably this is why King David asked for forgiveness for sins that were unknown to him, for errors that he did not understand (*Psa.* 19:12). Edwards helps us here by showing the real nature of what is required of us. He explains how the requirement of infinite love arises from the infinite perfections of God:

> God is in himself worthy of infinitely greater love, than any creature can exercise towards him: he is worthy of love equal to his perfections, which are infinite: God loves himself with no greater love than he is worthy of, when he loves himself infinitely: but we can give God no more than we have.[20]

It is particularly the 'infinitely great and wonderful' grace of God in our salvation that demands an infinite love of us:

> How great is the gratitude, that would become us, who are the subjects of so many and great benefits, and have such grace towards

---

[20] *Original Sin*, ed. by Clyde A. Holbrook, in *The Works of Jonathan Edwards* (New Haven: Yale University Press, 1970; repr. 1997), 3:141 (Hickman, 2:155).

poor sinful lost mankind set before us in so affecting a manner, as in the extreme sufferings of the Son of God, being carried through those pains by a love stronger than death, a love that conquered those mighty agonies, a love whose length and breadth and depth and height passes knowledge? But oh, what poor returns! How little the gratitude! How low, how cold and inconstant the affection in the best, compared with the obligation![21]

The infinite perfections and grace of God require us to love him completely: 'all that belongs to, or is comprehended within the utmost extent or capacity of our heart and soul, and mind and strength, is required.'[22] Every inch of us must be devoted, without any reservation, to loving God.

Think with Edwards for a moment. Compare your love for Christ with his love for you. The very comparison is ridiculous. Think of measuring his love and your love. Mathematically, it is apparently impossible to compare a finite thing with an infinity. Imagine trying: here is an infinite series of numbers starting from 1. Here is a finite series of ten numbers, from 1 to 10. Now take a measure and attach it to the *start* of each series. You may measure to the end of the line of ten numbers, but you can never even find the end of the infinite series to take a measure to see how great the difference is. Pile up the thoughts, words, and deeds in which your love for God is expressed. Lay them on top of one another. They are measurable, measurably small. Compare that small, wobbling pile with the immeasurable towering love of Christ seen in his thoughts, words, and deeds. There is no way of even beginning the comparison. The towering love of Christ requires of us an infinite love. And yet we see here the poverty of our love for him. Here is the first use of considering the infinite love of Christ: to expose, by the impossibility of the comparison, the paucity of our love for him.

Second use: showing why self-righteousness is ridiculous

The second use, one which Edwards himself draws out in the *History of the Work of Redemption*, is to see from the work of Christ how ridiculous self-righteousness is. The context in which he makes this application is important. By this point in the sermon series Edwards is on his seventeenth sermon. He has covered the definition of redemption; he has

[21] *Original Sin*, 3:142-3 (Hickman, 2:155).
[22] *Original Sin*, 3:141 (Hickman, 2:155, but text missing in Hickman ed.).

outlined the redeeming work of God from the fall through to the incarnation, and he has detailed the preparation for the coming of Christ. We have read of Abraham, Moses, and David; we have had a thorough account of the history of God's people. In fact by now there have been in the Yale edition of the text some 170 pages spent outlining the history of the work of redemption up to the incarnation. There have been another fifty pages on the atoning work of Christ himself in his humiliation. Edwards has described the labour of Christ to purchase his people, from his birth to his grave. This context of 220 pages is important because by now we have a clear impression of the sheer extent of the work of redemption, both in the preparation and in the incarnation itself. This lengthy account sets up the application which Edwards now makes. He points out that what we are saying when we are self-righteous is that we can undertake and accomplish this whole work of redemption by and for ourselves. If I trust in myself, I take it upon myself to accomplish this work. What I say when I trust in my own righteousness is that I can redeem myself. I say that I can do what God has done through this whole period of time from the fall up to the resurrection of Christ.

This, Edwards tells us, is a common delusion. The way he preaches suggests that he is addressing non-Christians, but this is a sin with which Christians continue to struggle. We too can take Edwards's words here and use them to expose the sinfulness of our sin. Edwards explains that it is 'a common thing with men to take it upon themselves to purchase salvation for themselves, and so to do that great work that Christ came into the world to do.'[23] He then presses home the folly of putting ourselves in the place of Christ:

> You take upon you to do the work of the great savior of the world. How great a thing that is that you take upon you. You trust in your own doings to appease God for your sins, and to incline the heart of God to you. Though you are poor, worthless, vile, polluted worms of the dust, yet so arrogant are you that you take upon you that very work; that very work that the only begotten Son of God did when upon earth, and that he became man to capacitate himself for, and in order to which God spent four thousand years in all the great dispensations of his providence in the government of the world through all that time, aiming chiefly at this, to make

---

[23] *History*, 9:334 (Hickman, 1:380).

way for Christ's coming to do this work. This is the work that you take upon yourself, and foolishly think yourself sufficient as if you were big enough for it, and as though your prayers and other performances were excellent enough for this purpose. Consider how vain is the thought you entertain of yourself. How must such arrogance appear in the sight of Christ, whom it cost so much to make a purchase of salvation, when it was not [to] be obtained even by him, though so great and glorious a person, at a cheaper rate than his wading through a sea of blood and passing through the midst of the furnace of God's wrath. And how vain must your arrogance appear in the sight of God when he sees you imagining yourself righteous enough, and your worthless, polluted performances excellent enough, for the accomplishing that work of his own Son, to prepare the way for which he was employed in ordering all the great affairs of the world for so many ages![24]

The challenge strikes home: when we are self-righteous, we make ourselves the Christ. We put ourselves in the place of that infinite being who stooped down from an infinite height and loved with an infinite love. We are mad enough to say in effect: 'We can do it! We can do what he did!'

Yet we are worse than that. We do not only make ourselves the Christ; we also make the work of Christ and God vain:

If you can do this by your prayers, Christ might have spared his pains; he might have spared his blood, he might have kept within the bosom of his Father without coming down into this evil world to be despised and reproached and persecuted to death. And God need not to have busied himself as he did for four thousand years together, causing so many changes in the state of the world all that while, in order to be bringing that about that you, as little as you are, can accomplish in a few days only, with the trouble of a few sighs, and groans, and prayers, and some other religious performances. Consider with yourself what greater folly could you have devised to have charged upon God than this, to do all those things before and after Christ came into the world so needlessly, when instead of all this he might only have called you forth and committed the business to you which you think you can do so easily.[25]

---

[24] *History*, 9:334-5 (Hickman, 1:580).
[25] *History*, 9:336 (Hickman, 1:580-1).

What does self-righteousness therefore say? It says that Christ and God are guilty of the greatest folly:

> Their self-righteousness does, in effect, charge Christ's offering up himself in these sufferings as the greatest instance of folly that ever men or angels saw, instead of being the most glorious display of divine wisdom and grace that ever was seen. Yea, self-righteousness makes all that Christ did through the whole course of his life, and all that he said and suffered for through that whole time, and his incarnation itself, and not only so, but all that God had been doing in the great dispensations of his providence from the beginning of the world to that time, as all nothing but a scene of the most wild, and extreme, and transcendent folly.[26]

Edwards presses the same point by arguing that claiming redemption for ourselves is even more arrogant than claiming that we could create the world by ourselves. Redemption is a greater work of God than creation, since creation involves no humiliation for God. If redemption is greater, then picture the folly of claiming even the lesser ability, the ability to create the world:

> To take on yourself to work out redemption is a greater thing than if you took it upon you to create a world. Consider with your-self what a figure you, a poor worm, would make if you should seriously go about to create such a world as God did, and should swell in your own conceit of yourself, and deck yourself with maj-esty, and should pretend to speak the word of power and call an universe out of nothing, intending to go on in order and say, 'Let there be light . . . [Let there be a firmament . . . Let the waters . . . be gathered together.]'
>
> But then consider that in attempting to work out redemption yourself, you attempt a greater thing than this, and are serious in it, and won't be beat off from it; but strive in it, and are full of the thought of yourself that you are sufficient for it, and always big with hopes of accomplishing of it.[27]

It is a telling spectacle. Picture yourself standing in the room you are in now as you read. You draw yourself up. You screw up your eyes in

---

[26] *History*, 9:337 (Hickman, 1:581).
[27] *History*, 9:336-7 (Hickman, 1:581).

concentration. You focus all of your will. And you speak the words, loudly, with authority, commanding the world to be: 'Let there be light.' We know what will not happen next. The picture is ridiculous. Would you do it? Of course you would not, because it is so obviously foolish. Edwards is saying that when we trust in our own righteousness, we are even more foolish than that. It may be more subtly done, it may happen silently in the heart; but when we trust in ourselves for our redemption, we are more stupid than any man who would stand before us and attempt to create a world.

Doctrine: the mind of Christ in his death

As you may have found, Edwards effectively exposes our conceits. His analysis of our lovelessness and pride is searching and disconcerting. Despite his reputation, however, he is not primarily a preacher of sin and condemnation. Edwards preached that sinners are in the hands of an angry God to point them to the mercy of that same God. We will look now at some of the doctrine of the cross from which he draws the comfort of the gospel.

In one of his *Miscellanies*, Edwards considers what Jesus saw in his mind as he suffered. Here we are touching holy things: there is a particular weightiness in considering what was going on in the mind of Christ as he suffered for us. Should we even do it? We will be in a better position to return to this question when we have seen exactly what Edwards teaches. He holds that for the Christ to be our mediator, for him to be our substitute, he actually needed to think certain thoughts as he suffered. More precisely, he needed to have in the view of his mind certain ideas. Edwards does not mean by 'idea' here something vague and speculative. For Edwards, 'idea' is a technical term describing the mental vision of a real thing. An idea is the perception of something real in our understanding. It need not of course be literally a picture, but it must be a clear *sense* of something. For example, I have no literal picture of my wife's love, but it is nonetheless something of which I have a clear 'idea'.

Edwards believes that Christ bore the punishment for sinners as he died, the punishment that they would have borne in hell. But he thinks that what Christ knew in his mind as he suffered was in one important sense different from what the lost suffer in hell. He explains that Christ had no sense of being personally hated by God. He knew, even as he suffered God's wrath against our sins, that his Father loved him as his only Son. This is how he puts it:

Christ suffered the wrath of God for men's sins in such a way as he was capable of, being an infinitely holy person who knew that God was not angry with him personally, knew that God did not hate him, but infinitely loved him. The wicked in hell will suffer the wrath [of God], as they will have the sense and knowledge and sight of God's infinite displeasure towards them and hatred of them; but this was impossible in Jesus Christ.[28]

Does Edwards go too far in speaking of God's hatred for sinners? He goes no further than Psalm 5:5: 'you hate all evildoers'. God does love sinners, but he also hates them, despite the popular saying that God 'hates the sin but loves the sinner'. Thus, unlike the lost, Jesus knew that he was loved and not hated. This does not contradict the view that Jesus bore God's wrath; it simply means that he viewed the wrath differently in his understanding.

Edwards strongly affirms that Jesus bore both sin and the effects of God's wrath against it. More than that, he adds that Jesus also had a clear sight of the hatefulness of sin and the wrath of God against it in his mind as he died. In other words, he did not just bear sin, he saw sin clearly as he bore it. He did not just bear wrath, he saw wrath clearly as he bore it. Edwards argues that this perception of sin and wrath was necessary for atonement to be made. It was only if he perceived sin and wrath clearly that Jesus could take them upon himself voluntarily (as he said he did in *John* 10:17, 18). If I am to do something voluntarily, then I must know exactly what I am doing. Imagine that we are on a walk and I undertake to carry your backpack up a mountain. To undertake the task voluntarily, I need to know about the backpack. If you decide to add rocks to the backpack as we go without telling me, then I might justly say that I have not undertaken to carry *this* backpack. To act voluntarily, I must make an undertaking with a clear sight of the task. Edwards argues that Christ must have known what he was doing in his death as he did it. Otherwise, Christ 'acted blindfold in giving so much'.[29] The sight of the hatefulness of sin and the weight of God's wrath needed to fill the mind of the Christ.

This is how Edwards explains the sense of being forsaken that Jesus expressed when he cried out the first verse of Psalm 22 from the cross. The Psalm is telling us something about what he saw in his mind's eye:

[28] *Miscellanies*, No. 1005, 20:329 (Hickman, 2:574).
[29] *Miscellanies*, No. 1005, 20:330 (Hickman, 2:574).

> Though Christ knew the love of God to him, and knew that he should be successful in those sufferings, yet when God forsook him, those dismal views, those gloomy ideas, so fixed and swallowed up his mind that, though he had the habitual knowledge of these, yet he could have comparatively but little comfort and support from them, for they could afford support no further than they were attended to, or were in actual view.[30]

Edwards is attempting to take measure here of the idea of Christ's forsakenness. Rather than thinking of the Trinity being ruptured (a modern theological absurdity), he thinks of Christ having his mind filled with what was being laid upon him. This explains how Christ voluntarily bore our sins and the wrath of God against them: he saw and understood the magnitude of what he was doing.

Doctrine: the love of Christ

We might well wonder how it was possible for Christ to endure if his mind was filled with such sight. Edwards has a wonderful explanation. Quite simply, the more he saw of sin and wrath, the more Christ resolved to obey because of his love. First and foremost, this was his love for the Father. The more he saw of the odiousness of sin, the more he willed to obey his Father rather than to fall into sin himself:

> The more lively his idea of the hatefulness and dreadfulness of sin was, which consists in disobedience to God, the more did it engage him not to disobey himself, in neglecting to obey that great command he had received of his Father, viz. that he should drink this cup and go through those sufferings.[31]

This is no speculation. Scripture teaches that the cross was the highest form of obedience: 'he humbled himself by becoming obedient to the point of death, even death on a cross' (*Phil.* 2:8). The Son was engaged in the most costly act of obedience ever, under the greatest weight of sin ever.

The love that sustained Christ was not only love for his Father. It was also love for his people. The clearer his sight of sin, the greater was Christ's desire to remove it from us. He knew the horror of sin and so willed to remove it from his people:

---

[30] *Miscellanies*, No. 1005, 20:331 (Hickman, 2:575).
[31] *Miscellanies*, No. 1005, 20:332 (Hickman, 2:575).

The more he had a sense what an odious and dreadful thing sin was, the more would his heart be engaged to do and suffer what was necessary to take away this odious, dreadful thing from those that his heart was united to in love, viz. those that the Father had given him.[32]

Christ saw not only the odiousness of sin, but also the wrath of God against it. As he saw God's wrath, so he longed to deliver us from it. His love and pity for his people 'engaged him to suffer for them, to deliver them from their deserved punishment that he had an idea of'.[33] Surely the more we would see of the wrath of God the more we would shrink from it. Not so with Christ. The more he saw of it, the more he willed to bear it for his people in their place. The clearer his sight of the wrath of God, the more his love for his people grew. Amazingly, therefore, the clear sight of sin and wrath in his mind actually furthered his resolve to suffer for us: 'hence we may see how the same things, the same ideas that distressed the soul of Christ, and brought his amazing sufferings, engaged him to go through them.'[34] Even as he tasted the bitterness of the cup by seeing the terrible sight clearly, so 'the tasting of that bitterness was the thing that engaged [him] to go on to drink up the cup'.[35] Here is the greatness of Christ's love: that he saw clearly what would come upon him, and yet he resolved to bear it.

Use: comfort in the love of Christ

Edwards has already shown us the smallness of our love when measured against the infinite love of Christ. Now he brings us the comfort of that same love of Christ. In the very love of God that demands our love we find the forgiveness for our lack of love. It is the infinite love of God which demands our love, and it is the infinite love of God which forgives our lack of love. Revisit the picture of your love and the love of Christ. See the small, low, tottering pile of your love. But then behold the immeasurable height of the love of Christ, an infinite tower stretching up with no end. And now meditate not on the smallness of your love, but on the greatness of the towering love of Christ that provides for you what you lack.

[32] *Miscellanies*, No. 1005, 20:332 (Hickman, 2:575).
[33] *Miscellanies*, No. 1005, 20:332 (Hickman, 2:575).
[34] *Miscellanies*, No. 1005, 20:332 (Hickman, 2:575).
[35] *Miscellanies*, No. 1005, 20:332 (Hickman, 2:575).

See it now not so that you can be brought low, but so that you can be lifted up, as you grasp afresh that this is his love for you that washes away the inadequacy of your own love and takes its place. This is the love that cleanses your conscience as it surrounds, consumes, and exhausts your sin. This is the flawless love for God that is substituted for your own lack of love for God. It is here, in this infinitely excellent love, that we find our rest. Let us say with Sarah Edwards: 'My God lives; and he has my heart. I am given to God; and there I am, and love to be.'

5

THE GRACE OF GOD:
AUGUSTINE OF HIPPO (354-430)

Augustine's context

By the year 300 A.D. the Christian church had grown at a phenomenal rate from the 120 recorded in Acts 1:15 to around five million Christians, out of a population of sixty million in the Empire. Humanly speaking, this happened largely through personal evangelism by ordinary Christians. During these first three centuries, the church engaged in reflection on many theological topics, with a particularly strong focus on the doctrine of the incarnation and the doctrine of the Trinity. This theological work was driven by the study of Scripture and the need to clarify the church's teaching in resisting wrong views of God and Christ. For much of its history up to 312, the church lived in a hostile environment. Some of the pagan Roman emperors left the Christians of the Empire alone, perhaps more than we ordinarily think. But others, such as Nero, Decius, and Diocletian, persecuted them harshly. When persecution came it was caused primarily by the religious challenge of the gospel to the Empire. If Christianity spread in a town and some disaster occurred, the Roman mind felt that the trouble was a sign of the anger of the gods at being displaced. For many inhabitants of the Empire, Christianity was a form of atheism, a denial of the true gods, and needed to be eradicated for the public good. This was the case when the Great Persecution began under Diocletian around the turn of the fourth century. Roman priests claimed that they could not discern the future through their religious rites because there were Christians present profaning them. The persecution that ensued was the worst the church had experienced.

In October 312 the unthinkable happened: the Emperor Constantine was converted. The next day he secured control of the western half of the Empire at the Battle of Milvian Bridge, and in 324 he gained control of the East as well. This extraordinary turn of events meant that Augustine of Hippo was born in an Empire Christianized by Constantine and his heirs. A last attempt at the re-paganization had been made by Julian the Apostate just after Augustine's birth, but his successors had undone it. By the time of Augustine's ministry the Empire was under serious threat from outside forces. Hippo, the town where he was bishop, was surrounded by Vandals as he was dying in 430. Carthage fell in 439, Rome in 455, and the whole western Empire in 476. Augustine thus lived in a Christianized Empire in its final days.

Augustine's influence

Augustine's contribution and influence extends through the history of the church down to the present day. He had an immediate impact in developing distinctively Christian ethics and politics to replace the popular classical approaches. The nineteenth-century Presbyterian Benjamin Warfield commented that Augustine 'was in a true sense the creator of the Holy Roman Empire', the European empire that would eventually emerge after the fall of classical Rome.[1] Some of Augustine's thinking stands behind Roman Catholicism, for example on purgatory, baptismal regeneration, and the nature of the church. But much of it stands behind the Protestant Reformation of the sixteenth century. The Reformation was the restoration of scriptural doctrine and practice to the church, and the reformers traced much of their teaching to Augustine, especially their understanding of God's grace and the Lord's supper. Warfield summarized Augustine's influence by stating that 'the Reformation, inwardly considered, was just the ultimate triumph of Augustine's doctrine of grace over Augustine's doctrine of the Church'.[2] Augustine's life is a fascinating story

---

[1] *Studies in Tertullian and Augustine*, in *The Works of Benjamin B. Warfield*, ed. by Ethelbert D. Warfield, William Park Strong, and Caspar Wistar Hodge, 10 vols (Oxford: Oxford University Press, 1930; repr. Grand Rapids, MI: Baker Book House, 1991), 4:126.

[2] *Studies*, 4:130.

in itself, and one could happily spend an entire scholarly career wrestling with the five million words he wrote. Here we will focus on the moment of Augustine's conversion and what it tells us about his understanding of the grace of God.

Augustine's conversion

Augustine was born in 354 in Thagaste in what is now Algeria. His mother Monica was a Christian, but his father Patricius was a pagan until shortly before he died. Augustine himself soon strayed from his mother's faith. He attended university in Carthage (today part of Tunis), where he took a mistress to whom he was faithful for fifteen years. He then pursued a career as a teacher of rhetoric in Thagaste, Carthage, Rome, and Milan. He was intensely caught up in literary pursuits and his own advancement. As he later explains it, he turned away from God and in upon himself and other created things: 'My sin consisted in this, that I sought pleasure, sublimity, and truth not in God but in his creatures, in myself and other created beings. So it was that I plunged into miseries, confusions, and errors.'[3] He expresses vividly the introverted spiritual barrenness that resulted: 'I became to myself a region of destitution.'[4]

Like other prominent converts in the early church, Augustine tried a variety of ancient philosophies before finding God—as he prayed in one of his most famous sayings, 'you have made us for yourself, and our heart is restless until it rests in you'.[5] Indeed, he believed that his failure to find satisfaction elsewhere was a sign that God had not abandoned him: 'you were always with me, mercifully punishing me, touching with a bitter taste all my illicit pleasures'.[6] For many years Augustine was a Manichaean. The Manichaeans, named after their third-century founder Mani, believed in a fundamental dualism in the universe of light against dark. A spark of the light is trapped in man and needs to escape. It can escape by means of ascetic living, including vegetarianism. But Manichaeism did not satisfy Augustine's spiritual hunger. He remained 'a vast problem' to himself: 'I had become to myself a place of unhappiness in which I could not

---

[3] *Confessions*, trans. by Henry Chadwick (Oxford: Oxford University Press, 1992), pp. 22-3.
[4] *Confessions*, p. 34.
[5] *Confessions*, p. 3.
[6] *Confessions*, p. 25.

bear to be; but I could not escape from myself.'[7] By the time he arrived in Milan (384) his philosophy was reduced to a form of scepticism, an ancient phenomenon as much as a modern one. Full-blown scepticism at this time meant a real, thorough-going doubt that questioned even the possibility of knowledge itself. Augustine never went this far, but he did live in a 'fluctuating state of total suspense of judgement'.[8] It did not last long. In 386 he encountered and soon embraced many of the ideas of the Neo-Platonists, followers of another third-century figure, Plotinus. Neo-Platonism was based on the ideas of Plato himself, but it was a highly religious philosophy involving the pursuit of mystical experience and a return from plurality to the One. While he would leave behind many of its key tenets when he became a Christian, Augustine would continue to use such Neo-Platonist concepts as he found to be compatible with the teaching of Scripture. In the *Confessions*, for example, he describes his departure into sin using Neo-Platonist vocabulary: 'I turned from unity in you to be lost in multiplicity.'[9] And yet he also notes that while there were many common ideas, he did not find in Platonism anything of the incarnation, the cross, or the mediatory work of Christ.[10]

It was while in Milan that Augustine heard the sermons of Bishop Ambrose. These began to answer his criticisms of the Bible. Nonetheless, he remained convinced that he could never actually manage to live as a Christian. He was pulled in two directions, toward God, and toward the flesh: 'I was caught up to you by your beauty and quickly torn away from you by my weight. With a groan I crashed into inferior things. This weight was my sexual habit.'[11] This sense of spiritual and moral inability is key to understanding Augustine's early years and conversion, which he narrates in detail in the first nine books of the *Confessions*, all of which are set out as a prayer to God. It is, as one suspicious modern biographer describes it, 'a self-conscious and stylized performance', but there is no doubt that the account of his conversion communicates the depth of his spiritual experience.[12] Stylization is not fabrication. It is manifest from the way that

[7] *Confessions*, pp. 57, 60.
[8] *Confessions*, p. 89.
[9] *Confessions*, p. 24.
[10] *Confessions*, pp. 121-2, 219.
[11] *Confessions*, p. 127.
[12] James J. O'Donnell, *Augustine: A New Biography* (New York: HarperCollins, 2006), p. 7.

it gripped him that Augustine's theology grew out of his experience of God's grace; he did not invent that experience in retrospect. Those who think that the Augustine of the *Confessions* is a cunning fabrication reveal more about their own attitudes than they do about him. Rather than thinking that we know better than the man himself, we will follow what happened to him in his own words.

In Book 8 of the *Confessions* we find him with a friend called Alypius in July 386. They are visited by another man called Ponticianus. Ponticianus spots a copy of Paul's letter to the Romans and congratulates Augustine on reading it. Ponticianus is a Christian, and he tells Augustine the story of the Egyptian monk, Anthony. He recounts how two of his own friends were converted through reading the *Life of Anthony* by Athanasius. Augustine tells us that as Ponticianus spoke, his thoughts turned to himself. He describes how God moved him so that he could not avoid confronting his own condition:

> This was the story Ponticianus told. But while he was speaking, Lord, you turned my attention back to myself. You took me up from behind my own back where I had placed myself because I did not wish to observe myself (Ps. 21:12), and you set me before my face (Ps. 50:21)[13] so that I could see how vile I was, how twisted and filthy, covered in sores and ulcers. And I looked and was appalled, but there was no way of escaping from myself. If I tried to avert my gaze from myself, his story continued relentlessly, and you once again placed me in front of myself; you thrust me before my own eyes so that I should discover my iniquity and hate it. I had known it, but deceived myself, refused to admit it, and pushed it out of my mind.[14]

Here we see Augustine's deep awareness of his own sinfulness and his unwillingness to confront it. He wanted to hide from himself, to suppress his awareness of sin so that he would not have to deal with it. But the Lord would not let him go. He puts it vividly: 'the day had now come

---

[13] Augustine refers here (and elsewhere) to the Old Latin translation of the Bible; the Bible references given in brackets have been changed to refer to an English translation. Augustine's reliance on the Latin also explains why the verses he quotes do not always seem to fit his purpose.

[14] *Confessions*, pp. 144–5.

when I stood naked to myself".[15] In the end Augustine's inner turmoil manifested itself in an outburst to his friend Alypius, even with physical manifestations:

> In the middle of that grand struggle in my inner house, which I had vehemently stirred up with my soul in the intimate chamber of my heart, distressed not only in mind but in appearance, I turned on Alypius and cried out: 'What is wrong with us? What is this that you have heard? Uneducated people are rising up and capturing heaven (Matt. 11:12), and we with our high culture without any heart—see where we roll in the mud of flesh and blood. Is it because they are ahead of us that we are ashamed to follow? Do we feel no shame at making not even an attempt to follow?' That is the gist of what I said, and the heat of my passion took my attention away from him as he contemplated my condition in astonished silence. For I sounded very strange. My uttered words said less about the state of my mind than my forehead, cheeks, eyes, colour, and tone of voice.[16]

Augustine then went out to the garden of their lodging to be by himself, but the worried Alypius followed him. Augustine records that in the garden he experienced an acute sense of the paralysis of his will. He found that he could move himself physically but not spiritually. He saw his need, yet he could not turn himself. He reflects on his spiritual inability:

> The mind commands the body and is instantly obeyed. The mind commands itself and meets resistance. The mind commands the hand to move, and it is so easy that one hardly distinguishes the order from its execution. Yet mind is mind, and hand is body. The mind orders the mind to will. The recipient of the order is itself, yet it does not perform it. What causes this monstrosity and why does this happen?

Augustine reflects that he was in some sense divided against himself. To an extent he longed to serve God, yet he did not fully will to serve God, because if he willed it he would do it. So he was both willing and unwilling. Augustine locates his problem within himself, but he traces its origin to the first man Adam:

[15] *Confessions*, p. 145.
[16] *Confessions*, p. 146.

This was not a manifestation of the nature of an alien mind but the punishment suffered in my own mind. And so it was 'not I' that brought this about 'but sin which dwelt in me' (Rom. 7:17, 20), sin resulting from the punishment of a more freely chosen sin, because I was a son of Adam.[17]

Here we find the heart of Augustine's doctrine of sin. He holds that his sin is his own problem. The division of his will is not something forced on him from without, something alien; it is thoroughly his. Nonetheless, his condition does ultimately come from another, from the progenitor of the human race, Adam. When Adam was made he had no inner conflict of will. In that sense, God made Adam free. But Adam fell into sin, and the punishment for his sin came not only on him but also on all of his progeny, resulting in every son and daughter of Adam being born with a fallen, paralysed will. This was the will that Augustine felt in the garden. In his Adamic condition he was trapped by the flesh and its desires:

Vain trifles and the triviality of the empty-headed, my old loves, held me back. They tugged at the garment of my flesh and whispered: 'Are you getting rid of us?' And 'from this moment we shall never be with you again, not for ever and ever'. And 'from this moment this and that are forbidden to you for ever and ever.' What they were suggesting in what I have called 'this and that'— what they were suggesting, my God, may your mercy avert from the soul of your servant! What filth, what disgraceful things they were suggesting![18]

At this point Augustine, in a literary device, pictures Lady Continence, source of control but never barren, appearing to him and encouraging him to come to the Lord. Her voice countered the voice of the vain trifles and triviality. Crucially, she pointed Augustine outside of himself for the strength to change, for the gift of continence:

From that direction where I had set my face and towards which I was afraid to move, there appeared the dignified and chaste Lady Continence, serene and cheerful without coquetry, enticing me in an honourable manner to come and not to hesitate. To receive and embrace me she stretched out pious hands, filled with numerous

[17] *Confessions*, p. 149.
[18] *Confessions*, p. 151.

good examples for me to follow. There were large numbers of boys and girls, a multitude of all ages, young adults and grave widows and elderly virgins. In every one of them was Continence herself, in no sense barren but 'the fruitful mother of children' (Ps. 113:9), the joys born of you, Lord, her husband. And she smiled on me with a smile of encouragement as if to say: 'Are you incapable of doing what these men and women have done? Do you think them capable of achieving this by their own resources and not by the Lord their God? Their Lord gave me to them. Why are you relying on yourself, only to find yourself unreliable? Cast yourself upon him, do not be afraid. He will not withdraw himself so that you fall. Make the leap without anxiety; he will catch you and heal you.'[19]

We see here Augustine's strong emphasis on dependence on God's grace. Lady Continence told him to stop looking within himself to solve the problem of his conflicted will. She could only be found as a gift from God.

Despite the exhortation, Augustine found himself paralysed. Increasingly, however, the burden of sin was too great for him to remain in that condition. He describes how he had before his eyes a heap of misery. Aware that the misery was about to come out in the form of a flood of tears, Augustine moved away from Alypius; he comments that 'solitude seemed to me more appropriate for the business of weeping'.[20] He threw himself on the ground, still paralysed, still gripped by the past but crying out words like the Psalmist's question 'How long, O Lord?'. As he wept, Augustine heard the voice of children singing 'Pick up and read, pick up and read'. Unable to recall a children's game with such a song, he interpreted the words as a command from God to take up and read the words of Paul. This he did, alighting on Romans 13: 'Not in riots and drunken parties, not in eroticism and indecencies, not in strife and rivalry, but put on the Lord Jesus Christ and make no provision for the flesh in its lusts.'[21] Augustine describes the immediate effect of these words of God: 'I neither wished nor needed to read further. At once, with the last words of this sentence, it was as if a light of relief from all anxiety flooded into my heart. All the shadows of doubt were dispelled.'[22] Augustine was now a Christian. He

[19] *Confessions*, p. 151.
[20] *Confessions*, p. 152.
[21] *Confessions*, p. 153.
[22] *Confessions*, p. 153.

told his friend and his mother about what had happened. Monica rejoiced and praised God: 'She saw that you had granted her far more than she had long been praying for in her unhappy and tearful groans.'[23]

From life to theology

This is a moving description. As we read the words and picture the scenes we are watching a man come to the Lord Jesus Christ, from death to life, from slavery to freedom. The description is also deliberate and theologically formed. Augustine's narrative is a narrative with a purpose, designed to describe his experience and to teach the Bible's theology of sin and grace. Several points stand out.

One is the role of Adam. The first man is the key to explaining the fallen condition in which Augustine and all the sons of Adam find themselves. Adam's fall results in every one of his children being born in a state of slavery to sin, captive to the desires of a will turned in upon itself, hiding from God. Adam was not created with a fallen nature. He himself chose this condition for us as the head of our race. As Augustine puts it elsewhere, Adam's sin was 'the original sin by which God's covenant was first broken'.[24] For Augustine, the whole race sinned in Adam: 'By the evil will of that one man all sinned in him, since all were that one man, from whom, therefore, they individually derived original sin'.[25] Augustine himself was never exactly sure how we are connected to Adam. Did it simply rest on a divine decree, with Adam appointed as our representative in the covenant? Or were our souls somehow present in Adam when he sinned, though not yet the souls of separate individual persons? He never resolved this question, but he knew for sure the fact of Adam's headship of the race and action on our behalf. Somehow, we were in Adam. We sinned in Adam. We died in Adam. This much Augustine knew from Paul in Romans 5:12-21 and 1 Corinthians 15.

Second, Augustine knew from both Scripture and experience that Adam's fall has left us in a state where we sin *voluntarily* but *necessarily*. This

---

[23] *Confessions*, p. 153.

[24] *The City of God*, ed. by John O'Meara, trans. by Henry Bettenson (London: Penguin Books, 1984), xvi. 27, p. 689.

[25] *On Marriage and Concupiscence*, in *Augustine: Anti-Pelagian Writings*, ed. by Benjamin B. Warfield, trans. by Peter Holmes and Robert Ernest Wallis, Nicene and Post-Nicene Fathers: First Series, 5 (New York: Christian Literature Publishing Company, 1887; repr. Peabody, MA: Hendrickson, 1994), ii. 15, p. 288.

sounds to our ears like a contradiction: how can something that is voluntary be necessary? On closer scrutiny it makes perfect sense. We have a will
that wills things. Augustine did not believe that we sin against our will, as if
someone else forced us to sin against our wishes. When we sin we do so as
a result of a choice that we make, that we will. It is not as if we are strapped
into a metal suit and our bodies are manipulated by someone else who
forces us to sin. When we sin, we decide with our own wills to sin, and so
we sin *voluntarily*. The Latin word for 'will' is *'voluntas'* which gives us our
word 'voluntary', so a voluntary sin is literally one that is willed. In willing,
we act voluntarily. Being fallen creatures, this is what we will always do,
apart from the grace of God. We have no power to turn ourselves away
from sin. In this sense, we sin voluntarily, using our wills, but also *necessarily*,
because we can will nothing else. The necessity is not external to us and
against our will; it is internal to us, arising from our fallen will. For Augustine, then, we do make voluntary choices, but apart from God's grace our
choices will necessarily be to reject God. Emma Scrivener expresses this
understanding of the bondage of the will powerfully:

> For centuries, Christian thinkers have spoken of our will as being
> 'bound'. They don't mean that we're robots and can't do what we
> want. It's a deeper imprisonment than this. The bondage of the
> will means that we *only* do what we want. We follow our desires all
> the way to the basement—and then we lock the door. *That's* our
> slavery.[26]

When we do turn to Christ it is because the grace of God recreates
and moves our wills. We come then willingly, but we cannot come by
ourselves. It is the Lord Jesus Christ who sets us free from sin. Note the
verse which broke through Augustine's paralysis in the garden: it urges
Augustine to put on Jesus Christ himself, to turn from himself to Christ,
to abandon self-confidence and to find in Christ the strength he needs.
One of Augustine's favourite verses was 1 Corinthians 4:7: 'What do you
have that you did not receive?' Apart from Christ we are dead in sin, so
that even the initial turning of our will to God is a gift. Faith itself is a gift
rather than something that we produce from within ourselves. Believing
is not a matter of summoning up inner resources. There are no inner
resources; the dead cannot resurrect themselves. Faith is a gift received, the
reception itself moved by the Spirit.

[26] *A New Name: Grace and Healing for Anorexia* (Nottingham: Inter-Varsity
Press, 2012), p. 121.

Like Paul in Romans 9, Augustine knew that his position raised theological questions and objections, and he spent a great deal of effort defending it from the Scriptures and refuting alternatives. Augustine was not shy of the technicalities of doctrine, but as much as he teaches us a theological position in his writings, he also models for us a spiritual disposition before the word of God, a readiness to accept what is revealed despite the difficulties that our minds generate. He was aware, for example, that the idea of faith as a gift raises the question why God does not give the gift to all fallen people. Alert to the question, he insists that we ask instead why *any* fallen creatures are given faith:

> Why it is not given to all ought not to disturb the believer, who believes that from one all have gone into a condemnation, which undoubtedly is most righteous; so that even if none were delivered therefrom, there would be no just cause for finding fault with God.[27]

There is no obligation on God to save any. The gift of faith to God's chosen people, the elect, is utterly gracious: 'He saved them for nothing', that is, because of nothing in them that made them fit for salvation.[28]

Reflecting on sin and grace

Augustine's conversion and his accompanying theology of sin and grace leaves
 us with several points for reflection. We may ask first of all about our perception of our natural state apart from the grace of God. It is always tempting to ascribe our salvation, or at least some of our salvation, to ourselves. Do I harbour in a corner of my mind the secret conviction that the difference between me and a non-Christian is that I got it right, that I made the right response to an offer because I am somehow better? Or am I aware of my total helplessness, my spiritually dead condition apart from the grace of God, my dependence on him for the beginning, middle, and end of my Christian life? Is my praise for salvation rendered solely, wholly, and entirely to God? If we maintain that we have free will to turn ourselves to God, then *we* make the difference. Even if we say that grace is necessary as a help but that we choose under our own power not to resist it, then *we* are still the ones who make the decisive difference by choosing

---

[27] *On the Predestination of the Saints*, in *Anti-Pelagian Writings*, xvi, p. 506.
[28] *On the Predestination of the Saints*, in *Anti-Pelagian Writings*, xi, p. 504.

not to resist. On such a view the grace of God is offered in one way to all, and we are the ones who have responded rightly compared to others who made the wrong response. If this were the case then we would be the ones to be praised for our salvation, or at least to share the praise with God. This is the consequence of the position that opposes the doctrine of Augustine, known after its later proponent Jacobus Arminius as Arminianism. In actual fact I know no Arminians who really do praise themselves, but by the logic of their own position they ought. They are saved from self-praise by their inconsistency. Against such a position we should, with Augustine, recognize from Scripture and from our knowledge of ourselves that as children of Adam we are by nature spiritually dead. A sovereign act of resurrection by the Spirit of God is our only hope.

This recognition leads us to a deeper awareness of our total dependence on the grace of God for all that we have received. All we have, we have received. Our trust in the Lord Jesus is not something that *we* have whipped up within us. It is wholly a gift for which God alone is to be praised. This is a wonderfully liberating position that fosters deep confidence: if we depend on Christ then the measure of our strength is *his* strength rather than our own. And his strength is immeasurable. Our security is his security, and it is total. He is perfectly powerful to do what we cannot, to be our refuge. This is the good news of the gospel for the children of Adam to which Augustine's theology and life point us.

6

JUSTIFIED BEFORE GOD'S THRONE: JOHN CALVIN (1509-64)

Theological OCD?

Christians are often tempted to become impatient with the fine distinctions drawn by theologians and preachers. Surely, we find ourselves wondering, it is enough for someone to trust in Jesus. Preachers who are always going on about nice points of doctrine may look to us as if they have a theological variant of Obsessive Compulsive Disorder, like a man who polishes his shoes with weird frequency. Is there not something unhealthy in a pernickety concern for the minutiae of theological formulae? Do we really need all of the logic chopping? This unease about precision is only worsened by the fact that there are theologians who do indeed go too far in their concern for precision, constantly finding errors where there are none and jousting with imaginary enemies like some theological Don Quixote. The ugly side of the Reformed theological world, evident at a click of the internet, is real, and it thrives on an exaggerated doctrinal concern married to an indifference to the command to love our brothers and sisters. Nor do the problems stop with battles against imagined enemies. Even when we fight real opponents of the truth on central matters we can fall into worldly methods of fighting and ungodly attitudes of heart. Everything in the Reformed garden is not rosy.

When we come across examples of unwarranted theological precisionism and ungodly conduct the danger is that we react into the opposite extreme. This is often how the history of theology proceeds: one position is rejected as a new school of thought reacts against it by denying even its valid concerns, sending the church ricocheting from one extreme to another down the corridors of history. Anti-intellectual pietism replaces dry orthodoxy, only to be replaced again by dry orthodoxy, and so forth. Over-reaction into doctrinal indifference is as much to be avoided as hyper-critical heresy hunting. Neither should be our disposition. Instead, we should seek to discern those matters where theological exactness matters, and those where there is more permissible disagreement. I do not mean that areas of disagreement do not matter, but they are not areas on which we must fight to the death as if heaven and hell were at stake.

There are, however, theological areas where heaven and hell are at stake. One of them is the doctrine of justification, the doctrine that explains how as sinners we can be made righteous in the sight of our holy God. In this chapter we will explore some very subtle distinctions drawn by John Calvin in his teaching on justification, and more briefly a single distinction drawn by his successor Francis Turretin. The aim is to show why theological precision on this doctrine is so important, and to see in their conduct an example of godly theological controversy. Obviously neither man was sinless. For example, Calvin sometimes sinned by carrying his zeal into vehemence. He himself acknowledged that this was one of his weaknesses. As he approached death it seems to have been on his mind. He thanked the gathered Genevan senators for bearing with him:

> I also certainly acknowledge, that on another account also I am highly indebted to you, viz., your having borne patiently with my vehemence, which was sometimes carried to excess; my sins, in this respect, I trust, have been pardoned by God also.[1]

In many respects, however, Calvin was a model in the way that he conducted himself.

The texts

We will consider two texts written by Calvin in the heat of the Reformation conflict. The first is his *Reply to Sadoleto*. In 1538 a dispute with the Genevan authorities resulted in Calvin and his fellow-reformer Guillaume Farel being expelled from the city. This left Geneva, still in the very early stages of reform, without her best theologians. Then, in March 1539,

[1] Cited in Beza, *Life*, 1:xc.

Cardinal Jacopo Sadoleto wrote a letter to the Genevans exhorting them to return to the Roman fold. This was part of the first wave of the Counter-Reformation attempt to regain territories lost to Protestantism. Having no one to reply, Geneva sent the letter to Berne, where the chief minister forwarded it to Calvin at Strasbourg. Remarkably, Calvin wrote his *Reply*, a classic of Reformation literature, during just six days in mid-August.

The second text is Calvin's 1547 *Antidote* to the Council of Trent. The Council was the central Roman Catholic effort to define a doctrinal position against the reformers and to address, on paper at least, the abuses within the Roman church. In practical matters the Council was to some extent an expression of a desire for reform that had been inherent within the church prior to the Reformation. In that regard it may be thought of as a 'Catholic Reformation' council. In doctrine, however, its decisions were explicitly formed as responses to the Protestant positions (both genuine and caricatured). In that regard it was a 'Counter-Reformation' council. Trent met intermittently from 1545 to 1563, so Calvin's *Antidote* was only a reply to the first seven sessions. These sessions were the vital ones, since they expressed the church's position on two key Reformation issues, Scripture and justification. Calvin's text is a brisk polemical walk through the decrees and canons Trent produced, highlighting where they deviate from Scripture. The *Reply to Sadoleto* and the *Antidote* together allow us to see Calvin's precise doctrine and godly character in the heat of theological controversy.

Justification and the judgement seat of Christ

We start with Sadoleto's invitation. He focuses on two main areas, justification and the unity of the church. His concern is typical of the problems that Roman Catholics had with the Protestant doctrine. Like the great Humanist scholar Desiderius Erasmus before him, Sadoleto fears that the Protestant position will inevitably entail antinomianism, the rejection of the need for obedience to God's law. He anticipates that this licentiousness would in turn cause moral meltdown and political anarchy. To many the reign of the Anabaptist revolutionaries in Münster during 1534–35, with its murders, polygamy, and theft, was the logical result of the Protestant denial of the role of good works as the ground of justification. The magisterial reformers, who did not believe in such revolution and who advocated the authority of the civil magistrate, were nonetheless tarred with the same brush as the revolutionaries.

At the end of his work Sadoleto depicts two men appearing before the throne of Christ on the day of judgement:

> This is the place, dearest brethren, this the highway where the road breaks off in two directions, the one of which leads us to life, and the other to everlasting death. On this discrimination and choice, the salvation of every man's soul, the pledges of future life, are at stake—whether is our lot to be one of eternal felicity, or of infinite misery? What, then, shall we say? Let us here suppose two persons, one of each class, that is, from each road, let them be placed before the dread tribunal of the Sovereign Judge, and there let their case be examined and weighed, in order to ascertain whether a condemnatory or a saving sentence can justly be pronounced.[2]

The two men come before Christ. One is a faithful son of the Church. He explains that he simply followed what his parents taught him. He revered the Church, following what everyone far and wide around the world followed, the ancient way. He admits that there were abuses by prelates and ecclesiastics, but these were not sufficient to draw him away from the Church. The other man is one who dissents from the Church. This man's speech begins with the manner of the clergy. He explains that seeing their corruption led him to condemn the Church. He taught justification by faith alone because Christ had paid the penalty for sin. He held that 'we, trusting to this our faith in thee, might thereafter be able to do, with greater freedom, whatsoever we listed'.[3] Whatsoever we listed (that is, wanted): here is Sadoleto's reading of the Protestant doctrine as a licence for immorality. The atonement means we can do what we want. What would the Lord's judgement on these men be? Sadoleto insists that the one who followed the Church will be saved, while the libertine will be condemned for trusting his own ideas, for dishonouring the Church, and for living as he pleased. Like Sadoleto, the Council of Trent also identifies a judgement seat setting for the doctrine of justification, at least implicitly. The decree on justification is followed by a series of canons which pronounce eternal anathemas on various Protestant positions, both authentic and caricatured, showing that for Rome the doctrine is a heaven or hell issue.

---

[2] *Sadolet's Letter to the Senate and People of Geneva*, ed. and trans. by Henry Beveridge and Jules Bonnet, in *John Calvin: Tracts and Letters*, 7 vols (Edinburgh: Calvin Translation Society, 1851; repr. Edinburgh: Banner of Truth, 2009), 1:16.

[3] *Sadolet's Letter*, 1:18.

Here is the challenge that Calvin faces. Interestingly, in his *Reply to Sadoleto* he accepts the judgement day scenario that Sadoleto depicts. Sometimes it is right to refuse the terms of a debate, but here Calvin accepts them: 'Since, towards the end, a person has been introduced to plead our cause, and you have cited us as defenders to the tribunal of God, I have no hesitation in calling upon you there to meet me'.[4] Calvin warms to the terrible theme:

> Let us turn our ears to the clang of that trumpet which even the ashes of the dead shall hear in their tombs. Let us direct our thoughts and minds to that Judge who, by the mere brightness of his countenance, will disclose whatever lurks in darkness, lay open all the secrets of the human heart, and crush all the wicked by the mere breath of his mouth.[5]

In other words, Calvin agrees with Sadoleto that justification is a heaven or hell issue. Eternity is at stake. The doctrine of justification concerns how we can stand on the last day, how sinful men can endure the presence of a holy God. For Calvin, Sadoleto's answer is wrong, but the way he contextualizes the issue is exactly right.

Were Sadoleto and Calvin correct about the status of the doctrine of justification? Some would argue that the Apostle Paul does not mean by justification what Calvin and Sadoleto mean, and that it is possible to be saved without believing in justification by faith alone. As N. T. Wright puts it, 'we are not justified by faith by believing in justification by faith'.[6] In one sense this statement is true. Our justifying righteousness, according to both Paul and Calvin, is Christ. No doctrine, no set of words, justifies us. As we resist the idea of our good works justifying, so we must resist the idea that a doctrinal formula justifies, like a magical mantra that can open the door to everlasting life. We are not justified by the merit of a doctrine, but by the merit of Christ. Furthermore, someone can be justified who has no grasp of the complexities of the doctrine of justification by faith alone. If someone trusts in Christ and not himself for justification, then he is justified, regardless of his knowledge of the formulae in which this doctrine has been expressed. But Wright's statement might also be used

---

[4] *Reply by Calvin to Cardinal Sadolet's Letter*, in *Tracts and Letters*, 1:55.

[5] *Reply*, 1:56.

[6] 'New Perspectives on Paul', in *Justification in Perspective: Historical Developments and Contemporary Challenges*, ed. by Bruce L. McCormack (Grand Rapids, MI: Baker Academic; Edinburgh: Rutherford House, 2006), p. 261.

to reduce the doctrine of justification to second-order status in a way that is intended to bypass the Reformation division. This is wrong. We are not justified by the merit of a doctrinal formula, but actual faith in Christ is the instrumental cause of our justification. If I deny the doctrine and believe that my works justify me, then I remain under the wrath of God. This is not because I deny a mantra with my lips, but because in my heart I deny the sufficiency of Jesus and trust in my own holiness, a denial manifested in my words. So the doctrine itself does not justify, but it is only by having what it describes, trust in Christ, that I can be justified. This is why in Galatians Paul pronounces an anathema on any who preach another gospel. For this reason the doctrine of justification is emphatically first-order and Sadoleto and Calvin were right about its last-day context.

Calvin as courageous advocate

We come now to consider Calvin's first strength in his reply: he was a courageous advocate of the truth. We can already see the basis for his courage in Sadoleto's point about the judgement day. The heaven or hell context of the issue shows its seriousness and demands plain speech. Calvin explains his compulsion to Sadoleto:

> I am compelled, whether I will or not, to withstand you openly. For then only do pastors edify the Church, when, besides leading docile souls to Christ, placidly, as with the hand, they are also armed to repel the machinations of those who strive to impede the work of God.[7]

Calvin felt that he had to resist one who resisted the Lord and his saving purposes. He rejected the idea that the debate over justification was mere pedantry: 'Is this a knotty and useless question? Wherever the knowledge of it is taken away, the glory of Christ is extinguished, religion abolished, the Church destroyed, and the hope of salvation utterly overthrown.'[8] Calvin's perception of the seriousness of the issue sustained his courage in the Reformation. He felt the great day looming, and so he was bold. We too must remember the seriousness of this doctrine. We must cling to Christ alone, and we must be courageous advocates of the truth. It is when we remember the last-day context that we will do this.

Even as we seek to speak courageously, we must remember *how* we should speak. While Calvin writes plainly and strongly to Sadoleto, he also

[7] *Reply*, 1:29.
[8] *Reply*, 1:41.

explains that he has endeavoured to write carefully:

> There will doubtless be some things which will sting, or, it may be, speak daggers to your mind, but it will be my endeavour, *first*, not to allow any harsher expression to escape me than either the injustice of the accusations with which you have previously assailed me, or the necessity of the case may extort; and, *secondly*, not to allow any degree of harshness which may amount to intemperance or passion, or which may, by its appearance of petulance, give offence to ingenuous minds.[9]

Gentleness, we may recall, is a requirement of Christian pastors like Calvin. It is commanded of Timothy by Paul: 'Pursue righteousness, godliness, faith, love, steadfastness, gentleness' (*1 Tim.* 6:11). Peter similarly warns elders not to be domineering (*1 Pet.* 5:3). But gentleness is also a fruit of the Spirit to be borne by all Christians (*Gal.* 5:22, 23), even if we never find ourselves writing letters to cardinals. Let us be clear on this: gentleness is a requirement. Even heaven and hell issues require grace and gentleness. We are not free to fight for the right cause in the wrong way. If we do, we fight for the wrong cause. Are we secretly energized by argument and conflict rather than saddened by it? It may be necessary, but it must be with tears. I know that I for one have shed too few of them.

Calvin as careful analyst

Second, Calvin was a careful analyst. He needed to be, because the doctrine of justification requires careful articulation. Of course the gospel is simple, and in one sense justification by grace alone through faith alone is simple. A small child, even an unborn child, can lean on Christ for salvation (*Psa.* 22:9, 10). In a world of obedience the task of stating the doctrine would not be complicated because it would have no opponents throwing up clouds of dust around it. But it is complicated in this fallen world. Calvin knew that it was, and in the *Antidote* he explains how the complexity came about: 'The doctrine of man's Justification would be easily explained, did not the false opinions by which the minds of men are preoccupied, spread darkness over the clear light'.[10] Calvin saw that it is man's pride that complicates the doctrine. The doctrine itself is simple,

[9] *Reply*, 1:28.
[10] *Canons and Decrees of the Council of Trent, with the Antidote*, in *Tracts and Letters*, 3:108.

but we try to squirm around it because we do not want to let go of our own role in justification:

> The principal cause of obscurity, however, is, that we are with the greatest difficulty induced to leave the glory of righteousness entire to God alone. For we always desire to be somewhat, and such is our folly, we even think we are.[11]

There is the cause of complexity: our desire for glory, 'to be somewhat'. This desire means that we seek subtle ways of giving our works a role in our justification, and thus create the need for more subtle explanations of the doctrine in response. This is why Calvin traces Trent's position on justification back to Rome's commitment to some element of human free will remaining after the fall.[12] Trent teaches only a weakened and not a dead will, and uses this position as the base for securing 'somewhat' for us: after the fall some power remains for us to choose the good.

Calvin's point here is important for the history of doctrine generally. Error has frequently prompted a more refined definition of a doctrine. In response to a subtle distortion in false teaching it is necessary for the church to make careful distinctions to exclude the error. The doctrine of the Trinity is a good example of this. The New Testament itself had none of the technical apparatus of the later doctrine, none of the language of persons, essence, and relations. Why? Not because the doctrine did not exist, but because although errors were beginning within the New Testament era, they became more subtle later. The pressure to respond with more precision increased over time as the errors became more sophisticated. In the *Institutes* Calvin explains that this was why the new language of the Trinity mattered: 'If anyone, then, finds fault with the novelty of the words, does he not deserve to be judged as bearing the light of truth unworthily, since he is finding fault only with what renders the truth plain and clear?'[13] An essentially simple doctrine becomes complex in order to distinguish truth from error.

---

[11] *Antidote*, 3:108.

[12] See *Antidote*, 3:108–109.

[13] *Institutes of the Christian Religion*, ed. by John T. McNeill, trans. by Ford Lewis Battles, 2 vols, *The Library of Christian Classics*, 20-21 (Philadelphia: The Westminster Press, 1960), I. xiii. 3, 1:124.

Is 'justification by faith alone' enough?

We will consider two examples of Calvin's careful analysis, to which we will add a third from Turretin. Consider three statements:

- We are justified by faith alone.
- We are justified by union with Christ.
- We are justified by the imputation (that is, the reckoning) of Christ's merit to us.

Which of these statements is so uniquely Protestant that it could never honestly be professed by a Roman Catholic? The answer may surprise you. Here is Sadoleto explaining in his letter how we can receive eternal life 'by faith alone':

> We obtain this blessing of complete and perpetual salvation by faith alone in God and in Jesus Christ. When I say by faith alone, I do not mean, as those inventors of novelties do, a mere credulity and confidence in God, by which, to the seclusion of charity and the other duties of a Christian mind, I am persuaded that in the cross and blood of Christ all my faults are unknown; this, indeed, is necessary, and forms the first access which we have to God, but it is not enough. For we must also bring a mind full of piety towards Almighty God, and desirous of performing whatever is agreeable to him; in this, especially, the power of the Holy Spirit resides. This mind, though sometimes it proceeds not to external acts, is, however, inwardly prepared of itself for well-doing, and shows a prompt desire to obey God in all things, and this in us is the true habit of divine justice. For what else does this name of justice signify, or what other meaning and idea does it present to us, if regard is not had in it to good works?[14]

Sadoleto states plainly that he believes in salvation 'by faith alone', but he then goes on to say that our good works are our 'justice'. The Latin noun for 'justice' that Sadoleto uses here also denotes what we term 'righteousness', so when Sadoleto talks about the 'justice' in us he is talking about the righteousness that justifies us. He is saying that our justice, our justifying righteousness, is a desire to obey God, and good works themselves. Justifying righteousness takes the form in us of a disposition to obey and actual deeds of obedience. How can Sadoleto square this with justification

[14] *Sadolet's Letter*, 1:9.

'by faith alone'? He can do so because he defines 'faith' to include within it the desire to obey and do good works. Faith for Sadoleto is not only confidence in God, but also a desire for good works and the good works themselves. By contrast, while Calvin believes that faith and good works are inseparable, good works are not a part of faith. The faith that justifies is never alone, but faith justifies alone.

This example shows why the doctrine of justification requires careful articulation. The reformers begin with a simple statement that we are justified by faith alone, but Rome can agree with that statement by defining faith to include works. The simple definition, in this context, will no longer suffice. The reformers need now to distinguish between faith defined as trust in Christ, and faith defined as trust *plus* the desire for good works and the works themselves. The subtlety is required to exclude the error.

Is 'justification by union with Christ' enough?

Our second example of careful analysis concerns the role of union with Christ in justification. We saw in Chapter 3 with John Owen how important the idea of union with Christ is for showing that the atonement did not involve Jesus dying for people to whom he was unrelated. It was not a case of me being here and Christ being there and there being no connection between us. When God reckoned my sin to Christ he was not charging the wrong man, because Christ took my sins from me on the basis of our union, decreed in eternity and realized in history by the bond of the Spirit. For Calvin too, union with Christ is a central theme. Nothing I am about to say is intended to diminish the importance of union with Christ for his doctrine of justification. Nevertheless, despite the importance of union with Christ, the concept is not by itself enough to secure a distinctively Protestant doctrine of justification. Rome too can honestly say 'We are justified by union with Christ'. The Council of Trent's statement on justification is full of the language of union with Christ: the love of God 'inheres in' the justified; a Christian is 'ingrafted' in Christ; with faith and hope and love a man is united with Christ and becomes a 'living member of his body'.[15] Trent teaches that Christ is in the believer and the believer is in Christ. In fact, even within Calvin's own theology a simple affirmation of union with Christ would not be enough to mark the distinction between our once-off justification and our progressive

---

[15] Calvin quotes the full text of Trent; for these statements see *Antidote*, 3:96.

sanctification, since he himself believed that sanctification is also the fruit of union with Christ. Union with Christ stands behind justification and sanctification. This is the point of Calvin's famous sun illustration:

> It is not to be denied, however, that the two things, Justification and Sanctification, are constantly conjoined and cohere; but from this it is erroneously inferred that they are one and the same. For example:—The light of the sun, though never unaccompanied with heat, is not to be considered heat.[16]

In Calvin's own theology, therefore, we cannot stop with union when explaining justification. We must ask: union for justification or for sanctification?

This raises the question of the two different ways in which union works in justification and sanctification. In justification the righteousness of Christ is imputed to us, reckoned to us on the basis of our union with Christ. In sanctification it is infused into us or imparted to us and takes the form of our ongoing good works. Both imputation and impartation are aspects of our union with Christ, but the difference between them is everything. Calvin sees that we need to maintain the external, alien aspect of justification to show that the righteousness that justifies is found in Christ, and not in our good works, even good works done by the power of the Holy Spirit. One sentence from his commentary on Romans shows this well: 'we are *in Christ* because we are out of ourselves'.[17] The pairing of 'in Christ' and 'out of ourselves' relates union to an imputed rather than an infused righteousness. We need to maintain this emphasis on imputed righteousness to show that our justifying righteousness is not infused in works. Many writers have suggested that the idea of union with Christ suffices to secure what needs to be secured in the doctrine of justification. We can now see that this is not the case. If we isolate the concept of union with Christ then it will not be clear whether the union results in a justifying righteousness that is imputed or one that is imparted. Union by itself cannot make that distinction. The traditional coupling of union with imputation must be maintained to mark the distinction between the Protestant and Catholic positions.

[16] *Antidote*, 3:115–16.
[17] *Commentaries on the Epistle of Paul the Apostle to the Romans*, ed. and trans. by John Owen, in *Calvin's Commentaries*, 22 vols (Edinburgh: Calvin Translation Society, n.d.; repr. Grand Rapids, MI: Baker Book House, 1993), 19:136, commenting on 3:21.

Is 'justification by the imputed merit of Christ' enough?

We have seen that the doctrine of justification by faith alone rests on a precise definition of faith, and that we must add to the idea of union with Christ the distinction of imputation from infusion. Yet even this was not enough to maintain clarity on the biblical doctrine. Here we move about a hundred years after Calvin to Turretin. In his *Institutes of Elenctic Theology*, we find that by the end of the sixteenth century Rome was even able to affirm justification by imputation. This emerges in the words of the Jesuit theologian Gabriel Vázquez (1549–1604), words which will need some careful explanation:

> We grant there are imputed to us for a certain effect, not only those things that are in us, as sin, faith and righteousness, but also some things that are without us, as the merit and obedience of Christ, because not only the things that are in us, but also those without, in view of which something is given to us, are said to be reckoned among our things for some effect, as if they were truly ours.[18]

Surprisingly, Vázquez here affirms an imputation of the alien merit of Christ to the believer. How can this be? Is imputation not *the* Protestant distinctive?

The Council of Trent assigns a key place to the merit of Christ in justification. It teaches that the merit of Christ in his obedient death moved the Father to give the Holy Spirit to the believer. Righteousness is then infused into the believer so that he does good works in the power of the Spirit. The infused righteousness of Christ is thus found in the believer's good works. In chapter 16 of its decree on justification, Trent teaches that these works merit eternal life on the last day. Thus Trent maintains that the merit of Christ purchases the gift of the Spirit by whom the believer does the good works that merit his justification. This background helps to explain how Vázquez can affirm justification by the imputed righteousness of Christ. On his reading, Trent teaches a process of justification that involves some kind of imputation of Christ's merit to the believer. When God is moved by the merit of Christ to give the Spirit to the believer, that merit is in a sense 'reckoned to' the believer, or imputed to him. Christ merits, but God gives the reward to the believer: he is treating the believer as if Christ's merit were his. As Vázquez puts it, Christ's merit is imputed to the believer 'for a certain effect'.

[18] Cited by Turretin in *Institutes*, XVI. iii. 13, 2:649-50.

An illustration may help. Imagine that some quality in me moves someone to give something to you. Perhaps a friend is so grateful to me for some help I gave him in his DIY[19] project that he offers to pay for my family holiday. In an act of generosity, I ask if he would consider paying for your holiday instead, since you are struggling financially at the moment. Vázquez is saying that my DIY skill is being imputed to you for an effect, your holiday. It is not directly imputed to you so as to become yours (I am the one who has helped with the DIY), but it is counted in some sense as sufficiently yours to bring you some other benefit, the holiday. So with the merit of Christ: according to Vázquez it is not directly imputed to the believer, but it is reckoned to him for an effect, for the infusion of righteousness. The righteousness that justifies remains the infused right-eousness in the believer's good works, but Vázquez can speak of an act of imputation prior to it. He has managed to square a species of imputation with Trent's doctrine of justification by good works done in the power of the Spirit.

Vázquez has identified an act of imputation, but the problem is that it is not the imputation of a justifying righteousness that is found only in Christ. The infused merit that justifies is within the believer and his deeds. The believer may give thanks for the imputed merit, but he does not lean on it exclusively for his justification. The imputation does not suffice for justification, it serves to cause something else that suffices. Turretin high-lights the difference: 'To what is that imputation made? To justification and life, as we maintain; or only to the infusion of internal grace and inherent righteousness, as they hold?'[20] For Vázquez, Christ's obedience is never directly, immediately imputed. It is remote from the believer, meriting from the Father the Christian's Spirit-led obedience by which satisfac-tion for sin is made. Turretin helpfully calls this 'mediate satisfaction' and explains what is wrong with it:

> This mediate satisfaction is unheard-of in Scripture, which never says that Christ satisfied that he might acquire for us the power to satisfy, but by himself made expiation for sins, and thus reconciled us to God and freed us from the curse of the law, being made a curse for us.[21]

---

[19] i.e., Do-It-Yourself.
[20] *Institutes*, XVI. iii. 13, 2:650.
[21] *Institutes*, XVI. v. 11, 2:662.

We see here how Roman Catholic theologians can, without dissimulation, say that they believe in justification by the imputed righteousness of Christ. Their position requires that we ask whether the imputation is immediate or mediate: is it for justification itself, or is it for the effect of infusion, and thereby justification?

We now have our three examples of careful analysis before us. We have seen that justification by faith alone needs a definition of faith that distinguishes it from works. Calvin provides this. We have seen that union with Christ needs a distinction between imputed and infused righteousness. Calvin also provides this. And we have seen that imputed righteousness needs a distinction between immediate and mediate imputation. Turretin provides this.

A fight over words?

Perhaps as the argument has become more subtle you have been wondering if it is just pedantry, the concern of the theologically uptight who have nothing better to do and ought to get out more to the coal-face of Christian living in the world. Calvin did not think so. He himself took no delight in arguing about definitions, but he knew when it mattered: 'I would be unwilling to dispute about a word, did not the whole case depend upon it.'[22] Turretin also defended the need for the debate: 'we have not here a mere dispute about words (as some falsely imagine), but a controversy most real and indeed of the highest moment'. Like Sadoleto and Calvin, he takes us forward to the day of judgement to explain why:

> This appears more clearly when we come to the thing itself and the controversy is not carried on coldly and unfeelingly in scholastic cloud and dust (as if from a distance), but in wrestling and agony—when the conscience is placed before God and terrified by a sense of sin and of the divine justice, it seeks a way to stand in the judgment and to flee from the wrath to come. It is indeed easy in the shades of the schools to prattle much concerning the worth of inherent righteousness and of works to the justification of men; but when we come into the sight of God, it is necessary to leave such trifles because there the matter is conducted seriously and no ludicrous disputes about words (*logomachia*) are indulged.[23]

[22] *Antidote*, 3:115.
[23] *Institutes*, XVI. ii. 7, 2:639.

When we stand before God all talk of the justifying righteousness of good works will be silenced. That is why the careful distinctions matter, because they exclude in the present what will be excluded in the future. If they are not upheld, then the proclamation of Christ and his justifying righteousness is at best clouded, and at worst obscured entirely. And without the gospel, men, women, and children cannot be saved. If the distinctions are pedantic, it is the pedantry of heaven and hell.

Careful analysis and courageous advocacy

We urgently need both of Calvin's virtues, careful analysis and courageous advocacy. Careful analysis without courage is fruitless. It is very tempting to analyze carefully and then to keep quiet about the results for the sake of an easy life, but right understanding without action will never protect the church. We cannot identify error and then do nothing about it. My own experience has been that careful analysis is usually welcome whereas joining up the dots to courageous advocacy is not. There are some who are unduly belligerent, but many of us find the advocacy much harder than the analysis, perhaps increasingly as we mellow with age. Nevertheless, the health of the church requires that, when once we have carefully identified serious error, we courageously resist it.

If we are worried about the possibility of engaging in futile theological battles against imaginary enemies, then it is actually careful analysis that will guard us against it. The risk of misapplied theological zeal is a risk that demands rather than excludes careful doctrinal analysis. When unnecessary battles have been fought it has been because the analysis—if there has been any—has gone wrong, not because it has been done too carefully. We need careful doctrinal analysis to avoid misdiagnosing error. Wrong diagnosis can mean wrong treatment. In the context of the church when done by elders and pastors this can lead to church discipline wrongly carried out against the innocent. The red haze descends as we ride out into battle, slashing indiscriminately. The result is not pastoring of the sheep but butchery, not leadership but abuse.

But it would be naive for church members to think that this is only a temptation for their leaders. I have met more church members who have misdiagnosed minor issues as major ones than I have church leaders. To be accurate I have met more ex-church members, since their peculiar doctrinal obsessions have isolated them from any regular involvement in a fellowship of the Lord's people. Such courage based on poor analysis is a temptation for all Christians because it throws the fuel of apparent zeal on to the fire of pride. Between individual church members and amid families it can lead to painful and permanent sundering. And in the internet age it can even affect total strangers on the other side of the world as a sentence pronounced by a self-appointed cyber-judge goes viral. This is very serious: we find the hideous spectacle of one limb wielding the knife against another in the self-harming body of Christ. We can only begin to imagine what the loving head of the body thinks as he feels his own limbs tearing themselves apart. As people and pastors alike, will we be courageous advocates *and* careful analysts? Will we distinguish central doctrines from matters on which we may disagree and remain in fellowship? Will we stand for the biblical doctrine of justification with all necessary subtlety, but will we do so with tears of love like the good shepherd himself?

ON THE CHRISTIAN LIFE

7

LOVING GOD WITH ALL YOUR HEART: THE PURITAN PSYCHOLOGY

How do you feel?

What does it mean to love God with all your heart (*Matt.* 22:37)? Does it mean that our love for God should be something we feel? Preachers and pastors often tell us to be wary of our feelings. Unlike the facts on which our faith rests—the facts of the incarnation, death, and resurrection of Jesus Christ—our feelings come and go, often unpredictably. We are warned that if we live our Christian lives by our feelings, then our walk with the Lord will be unstable and we will be left spiritually vulnerable. This is surely good counsel, but I wonder if the fact that it is sometimes the only thing we are told about our feelings leaves us thinking that they are to be treated with nothing but suspicion, as if they are only capable of causing trouble. If that is what we are led to think then we will be spiritually vulnerable in a quite different way: not to the rise and fall of our emotions, but to a mistaken vision of the true Christian life as one of cold emotional detachment.

The Bible teaches that there is more to our feelings than trouble, and we find among the Puritans a rich vein of reflections on the place of religious affection in the Christian life. The Puritans do not mean by 'affection' exactly what we mean by 'feeling' or 'emotion' (as we will see in due course), but there is enough of an overlap for their understanding of the affections to provide us with a proper understanding of the place of religious feeling in the Christian life, and even to encourage us to think more about the deep affections than we do about superficial emotions.

Psychology? Puritan?

Please dismiss from your mind some of the connotations of the term 'psychology' as it is used today: rats, shrinks, and couches. I intend the term in its etymological sense: speaking about the human *psyche*, our life and soul. Our main Puritan conversation partners will be men we have met before, John Owen and Jonathan Edwards. Theirs was not the only religious psychology among the Puritans, but it was perhaps a dominant strand.

No one would question that Owen was a Puritan, but the use of the term for Edwards is disputed. There are some who argue that we cannot treat Edwards as a Puritan, at least on this topic, because it was here that he broke from the Puritan tradition. Perry Miller is one of the giants of scholarship on Edwards. He wrote a rightly renowned biography and contributed greatly to the revival of interest in Edwards, especially as editor of the definitive Yale University Press edition of his works. Miller was an exceptionally brilliant writer of English prose; reading his works reminds me of A. J. P. Taylor's comment about his fellow-historian Hugh Trevor-Roper: 'When I read one of Trevor-Roper's essays tears of envy stand in my eyes.'[1] For Miller, Edwards was an innovator in his account of the human person and the religious affections. Miller argues that the Puritans were trapped within a 'faculty psychology', a model that sharply divided the faculties of the human soul and viewed them as independently acting substances. Miller traces this model to the Greek philosopher Aristotle and the mediaeval theologian Thomas Aquinas. He maintains that it left the Puritans with a low estimate of the affections because they identified them as part of the animal aspect of human nature, the aspect concerned with sensual experiences. Edwards supposedly broke out of this Puritan model with a more integrated view of the human faculties and, as a result, a higher place for the affections.[2]

If Miller is right, then Edwards should not appear in a chapter on Puritan psychology. But for all the brilliance of his writing, Miller gets Edwards wrong in a number of important ways, and this is one of them. Rather than setting out arguments here to show you why we can rightly

---

[1] Cited in Adam Sisman, *Hugh Trevor-Roper: The Biography* (London: Weidenfeld & Nicolson, 2010), p. 466.

[2] See *Jonathan Edwards* (New York: Meridian Books, 1959), p. 251ff.

look to Edwards as a Puritan psychologist, I will, as we proceed, introduce evidence from Owen to show that Edwards stood in a long line of
Puritan thinking on the affections. When you read that evidence, you are
seeing why Miller is wrong about Edwards and why Edwards can rightly
be classed as a Puritan on this issue. I do not mean to imply that there is
nothing new in Edwards on the affections, but the novelty is more the
novelty of refinement than revolution, as Brad Walton argues:

> It is arguably the special accomplishment of Edwards that he
> organized, for the first time since Augustine, Bernard, William
> of St. Thierry and William Ames, and in a manner perhaps more
> exhaustive than any of them, a systematization of traditional heart-
> language into a thorough, clearly defined and fairly coherent
> analysis of religious interiority.[3]

There is a new level of organisation in Edwards, but it is the organisation
of an existing tradition.

I should also note at the outset that we will not be going into detail
on what is actually the burden of the second and third parts of Edwards'
great work, the *Treatise Concerning the Religious Affections*. In those parts
he explores the criteria for discerning genuine religion. He relentlessly
argues that the only true proof of genuine affections is persevering, filial
obedience to God. He uses the purging of Achan and his family from the
Israelite camp in Joshua 7 to illustrate how we need to put sin to death in
order to obtain assurance:

> The accursed thing is to be destroyed from their camp, and Achan to
> be slain; and till this be done they will be in trouble. 'Tis not God's
> design that men should obtain assurance in any other way, than by
> mortifying corruption, and increasing in grace, and obtaining the
> lively exercises of it.

Thus, he concludes, the Christian finds assurance not so much in thinking
as in doing: 'Assurance is not to be obtained so much by self-examination,
as by action.'[4] While Edwards concedes the possibility of early assurance

---

[3] *Jonathan Edwards, 'Religious Affections' and the Puritan Analysis of True Piety,
Spiritual Sensation and Heart Religion, Studies in American Religion*, 74 (Lewiston, NY:
Edwin Mellen, 2002), p. 181.

[4] *Religious Affections*, ed. by John E. Smith, in *The Works of Jonathan Edwards*
(New Haven: Yale University Press, 1959), p. 195. (Hickman ed. [Edinburgh: Banner of Truth, 1974], 1:263).

given by God, his emphasis is elsewhere:

> I think it to be abundantly manifest, that Christian practice is
> the most proper evidence of the gracious sincerity of professors,
> to themselves and others; and the chief of all the marks of grace,
> the sign of signs, and evidence of evidences, that which seals and
> crowns all other signs.[5]

The Bible certainly teaches that obedience brings assurance, but I think
Edwards underestimates the role of immediate assurance by the application of the promises of God to the heart in the power of the Holy Spirit.
I register the disagreement, but this will not be our concern here. We are
interested in the Puritan psychology of religious affection, not the Puritan
doctrine (or perhaps doctrines) of assurance.

A shared concern

Edwards ministered and wrote in a different land and a different century
from Owen, but they faced similar pressures. Remembering the similar
challenges they faced will help us understand them, and it will also be
useful as we seek to apply their thinking to our own times. Edwards was
concerned to defend the religious revival of the Great Awakening against
both criticism from outside and excess from within. The criticism came
from rationalists who dismissed the revival as a lot of heat without light.
Chief among them was Charles Chauncey, minister of First Church,
Boston. Against Chauncey, Edwards insisted that the revival was a genuine work of the Holy Spirit. To do this he defended the movement as a
whole by analysing the experience of the individual. This approach made
good sense: for the Awakening to be genuine, the experience of people
within it had to be genuine. As Ava Chamberlain explains, the inquiry
'was transferred from the microcosm of personal experience to the mac-
rocosm of God's action in history as the colonists attempted to answer
the "grand Question" concerning the awakening'.[6] On the other hand,
Edwards needed to show why he was not simply accepting all the excesses
of the revival advocated by a man like James Davenport, and how he could
account for the many instances of shallow professions of faith that had
not proved genuine. Hence he sought to set out strict biblical criteria that
would distinguish true religious affections.

[5] *Affections*, p. 443 (Hickman, 1:331).
[6] 'Self-Deception as a Theological Problem in Jonathan Edwards's "Treatise
Concerning Religious Affections"', *Church History*, 63 (1994), p. 545.

Owen too had faced the challenge of defending against both rationalism and excessive 'enthusiasm' (as it was called). His opponents denied the regenerative work of the Spirit and any claim to have experienced it:

> This whole doctrine, with all the declarations and applications of it, is now, by some among ourselves, derided and exposed to scorn, although it be known to have been the constant doctrine of the most learned prelates of the church of England. And as the doctrine is exploded, so all experience of the work itself in the souls of men is decried as fanatical and enthusiastical.[7]

Faced with a choice between excess and sterility, Owen knew which he would choose:

> I had rather be among them who, in the actings of their love and affection unto Christ, do fall into some irregularities and excesses in the manner of expressing it (provided their worship of him be neither superstitious nor idolatrous), than among those who, professing themselves to be Christians, do almost disavow their having any thoughts of or affection unto the person of Christ. But there is no need that we should foolishly run into either of these extremes. God hath in the Scripture sufficiently provided against them both. He hath both showed us the necessity of our diligent acting of faith and love on the person of Christ, and hath limited out the way and means whereby we may so do.[8]

With this understanding of the pressures that Owen and Edwards faced, we will now explore a synthesis of some of the most significant points that we find in their Puritan psychology of the religious affections.

The believer's love rests on God's prior love

We begin with Owen, who begins with the triune God himself. In his work *Christologia* Owen makes the profoundly important point that love has its origin within the Godhead:

> No small part of the eternal blessedness of the holy God consisteth in the mutual love of the Father and the Son, by the Spirit. As he is

[7] *A Discourse Concerning the Holy Spirit*, in *The Works of John Owen*, ed. by William H. Goold, 16 vols (Edinburgh: Banner of Truth, 1965-68), iii. 6, 3:366.

[8] ΦΡΟΝΗΜΑ ΤΟΥ ΠΝΕΥΜΑΤΟΣ: *Or, the Grace and Duty of Being Spiritually Minded*, in *Works of John Owen*, i. 7, 7:346.

the only-begotten of the Father, he is the first, necessary, adequate, complete object of the whole love of the Father.[9]

How then does love come to us from God? Owen finds his answer in John 17:26 where Jesus asks the Father 'that the love with which you have loved me may be in them'. Owen explains:

> The love of the body is derived unto it from the love unto the Head; and in the love of him does God love the whole church, and no otherwise. He loves none but as united unto him, and participant of his nature.[10]

The intratrinitarian love is thus the source of God's love for the church because Christ is the head of the church. As the Father loves Christ the head, so his love embraces Christ's body the church. The love passes from the Father through the Son to his people. We are caught up in the Father's love for the Son.

God is therefore not only the one we love: he is first the one from whom love comes. He is the source and goal of all love. As Owen puts it, 'all *spiritual things do proceed from and are resolved into an infinite Fountain of goodness'*.[11] Love flows from God and returns to him. The very reason for creation was the expression of God's triune love:

> For God's love of himself—which is natural and necessary unto the Divine Being—consists in the mutual complacency of the Father and the Son by the Spirit. And it was to express himself, that God made any thing without himself.[12]

Here we see the roots of our love in the eternal, prior, initiating love of God.

The centrality of love and affection to the Christian life

With this connection to the doctrine of God in place, we can see why for Owen, and for Edwards, love is so important. Owen gives it a preeminent place in the soul: 'Love is the most ruling and prevalent affection in the

---

[9] ΧΡΙΣΤΟΛΟΓΙΑ: *Or, A Declaration of the Glorious Mystery of the Person of Christ—God and Man*, in *Works of John Owen*, 1:144.

[10] *Glorious Mystery*, 1:146.

[11] *Grace and Duty*, ii. 19, 7:478.

[12] *Glorious Mystery*, 1:145.

whole soul'.[13] Because of its 'constant exercise', love is the 'spring unto all other affections'.[14] Edwards agrees: 'Christian love is the fountain of all gracious affections'.[15]

If love is central to the Christian life, then affection is clearly central, because love is an affection. For Owen spiritual affections are the *peculiar spring and substance of our being spiritually minded*. It is ultimately affection that God wants of us: 'The great contest of heaven and earth is about the affections of the poor worm which we call man.' Again: 'It is our affections he asketh for, and comparatively nothing else.'[16] Conversely, in their opposition to God the world and the devil seek to capture our affections:

> On the other side, all the artifices of the world, all the paint it puts on its face, all the great promises it makes, all the false appearances and attires it clothes itself withal by the help of Satan, have no other end but to draw and keep the affections of men unto itself.[17]

Certainly then Edwards was not the inventor of the idea of the priority of the affections when he likewise stated that 'true religion, in great part, consists in holy affections.'[18] Given who God is, the strong inclination of affection toward him is necessary: 'The things of religion are so great, that there can be no suitableness in the exercises of our hearts, to their nature and importance, unless they be lively and powerful.'[19]

The human person is unitary rather than composite

We turn now to consider the make-up of the human person and the 'location' of the affections. Here it is Edwards who produces the most sustained and thought-through account. He strongly insists that the human soul is not divisible into different faculties. His term for the unitary person is 'soul' or 'mind'. He does believe in *distinguishable* faculties of the soul, but they are not to be understood as *divisible* components, let alone as distinct substances. Rather, they denote the soul as it is 'capable of' different activities. The 'understanding' is the faculty by which the soul perceives,

---

[13] *Grace and Duty*, ii. 19, 7:475.
[14] *Glorious Mystery*, c. 13, 1:150.
[15] *Affections*, p. 240 (Hickman, 1:275).
[16] *Grace and Duty*, ii. 11, 7:395.
[17] *Grace and Duty*, ii. 11, 7:395-96.
[18] *Affections*, p. 95 (Hickman, 1:236).
[19] *Affections*, pp. 99-100 (Hickman, 1:238).

speculates, discerns, views, and judges. The 'inclination' is the faculty by which the soul likes or dislikes, approves or rejects something which it perceives. When we speak of the inclination actually making a choice it is to be termed the 'will'.[20] This psychology can be represented diagrammatically thus (Diagram 1):

Diagram 1

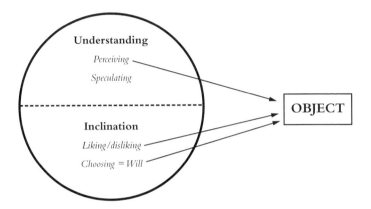

There is no third faculty of the soul alongside or beneath the understanding and inclination. The affections, therefore, are to be understood within this model, not as an additional component alongside it. In particular, they are not distinct as a part of the lower animal aspect of the human person (as they are for Thomas Aquinas), but are identified by Edwards as an aspect of the will:

> The will, and the affections of the soul, are not two faculties; the affections are not essentially distinct from the will, nor do they differ from the mere actings of the will and inclination of the soul, but only in the liveliness and sensibleness of exercise.[21]

The affections are simply 'the more vigorous and sensible exercises of the inclination and will of the soul'.[22] The diagram can be supplemented thus (Diagram 2):

[20] For these definitions, see *Affections*, p. 96 (Hickman, 1:237).
[21] *Affections*, p. 97 (Hickman, 1:237).
[22] *Affections*, p. 96 (Hickman, 1:237).

Diagram 2

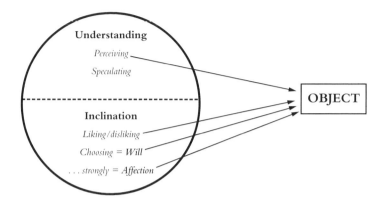

When Edwards speaks of the person perceiving and choosing, he sometimes prefers the term 'heart'. The heart is thus the whole person (the 'soul' or 'mind') engaged in acting toward an object with the full range of its capabilities. Brad Walton rightly describes the activity of the whole soul denoted by the term 'heart' as the 'cognitive-volitional-affective complex'.[23] This is not the most simple or succinct label, but it does express the unifying idea of the heart.

One consequence of the integrated nature of Edwards's psychology is that he thinks that bodily expressions of affections are appropriate. He does not think that physical manifestation proves the genuineness of a religious affection, but it is appropriate for it to accompany a genuine affection. Hence, even as he categorizes physical effects as one of the signs that do not prove the genuineness of an affection, he explains why they do and should occur: 'Such is our nature, and such are the laws of union of soul and body, that the mind can have no lively or vigorous exercise, without some effect upon the body.'[24]

While the unitary understanding of the 'heart' as the whole person in action is more developed in Edwards, it is an understanding of the term anticipated in Owen, because both men find it in the Bible:

> The heart in the Scripture is taken for the whole rational soul, not absolutely, but as all the faculties of the soul are one common

[23] *Jonathan Edwards*, p. 209.
[24] *Affections*, p. 132 (Hickman, 1:246).

principle of all our moral operations. Hence it hath such properties assigned unto it as are peculiar to the mind or understanding, as to see, perceive, to be wise, and to understand; and, on the contrary, to be blind and foolish; and sometimes such as belong properly to the will and affections, as to obey, to love, to fear, to trust in God.[25]

In fact the picture of understanding, will, and affections that we find in Edwards is anticipated in Owen. Speaking of how man functioned in Eden, he explains a pattern that is close to that stated by Edwards:

God created them all in a perfect harmony and union. The mind and reason were in perfect subjection and subordination to God and his will; the will answered, in its choice of good, the discovery made of it by the mind; the affections constantly and evenly followed the understanding and will. The mind's subjection to God was the spring of the orderly and harmonious motion of the soul and all the wheels in it.[26]

It is in the details of the location of the affections that Edwards most refines and clarifies the position of Owen. For example, in his work on the Holy Spirit Owen has a more fluid conception of the relationship between the mind, will, and affections. He can identify the affections as part of the mind (from which he excludes the will):

The *mind* of man, which is the subject of this work of conviction, hath two things distinctly to be considered in it:—first, The *understanding*, which is the *active*, *noetical*, or *contemplative* power and faculty of it; second, The *affections*, wherein its passive and sensitive power doth consist.[27]

But he can also pair the affections with the will rather than the mind, distinguishing in the unregenerate between 'the corruption and depravation of the *mind*' and 'the depravation of the *will* and *affections*'.[28] Or he can even separate them from both mind and will, describing those in whom there is 'a change wrought upon the affections only, whilst the mind, will, and

---

[25] *Discourse*, iii. 5, 3:326.

[26] *The Nature, Power, Deceit, and Prevalency of the Remainders of Indwelling Sin in Believers*, in *Works of John Owen*, c. 3, 6:173.

[27] *Discourse*, iii. 6, 3:350.

[28] *Discourse*, iii. 3, 3:244.

conscience, have been totally unsanctified'.[29] This is the kind of fluidity that Edwards resolves.[30]

Religious affections are new senses, not new faculties

What changes in the soul when the new birth occurs? Does it receive new faculties with which to love God? Owen explains that when a person is given new birth his faculties are not annihilated with new ones created out of nothing. Rather, the affections remain in nature, but are renewed by grace: 'Our affections continue the same as they were in their nature and essence; but they are so cured by grace as that their properties, qualities, and inclinations, are all cleansed or renewed.'[31] There is a wider theological principle at work here: as Thomas Aquinas said in a different context, 'grace does not destroy nature, but perfects it'.[32] There are also parallels to the way in which the resurrection body is the old body transformed rather than a new one created out of nothing, and the way in which the entire creation will be made new at Christ's return. Yet just as a right emphasis on continuity should not lead us to downplay the newness of the resurrection body and the new earth, so it should not lead us to downplay the newness of the new birth. Indeed, even as Owen insists on continuity, he maintains that it is essential to believe in a new principle at work in the believer: 'And to deny such a quickening principle of spiritual life, superadded unto us by the grace of Christ, distinct and separate from the natural faculties of the soul, is, upon the matter, to renounce the whole gospel'.[33]

Similarly, Edwards explains that regeneration does not involve the creation of a whole new set of faculties, but a new spiritual sense in the existing faculties:

This new spiritual sense, and the new dispositions that attend it, are no new faculties, but are new principles of nature. I use the word 'principles,' for want of a word of a more determinate signification. By a principle of nature in this place, I mean that foundation which

[29] *Grace and Duty*, ii. 12, 7:413.
[30] On the comparison with Owen, see Walton, *Jonathan Edwards*, pp. 104-116.
[31] *Grace and Duty*, 7:415.
[32] *Summa Theologica*, trans. by Fathers of the English Dominican Province, 5 vols (Westminster, MD: Christian Classics, 1948; repr. 1981), 1a. 1. 8, 1:6.
[33] *Discourse*, iii. 4, 3:287. Cf. iii. 5, 3:336-37.

is laid in nature, either old or new, for any particular manner or kind of exercise of the faculties of the soul.[34]

Like Owen, Edwards does not wish to downplay the newness here: his explanation of 'principle' shows that he envisages a deep change in the person. He is clear that the new sense is qualitatively unlike anything the person has known before:

> In those gracious exercises and affections which are wrought in the minds of the saints, through the saving influences of the Spirit of God, there is a new inward perception or sensation of their minds, entirely different in its nature and kind, from anything that ever their minds were the subjects of before they were sanctified.[35]

While Edwards uses a technical term derived from the philosopher John Locke ('new simple idea') to describe what is created in the believer, he spends much more time unpacking the biblical metaphors:

> Hence the work of the Spirit of God in regeneration is often in Scripture compared to the giving a new sense, giving eyes to see, and ears to hear, unstopping the ears of the deaf, and opening the eyes of them that were born blind, and turning from darkness unto light.[36]

These metaphors state both the continuity and the discontinuity of the new sense: it is new because what is seen and heard has not been seen and heard before, but it is the eyes and ears that already existed which are now renewed.

Religious affections are not the same as emotions

We have seen that for Edwards the affections are the heightened inclinations of the will. But what exactly does this mean? In particular, does he mean by 'affection' what we mean by 'emotion'? This is important because if affection is the same as emotion, then all that Edwards writes on the subject may amount to nothing more than a defence of emotionalism. This is what Paul Helm thinks:

[34] *Affections*, p. 206 (Hickman, 1:266).
[35] *Affections*, p. 205 (Hickman, 1:266).
[36] *Affections*, p. 206 (Hickman, 1:266). The Lockean term is used on p. 205 (Hickman, 1:266).

The *Religious Affections* is an important book, but in my view it would be unwise to take its teaching on what true religion consists in very seriously. It is a book about the importance of emotion, expressed in a public, visible way, being the measure of true religion.[37]

Helm rightly points out that by contrast the New Testament has a place for quiet, diligent, calm religion:

A person may be affected by the work of the Holy Spirit, possessing his fruit, in ways that are focused and undemonstrative, which lead to restraint and constraint, which lead to the development of an undeviating routine.

Helm is wrong, however, in his reading of Edwards. His mistake is to identify what Edwards terms 'the more vigorous and sensible exercises of the inclinations and will of the soul' with what he himself describes as 'self-consciousness and exhibitionism'. The first description, 'self-consciousness', is accurate if read in a technical sense. Edwards does speak of '*sensible* exercises of the inclination and will'.[38] 'Sensible' here denotes awareness, as when Edwards refers to 'inward experience or sensible perceiving of the immediate power and operation of the Spirit of God'.[39] Self-conscious affection is an element of what Edwards means to defend. But he does not intend this in the modern pejorative sense of self-consciousness, the kind of self-consciousness that goes with exhibitionism, and the kind that Helm seems to have in mind. For example, Edwards is careful to distinguish affection from *passion*, which would be closer to what Helm describes:

The *affections* and *passions* are frequently spoken of as the same; and yet, in the more common use of speech, there is in some respect a difference; and affection is a word, that in its ordinary signification, seems to be something more extensive than passion; being used for all vigorous lively actings of the will or inclination; but passion for those that are more sudden, and whose effects on the animal spirits

[37] 'Edwards on True Religion', *Helm's Deep* <http://paulhelmsdeep.blogspot.com/2011/04/edwards-on-true-religion.html#links > [accessed 29 June 2011].

[38] *Affections*, p. 96, my italics (Hickman, 1:237).

[39] *Affections*, p. 138 (Hickman, 1:248). Among other examples, see pp. 84, 141, 147, and 361 (Hickman, 1:234, 248, 308).

are more violent, and the mind more overpowered, and less in its own command.[40]

The term 'affection', therefore, includes much more than just uncontrolled emotion.

In an important passage, Edwards explicitly rejects the idea that true religion can be correlated with a particular heightened emotional state. The passage is significant because it shows that while Edwards can freely interchange the terms 'emotion' and 'affection', he actually thinks that it is the deeper stratum of affection that matters rather than its transitory expression in emotion:

> I think it clearly and abundantly evident, that true religion lies very much in the affections. Not that I think these arguments prove, that religion in the hearts of the truly godly, is ever in exact proportion to the degree of affection, and present emotion of the mind. For undoubtedly, there is much affection in the true saints which is not spiritual: their religious affections are often mixed; all is not from grace, but much from nature. And though the affections have not their seat in the body, yet the constitution of the body, may very much contribute to the present emotion of the mind. And the degree of religion is rather to be judged of by the fixedness and strength of the habit that is exercised in affection, whereby holy affection is habitual, than by the degree of the present exercise: and the strength of that habit is not always in proportion to outward effects and manifestations, or inward effects, in the hurry and vehemence, and sudden changes of the course of the thoughts of the mind.[41]

Edwards here shows his analytical subtlety. Rather than giving credence to the transitory emotional state, he is alert to the role that natural affection and the body can play in the emotions. He is not interested in the frothy ephemera of the emotional life, intense public manifestations, or momentary inward feelings. It is the underlying habit of holy affection that matters.

Gracious affections are also marked by their abiding effects. Edwards is clear that the characteristic of true affection is not its emotional height, but its enduring depth:

[40] *Affections*, p. 98 (Hickman, 1:237).
[41] *Affections*, pp. 118-9 (Hickman, 1:243).

There is a sort of high affections that some have from time to time, that leave them without any manner of appearance of an abiding effect. They go off suddenly; so that from the very height of their emotion, and seeming rapture, they pass at once to be quite dead, and void of all sense and activity. It surely is not wont to be thus with high gracious affections; they leave a sweet savor and relish of divine things on the heart, and a stronger bent of soul towards God and holiness.[42]

Edwards evidently does not mean by affection what we normally mean when we speak of transitory emotion or self-conscious exhibitionism.

Religious affections are responses to the realities of the gospel

True religious affections do not arise from just anywhere; they are responses to realities perceived through the word of the gospel. The word of the gospel is primarily the word of the cross: 'I decided to know nothing among you except Jesus Christ and him crucified' (*1 Cor.* 2:2). Owen emphasises the sanctifying power of focusing our affections on the cross: 'As to the object of your affections, in an *especial manner*, let it be the cross of Christ, which hath exceeding efficacy towards the disappointment of the whole work of indwelling sin'.[43] Edwards likewise teaches that it is God who is supremely attractive, and that he is seen most clearly in the cross:

> The glory and beauty of the blessed Jehovah, which is most worthy in itself, to be the object of our admiration and love, is there exhibited in the most affecting manner that can be conceived of, as it appears shining in all its luster, in the face of an incarnate, infinitely loving, meek, compassionate, dying Redeemer.[44]

Religious affections terminate on God himself, not his benefits

Now that he has stated that our affections should respond primarily to the cross, the next point may initially seem surprising, even contradictory. It is stated forcefully by Edwards. He argues that we are not to rest our delight in the gifts and benefits that God gives us, such as our salvation: 'The first

[42] *Affections*, p. 344 (Hickman, 1:303).
[43] *Indwelling Sin*, c. 11, 6:250.
[44] *Affections*, p. 123 (Hickman, 1:244).

objective ground of gracious affections, is the transcendently excellent and amiable nature of divine things, as they are themselves; and not any conceived relation they bear to self, or self-interest.'[45] Edwards does not mean that the blessings we receive provoke no affection. Instead, he means that the blessings must carry us beyond themselves to delight in the God who gives them. We delight in the benefits of the cross, but they point us to the God who sent his Son to win salvation for us. Edwards has a helpful illustration that shows how the blessings do evoke affection, but are not its terminus:

> How can a man truly and rightly love God, without loving him for that excellency in him, which is the foundation of all that is in any manner of respect good or desirable in him? They whose affection to God is founded first on his profitableness to them, their affection begins at the wrong end; they regard God only for the utmost limit of the stream of divine good, where it touches them, and reaches their interest; and have no respect to that infinite glory of God's nature, which is the original good, and the true fountain of all good, the first fountain of all loveliness of every kind, and so the first foundation of all true love.
>
> A natural principle of self-love may be the foundation of great affections towards God and Christ, without seeing anything of the beauty and glory of the divine nature.[46]

As well as the fountain, Edwards has another illustration that shows the instrumental function of the blessings we receive in pointing us beyond themselves to God:

> God's kindness to them is a glass that God sets before them, wherein to be behold [sic] the beauty of the attribute of God's goodness; the exercises and displays of this attribute, by this means, are brought near to them, and set right before them.[47]

Edwards is clearly warning against delighting in being saved *as opposed to* the Saviour, against being interested only in what we can get out of God and not in God himself. His warning is sharp: 'a dog will love his master that is kind to him'.[48]

[45] *Affections*, p. 240 (Hickman, 1:274).
[46] *Affections*, p. 243 (Hickman, 1:275).
[47] *Affections*, p. 248 (Hickman, 1:277).
[48] *Affections*, p. 243 (Hickman, 1:275).

Edwards explains that it is particularly the beauty of God's holiness on which true affection terminates, a point he draws from verses in the Psalms that speak about worshipping the Lord 'in the splendour of holiness' (for example 29:2 and 96:9). He singles out holiness because it is the perfection of God's other attributes, for example his wisdom, majesty, and immutability:

> 'Tis the glory of God's wisdom, that 'tis a holy wisdom, and not a wicked subtlety and craftiness. This makes his majesty lovely, and not merely dreadful and horrible, that it is a holy majesty. 'Tis the glory of God's immutability, that it is a holy immutability, and not an inflexible obstinacy in wickedness.
>
> And therefore it must needs be, that a sight of God's loveliness must begin here.[49]

In one passage, Owen might sound as if he is saying something different from Edwards about the terminus of our affections:

> They are but empty notions and imaginations, which some speculative persons please themselves withal, about love unto the divine goodness absolutely considered. For however infinitely amiable it may be in itself, it is not so really unto them, it is not suited unto their state and condition, without the consideration of the communications of it unto us in Christ.[50]

This might suggest that our affections do not have regard to God in himself, but Owen only really intends to remind us that God's being is not directly accessible to us apart from his works. Like Edwards, Owen maintains that our love must ultimately terminate on who God is. In the order of our knowing, God's acts come first so that he must and can only be known through them; in the order of being, he is prior and must therefore be the ultimate goal of our love. This is clear when in the next chapter Owen speaks of how we love and know God: 'We love him principally and ultimately for what he is; but nextly and immediately for what he did. What he did for us is first proposed unto us, and it is that which our souls are first affected withal.'[51]

---

[49] *Affections*, p. 257 (Hickman, 1:279).
[50] *Glorious Mystery*, c. 13, 1:152.
[51] *Glorious Mystery*, c. 14, 1:162.

Affections must be universally renewed

Owen teaches that there must be a double universality in the renewed religious affections of the believer. There must be a universal renewal of *all* of the affections in a believer. This obviously does not mean a perfect renewal; it means simply that the whole person is changed in regeneration, not just a part. Also, the affections must be fixed on *all* objective spiritual things, in their due proportions:

> Affections spiritually renewed do fix themselves upon and cleave unto all spiritual things, in their proper places, and unto their proper ends: for the ground and reason of our adherence unto any one of them is the same with respect unto them all,—that is, their relation unto God in Christ.[52]

Edwards similarly insists that there must be a right proportioning of the affections to their different objects: 'In the truly holy affections of the saints is found that proportion which is the natural consequence of the universality of their sanctification.'[53] This means, for example, that the affections must not be hypocritically directed toward some while being withheld from others:

> Some shew a great affection to their neighbors, and pretend to be ravished with the company of the children of God abroad; and at the same time are uncomfortable and churlish towards their wives and other near relations at home, and are very negligent of relative duties.[54]

Again, Edwards warns of a public-private disproportion:

> Some are greatly affected from time to time, when in company; but have nothing that bears any manner of proportion to it, in secret, in close meditation, secret prayer, and conversing with God, when alone, and separated from all the world.[55]

---

[52] *Grace and Duty*, ii. 13, 7:420.
[53] *Affections*, p. 365 (Hickman, 1:310).
[54] *Affections*, p. 368 (Hickman, 1:310).
[55] *Affections*, p. 374 (Hickman, 1:311).

Ministry must be designed to heighten affections

Given all that we have seen, it is no surprise to find that Edwards sought to cultivate the affections:

> If it be so, that true religion lies much in the affections, hence we may infer, that such means are to be desired, as have much of a tendency to move the affections. Such books, and such a way of preaching the Word, and administration of ordinances, and such a way of worshipping God in prayer, and singing praises, is much to be desired, as has a tendency deeply to affect the hearts of those who attend these means.[56]

It should be obvious that Edwards is not advocating whipping people up into an emotional frenzy by any means available. He has not forgotten his own point about true affections being responses to the realities of the gospel. The two points must be held together: such means are to be used as move the affections by most clearly setting forth the beautiful reality of Jesus. Perhaps Edwards also intends that in addition to setting forth the realities of the gospel plainly, a pastor should deliberately minister to the affections, calling for a response of love rather than just informing the congregation.

Applications

Here then are some of the key elements in a Puritan psychology of the religious affections. What can we learn from them? No doubt many things, but I highlight five.

First and most obviously, our affections matter. We should not think that God is indifferent to how we relate to him with our whole heart. He is interested in our understanding, but he also wants us to desire him with the strong inclination of our will, to find abiding joy and delight in him. This is not to reduce the Christian life to emotionalism. As we saw with Edwards, our affections go deeper than our emotions. Indeed, it would be possible for our superficial emotions to be quite out of sync with and in conflict with our deep affections. My feelings can be careering all over the place while my soul remains anchored in Christ. Nor is it to demand a perfection of affections: we are justified by faith, not by love. But we should pray for and seek to cultivate an abiding disposition of delight in

---

[56] *Affections*, p. 121 (Hickman, 1:244).

God, and we should look to be affected by the means of grace in public worship. This looks different in diverse people, but it should be real for everyone. The unmoved Christian is an example of tragic spiritual malfunction, not heroic stoic nobility.

Second, we should understand that our predicament is and always will be that of Owen and Edwards, and learn from them how to address it. It is no coincidence that they faced the same challenges, since the dual pull of dry rationalism on the one hand and excessive enthusiasm on the other is perennial. Where is the answer? Is it to aim for some kind of *via media* between the two? Take the 'worship wars' as an example. Should we avoid the excesses of contemporary worship on the one hand and repressed formalism on the other by trying to find a happy medium between them? Should we be as contemporary as we can be, in order to draw in the young, or as conservative as can be, in order to flee compromise? None of these approaches is right, because they are all ultimately pragmatic on a question where pragmatism should not be our guide. Owen and Edwards show us a better way, which is to think theologically about the issues we face. Their psychology reminds us of both the crucial role played by the understanding, and the importance of the affections. We cannot be contented with either mindless modernity or dry orthodoxy, not because we want to find a middle way, but because both deny an aspect of biblical psychology: one denies the understanding and the other denies the affections. The errors of deadness and excess that we commit are not errors of failed balance, but of failed theology; specifically, of failed psychology and anthropology. If we recall that all affection is reliant on the understanding, then we will see the problems with sung worship that is emotive but lacks theological content. If we recall that all understanding should result in affection, then we will fear dry worship as much as we fear enthusiasm, perhaps more. The test for a Christian hymn or song is not its age or its style, but its ability to focus the understanding on the word of truth and evoke affection in the heart.

Third, the Puritan example helpfully warns us against thinking about human affections apart from the rest of our theology. The risk is that we do the theology, and then leave it behind as we start to think about our anthropology, about who we are as human persons. If we do that, then we may well turn to secular resources as our principal authority for understanding ourselves. By contrast, Owen's emphasis on the rooting of our affections in the love of God wonderfully locates anthropology right at the heart of theology proper, since man is caught up in the overflowing love of the Holy Trinity. We ask who we are by asking who God is.

Fourth, I am personally struck by the challenge to delight in God himself, not just in his benefits. Am I a dog loving my master just because of his benefits? Or do I love him for what his benefits reveal of who he is? Reading Owen and Edwards on this has made me wonder if we sometimes fall into a superstitious, talismanic relationship to the cross. I am not thinking of making the sign of the cross or going out of our way to adorn our buildings with crosses. But perhaps we can so think and speak of 'the cross' as an object and event that we forget that it is the Christ of the cross who matters. It is Christ dying on the cross, not the cross itself that saves. The cross is not love and mercy, Christ crucified is love and mercy. If asked what we mean by 'the cross' we would of course explain that we use the term as shorthand for the Christ of the cross, but do we always remember that? It is the action of the person that matters. Perhaps we depersonalize the cross because we think of it as a thing that happened *to* the person Christ, rather than as an action *of* the person. As the great nineteenth century Scottish theologian Hugh Martin emphasises: '*the Doctrine of the Atonement ought not to be discussed apart from the idea of Christ's Priestly* ACTION *in His death.*'[57]

Finally, I am struck by the challenge to hypocrisy in the requirement of universal affections. If you are a minister or an elder, are you most interested in the useful members of the congregation, the ones who might take on some role or do some job? Do you make an effort to cultivate a relationship with those who might seem to offer the church nothing? Are you interested in the lives of the people themselves, or only in them as instruments to the church's ends? This is not just a problem for ministers: we are all prone to loving only those we find easy to love. How readily we gravitate to fellow Christians who are People Like Us. Exactly what kind of newcomers do we most warmly welcome at church? Perhaps we are not so crass as to attend most to the richly adorned (*James* 2:1-7), but do we favour those who are socially competent and easy to talk to? Do we avoid those who look more likely to be needy? We are fortunate that Jesus did not do that.

---

[57] Hugh Martin, *The Atonement: In Its Relations to the Covenant, the Priesthood, the Intercession of Our Lord* (Greenville, SC: Reformed Academic Press, n.d.), p. 77.

8

TRUSTING GOD IN TRIALS: JOHN CALVIN (1509-64)

Introduction

Though a Calvinist, I have betrayed John Calvin. We all have. We betray Calvin every time we talk about him, because Calvin did a lot to stop people talking about him. He writes to Cardinal Sadoleto: 'I am unwilling to speak of myself, but since you do not permit me to be altogether silent, I will say what I can consistent with modesty'.[1] He was buried, at his own request, in an unmarked grave. Nonetheless, on this count (if on few others!) it is in our best interests to betray him. As Calvin's colleague Théodore Beza puts it in his *Life of Calvin*:

> Nobody, I presume, will deny, that of all the works of God, men best deserve to be known and observed, and of men, those of them who have been distinguished at once for learning and piety. It is not without cause Daniel (Dan. 12:3) compares holy men of God to stars, since they by their brightness show the way of happiness to others. Those who allow that brightness to be entirely extinguished by their death, deserve to be themselves plunged in thicker darkness than before.[2]

The images that we know of Calvin the man suggest a certain austerity. The contrast with Martin Luther is telling. Luther is large, bullish, full of

[1] *Reply*, 1:30.
[2] *Life*, 1:20-21.

life, full of German beer. Calvin is long, thin, precise, reserved, unflinching. He can also appear in our minds as an essentially successful man, a colossus. Perhaps we remember his works, the *Institutes*, the treatises, the commentaries. Perhaps we recall Geneva itself under his reforms—the 'most perfect school of Christ' as John Knox called it. And then there is his influence in France, Scotland, Poland, Germany, and even England. He appears as a giant effortlessly striding across the stage of sixteenth-century Europe.

Perhaps it is just me, just a side-effect of being a church historian, but do you ever day-dream about being there in the Reformation, perhaps in Geneva itself? To go, to see first hand the light of the gospel breaking forth? Even to be involved, to join the *Compagnie des pasteurs*? What would Calvin say to such a fantasy? I think we know. He would say a loud and clear '*Non*'! He would say: 'Whatever you do, do not come here. This is the last place on earth to which you should come. Choose a hundred other afflictions, but do not come here.' This is because Calvin was not the unflustered reformer we are tempted to imagine, effortlessly masterminding the evangelization of Europe. No, he was the suffering reformer. I want here to consider the extent of Calvin's sufferings, and to encourage you with an account of how he endured, and how any other Christian can therefore endure. Calvin was not in a class of his own. There are no such classes in the kingdom of God. He was a normal Christian who had available to him exactly the same spiritual resources you and I have.

In some respects Calvin was like Job. Recall how Satan claims that Job only fears God because God has protected him: 'Does Job fear God for nothing? . . . Have you not put a hedge around him and his household and everything he has?' (*Job* 1:10). In the verses that follow Job's hedge is torn down, piece by piece: his oxen, donkeys, sheep, camels, servants, children, and health are all taken from him. Then he suffers his wife's dangerous advice and the relentless counsel of his unhelpful friends. It is striking that Job himself then uses the language of being hedged in, but quite differently: 'Why is life given to a man whose way is hidden, whom God has hedged in?' (3:23). For Job it is not the hedge of protection that has been taken away but the hedge of trouble that now surrounds him. From every side he is hemmed in by Satan's attacks. This is the point of comparison with Calvin. Like Job, Calvin faced hostility on every side, in his public and personal life. Here is his testimony:

> I say nothing of fire and sword and exiles and all the furious attacks
> of our enemies. I say nothing of slanders and other such vexations.

How many things there are within that are far worse! Ambitious men openly attack us. Epicureans and Lucianists mock at us, impudent men insult us, hypocrites rage against us, those who are wise after the flesh do us harm, indirectly, and we are harassed in many different ways on every side. It is in short a great miracle that, weighed down by the burden of such a heavy and dangerous office, any one of us should persevere.[3]

'In many different ways on every side': what were the hedges that surrounded John Calvin?

Surrounded on every side

First of all, death impinged constantly on Calvin. It is obvious that in his time there was a greater and more immediate awareness of death than there is today. This meant that Christian spirituality was more markedly shaped by death. Calvin is an example of this. He lived with a constant and acute awareness of the vulnerability of the human condition. He writes this extraordinary passage in the *Institutes*:

Innumerable are the evils that beset human life; innumerable, too, the deaths that threaten it. We need not go beyond ourselves: since our body is the receptacle of a thousand diseases—in fact holds within itself and fosters the causes of diseases—a man cannot go about unburdened by many forms of his own destruction, and without drawing out a life enveloped, as it were, with death. For what else would you call it, when he neither freezes nor sweats without danger? Now, wherever you turn, all things around you not only are hardly to be trusted but almost openly menace, and seem to threaten immediate death. Embark upon a ship, you are one step away from death. Mount a horse, if one foot slips, your life is imperilled. Go through the city streets, you are subject to as many dangers as there are tiles on the roofs. If there is a weapon in your hand or a friend's, harm awaits. All the fierce animals you see are armed for your destruction. But if you try to shut yourself up in a walled garden, seemingly delightful, there a serpent sometimes lies hidden. Your house, continually in danger of fire, threatens in the daytime to impoverish you, at night even to collapse upon

[3] Cited in William J. Bouwsma, *John Calvin: A Sixteenth Century Portrait* (Oxford: Oxford University Press, 1988; repr. 1989), pp. 25-6.

you. Your field, since it is exposed to hail, frost, drought, and other calamities, threatens you with barrenness, and hence, famine. I pass over poisonings, ambushes, robberies, open violence, which in part besiege us at home, in part dog us abroad. Amid these tribulations must not man be most miserable, since, but half alive in life, he weakly draws his anxious and languid breath, as if he had a sword perpetually hanging over his neck?[4]

For Geneva the threat of military attack was real. In a letter following the Peace of Cateau-Cambrésis in 1559 between France and Spain, a peace that left Geneva more vulnerable, Calvin indicates his own sense of coming trouble: 'It is true that at this time I speak from outside the battle, but not very far, and I do not know for how long, since as far as one can judge our turn is indeed near.'[5] There was also physical danger closer to home, including politically and theologically motivated murder within Geneva itself. For Calvin, death pressed in on many sides.

Second, there was the fact that Calvin was a refugee. He had fled from his beloved home country France. As he expresses it, 'His native soil is sweet to everyone, and it is sweet to dwell among one's own people.'[6] This, from 1534 in his mid-twenties, Calvin could never do. He felt the loss acutely, and comments that it is 'a wretched safety when men cannot otherwise make provision for it than by inflicting a voluntary exile on themselves.'[7] As one historian puts it, 'Calvin in Geneva was a Frenchman who dreamed of his country.'[8]

Calvin was not only an unwilling refugee, he was also an unwilling settler. Here is the story of his attempt to pass quietly by the city of Geneva in pursuit of a quiet life of 'privacy and obscurity', found in one of his rare autobiographical passages:

[Guillaume] Farel, who burned with an extraordinary zeal to advance the gospel, immediately strained every nerve to detain me. And after having learned that my heart was set upon devoting myself to private studies, for which I wished to keep myself free from other pursuits, and finding that he gained nothing by

[4] *Institutes*, I. xvii. 10, 1:223.

[5] Cited in Bernard Cottret, *Calvin: A Biography*, trans. by M. Wallace McDonald (Grand Rapids, MI: William B. Eerdmans; Edinburgh: T&T Clark, 2000), p. 246.

[6] Cited in *Portrait*, p. 16.

[7] Cited in *Portrait*, p. 16.

[8] J. Viénot cited by Cottret in *Biography*, p. 157.

entreaties, he proceeded to utter an imprecation that God would curse my retirement, and the tranquillity of the studies which I sought, if I should withdraw and refuse to give assistance, when the necessity was so urgent. By this imprecation I was so stricken with terror, that I desisted from the journey which I had undertaken.[9]

Having settled under duress in Geneva, Calvin then suffered another exile following a dispute with the city authorities. This time he ended up in Strasbourg where he was greatly influenced by Martin Bucer. When in 1540 the possibility of his return to Geneva emerged, Calvin again came unwillingly: 'rather would I submit to death a hundred times than to that cross, on which one had to perish daily a thousand times over.'[10] We find a double-exiled Calvin with a double settlement in Geneva, both times not wanting to be there.

Third, there were the sheer demands of his ministry. The pressures he faced were enormous and relentless. Within just six weeks of returning to the city he could write: 'I am entangled in so many employments, that I am almost beside myself.'[11] But even without the additional controversies and conflicts that beset him, the ordinary duties of Calvin's ministry were extraordinary by any normal measure. Like Luther, Calvin had a phenomenal capacity for work. He preached twice on the Lord's day and every other week he preached each morning at 6 or 7 A.M. on the Old Testament, often totalling eight sermons in a week. He preached in all around 4,000 sermons after his return, averaging over 170 sermons each year. Then there were other services; in the 1550s, for example, there were 270 weddings and 50 baptisms.[12] Beza tells us in his *Life of Calvin* that alongside this the reformer lectured every third day on theology, met with the presbytery, and taught in the conference on Scripture that met every Friday.[13] If a man was ever hemmed in by sheer activity, it was John Calvin. Nor were his colleagues any help after his return from Strasbourg. As he describes them, one was 'of a touchy, or rather savage, character', the other 'wily and sly': 'they had not thought, even in dreams, about what it means to direct a church'.[14]

---

[9] *Commentary on Psalms*, preface, pp. xlii–xliii.
[10] *Tracts and Letters*, 4:175.
[11] *Tracts and Letters*, 4:294.
[12] For these details see *Portrait*, p. 29.
[13] *Life*, 1:xxxix.
[14] Cited in *Biography*, p. 158.

Fourth, there was trouble from enemies within the city. These fell into two main groups. There was trouble from among the refugees and visitors who came to the city, and from the Libertines, established citizens who were unhappy with Calvin's reforms. Geneva was largely a city of refugees and asylum seekers. An anonymous writer in 1584 criticised the city saying that people came to it from all parts of the world,

> as to an asylum and place of safety, all the criminals and evildoers, lost and abandoned people, thieves, robbers, brigands, homicides, murderers, assassins, sorcerers, enchanters, poisoners, arsonists, counterfeiters, and the whole band of outlaws and pillagers, because no other country has been willing to endure them, either among the Christians or even among the Turks.[15]

I suspect that in his bleaker moments Calvin would have agreed with this verdict.

As a place of safety from Rome, Geneva attracted not only mainstream supporters of the Magisterial Reformation from elsewhere, but also radical reformers from different countries, men like Michael Servetus. Calvin was repeatedly attacked by opponents of God's sovereign grace like Jerome Bolsec. Such visitors meant that Calvin faced doctrinal battles from within. And then of course there were enemies without, such as the Roman Catholic theologian Albertus Pighius. Calvin even found himself in lengthy and painful disputes with Lutherans, both the more orthodox over the Lord's supper, and the less, such as Andreas Osiander, over justification. The list goes on. It was Luther himself who commented that it is vital to fight where the battle is, and this Calvin certainly did. As Beza puts it: 'There will be found no heresy ancient or revived, or newly founded in our time, which he did not destroy down to its foundations'.[16]

The Libertines, the old Genevan leaders of the city, hated the way in which Calvin was reforming their hometown. Their opposition was ongoing, but it reached a peak when in 1552 Ami Perrin became first syndic, the senior leader of the city. Calvin writes to Bullinger on 7 September 1553 that the Council in Geneva 'have reached such a pitch of folly and madness, that they regard with suspicion whatever we say to them. So much so, that were I to allege that it is clear at mid-day, they would forthwith begin to doubt of it'.[17] The tensions reached a height when

---

[15] Cited in *Biography*, p. 108.
[16] Cited in *Biography*, p. 3.
[17] *Tracts and Letters*, 5:427.

the Consistory excommunicated an assistant judge from an old Genevan family, Philibert Berthelier, but the Council authorised him to participate in the Supper. In the midst of the crisis Calvin asked to be allowed to resign but was refused permission. Even as he preached on 3 September, he expected Berthelier to force the issue by presenting himself for communion. Calvin was determined not to compromise whatever the cost: 'if anyone wants to intrude at this holy table to whom it has been forbidden by the consistory, it is certain that I will show myself, at the risk of my life, what I should be.' He explains his resolve: 'I would rather have been killed than have offered the holy things of God with this hand to those declared guilty as scorners.'[18] As it happened Berthelier had been counselled not to appear on that occasion, but the trouble continued. Calvin comments in a sermon in December 1554: 'If it were up to me, I would want God to remove me from this world, and that I should not have to live here three days in such disorder as there is here'.[19] The great conflict with the Libertines was only finally resolved when the elections of February 1555 returned four syndics who supported Calvin. The syndics were then able to push through further changes to the city's councils. This turn-around only happened because a large number of French refugees had become citizens and were permitted to hold office on the Council of Sixty and the Council of Two Hundred. In frustration some of the Libertines took up arms against a house full of Frenchmen, and Perrin seized the baton of office from one syndic. This insurrection led to the leaders of the Libertines taking flight or being executed.

Perhaps the streets of Geneva were places of trouble but was not Calvin's home an oasis? In fact his home life formed the fifth side of the hedge that surrounded him. Just as the political troubles ended in 1555, so the domestic difficulties intensified. Calvin was deeply affected when his brother's wife committed adultery, all the more because the family lived together in the same house. She had previously been accused in 1548 but acquitted. Then in 1557 she was caught with Calvin's servant Pierre Daguet, and it was soon after discovered that Daguet had also been stealing from his master. In February Calvin writes to Farel:

> Besides open contentions, you can have no idea, my dear Farel, with how many ambushes and clandestine machinations Satan daily assails us. So then, though the state of public affairs be tranquil, it

[18] Cited in *Biography*, p. 196.
[19] Cited in *Biography*, p. 194.

is not allowed, for all that, to every body to enjoy repose. . . . we are weighed down by a load of domestic affliction. Of the city I say nothing, for our private calamity almost completely absorbs us. The judges find no way of disengaging my brother. I interpret their blindness as a just punishment for our own, because for upwards of two years though I was pillaged by a thief, I saw nothing. My brother perceived neither the thief nor the adulterer.[20]

What about his immediate family? Calvin married Idelette de Bure in 1540 and from the little we know they were very happily married. Yet their only son Jacques died shortly after he was born on 28 July 1542. Calvin expresses his grief to Pierre Viret: 'The Lord has certainly inflicted a severe and bitter wound in the death of our infant son. But he is himself a Father, and knows best what is good for his children.'[21] In 1545 Idelette herself became ill, and in March 1549, after just nine years of marriage and with Calvin still under forty, she died. Calvin writes to Viret just over a week later:

> Truly mine is no common source of grief. I have been bereaved of the best companion of my life, of one who, had it been so ordered, would not only have been the willing sharer of my indigence, but even of my death. During her life she was the faithful helper of my ministry. From her I never experienced the slightest hindrance. She was never troublesome to me throughout the entire course of her illness; she was more anxious about her children than about herself.[22]

A few days later he writes to Farel: 'I do what I can to keep myself from being overwhelmed with grief.'[23]

Sixth, Calvin suffered from ill health. Beza speculates that this was the result of over-doing his studies earlier in life:

> By these prolonged vigils he no doubt acquired solid learning, and an excellent memory; but it is probable that he also contracted that weakness of stomach, which afterwards brought on various diseases, and ultimately led to his untimely death.[24]

---

[20] *Tracts and Letters*, 6:314–15.
[21] *Tracts and Letters*, 4:344.
[22] *Tracts and Letters*, 5:216.
[23] *Tracts and Letters*, 5:217.
[24] *Life*, 1:xxiii.

Throughout his life Calvin had terrible migraines; he probably had pleurisy in the mid-1550s; he was room-bound in 1558 for several months; in 1559 he could hardly speak and spat blood; he suffered also from haemorrhoids, gout, and in later years kidney stones. In February 1564 he writes graphically to the physicians of Montpellier about his struggle to pass a kidney stone that lacerated his urinary canal. Having listed some of his illnesses he notes how 'at present all these ailments as it were in troops assail me'.[25]

In sum then: Calvin was often ill; he lived through the death of his son and his wife; he was opposed by natives and strangers to Geneva alike; at the start his colleagues were incompetent; he had an extraordinary workload, and he lived under the shadow of death. On every front he was a man hedged in. What kept him going in the face of such encompassing hardship?

Calvin's sustaining convictions

In short, Calvin was a Calvinist, but not just theologically. His was a lived Calvinism. His convictions concerning the sovereign purposes of God wrought within him a number of dispositions that allowed him to see his situation differently. Calvin is a good example of how there is no necessary causal link between affliction and a response of unbelief. Many of today's so-called 'new atheists' speak as if an awareness of suffering *compels* unbelief. I suspect that many young Christians who have not endured hardship of any kind can fear it too. But there is no necessary link. Calvin viewed the world through biblical eyes, and he therefore reacted in godly ways.

First of all, he expected suffering. In November 1559 he wrote to the French brethren following the accession of the young Francis II who was under the influence of the Catholic Guise family. He explained in the letter that suffering is a consequence of the believer's union with Christ. If we are united to Christ, then we must be united to him in his death. This is the will of the Father: 'above all by sufferings he wishes us to be conformed to the image of his Son, as it is fitting that there should be conformity between the head and the members.'[26] This is obvious for Calvin, and he finds refusal of it hard to comprehend: 'It is horrible that those who call themselves Christians should be so stupid, or rather brutalized, as to

---

[25] *Tracts and Letters*, 7:358–59.
[26] *Tracts and Letters*, 7:84–85.

renounce Jesus Christ as soon as he displays his cross'.[27] How can anyone be a Christian, Calvin asks, and not expect a cross?

Second, in the face of suffering Calvin was encouraged by God's providence. The long passage about death waiting around every corner that I cited above occurs in his discussion of divine providence in the *Institutes*. Immediately after expressing his anxieties he counters them:

> Yet, when that light of divine providence has once shone upon a godly man, he is then relieved and set free not only from the extreme anxiety and fear that were pressing him before, but from every care. For as he justly dreads fortune, so he fearlessly dares commit himself to God.[28]

Calvin constantly drew strength from the providential rule of God. As he puts it to Farel in 1553 during the proceedings against Servetus:

> Although we may be severely buffeted hither and thither by many tempests, yet, seeing that a pilot steers the ship in which we sail, who will never allow us to perish even in the midst of shipwrecks, there is no reason why our minds should be overwhelmed with fear and overcome with weariness.[29]

We may reinforce the significance of this confidence by contrasting Calvin's convictions with those of today's 'open theists' who deny the exhaustive sovereignty of God. Open theists think they are helping people by saying that when things go wrong for us God regrets his leading, even though it seemed good at the time given what he could foresee. Gregory Boyd, a popular open theist writer, recounts the tragic story of Suzanne, a young woman who took extensive counsel and concluded that the Lord wanted her to marry a particular man. She married, but then her husband committed adultery. Eventually he left her, only for her to discover that she was expecting his child. Boyd records that he began by trying to emphasise to Suzanne that the outcome was her ex-husband's fault. But she argued that God knew exactly what would happen, and so was responsible. Boyd then suggested instead that God had led her into the marriage, but that the outcome was unknown to him at the time because of human liberty: 'Because her ex-husband was a free agent, however, even the best decisions can have sad results.' Boyd believes that this helped Suzanne:

[27] *Tracts and Letters*, 7:86.
[28] *Institutes*, I. xvii. 11, 1:224.
[29] *Tracts and Letters*, 5:416-17.

By framing the ordeal within the context of an open future, Suzanne was able to understand the tragedy of her life in a new way. She didn't have to abandon all confidence in her ability to hear God and didn't have to accept that somehow God intended this ordeal 'for her own good.' Her faith in God's character and her love toward God were eventually restored and she was finally able to move on with her life.[30]

Here we have a picture of God not knowing what will happen, acting on his ignorance, and making terrible (albeit well-meaning) mistakes. As the evil surprises him he cannot have intended it for good. This is not the God of the Joseph who said to his brothers: 'you meant evil against me, but God meant it for good' (*Gen.* 50:20).

Witness Calvin's contrary position and its pastoral power in his own life. What did he say following the death of Jacques? Not 'It was beyond God's control'. Rather: 'The Lord has certainly inflicted a severe and bitter wound in the death of our infant son.' The Lord who inflicts is not an out of control Satan or a human free agent surprising an ignorant God with suffering. No, the Lord who inflicts is God himself. But, vitally, the Lord who inflicts is also, as Calvin says, a Father, our Father, who 'knows best what is good for his children'. Lord and Father: Calvin often conjoins these two titles for God. He knows the pastoral power of this combined description. We see him using it here with himself, and elsewhere with others too. In the *Institutes* we read that the believer's solace 'is to know that his Heavenly Father so holds all things in his power, so rules by his authority and will, so governs by his wisdom, that nothing can befall except he determine it.'[31] See the pairing again: 'Father' with terms expressing sovereignty. Our Father has total power over everything, to order all to our good. It is awareness of God as our Father that keeps us from thinking that we are victims of a cruel tyrant, 'as if God were making sport of men by throwing them about like balls'.[32] Calvin held together knowledge of God as Lord and as Father. He writes to the French brethren:

> Since it is our duty to suffer, we ought humbly to submit; as it is the will of God that his church be subjected to such conditions that even as the plough passes over the field, so should the ungodly have

[30] *God of the Possible: A Biblical Introduction to the Open View of God* (Grand Rapids, MI: Baker Books, 2000), p. 106.

[31] *Institutes*, I. xvii. 11, 1:224.

[32] *Institutes*, I. xvii. 1, 1:211.

leave to pass their sword over us all from the least to the greatest. According then to what is said in the psalm, *we should prepare our back for stripes*. If that condition is hard and painful, let us be satisfied that our heavenly Father in exposing us to death, turns it to our eternal welfare. And indeed it is better for us to suffer for his name, without flinching, than to possess his word without being visited by affliction. For in prosperity we do not experience the worth of his assistance and the power of his Spirit, as when we are oppressed by men. That seems strange to us; but he who sees more clearly than we, knows far better what is advantageous for us. Now when he permits his children to be afflicted, there is no doubt but that it is for their good. Thus we are forced to conclude that whatever he orders, is the best thing we could desire.[33]

This is astonishing when we consider some of the suffering that Calvin endured. It is a conviction only possible through the work of the Holy Spirit. And it is true that 'whatever he orders, is the best thing we could desire': the best thing, not necessarily the most comfortable. We have a kind Father and a sovereign Lord, so we submit because he is sovereign, and we trust because he is our loving Father working for our good. Losing these convictions, or rejecting them as the so-called 'open theists' have done, is a pastoral disaster. As Calvin puts it: 'ignorance of providence is the ultimate of all miseries; the highest blessedness lies in the knowledge of it'.[34]

Third, Calvin knew that no matter what their trials, Christians never lose, are never defeated, and are never poor. We are always wealthy conquerors because we have the Lord Jesus Christ. He writes in September 1545 to one Monsieur de Falais who was suffering imperial displeasure:

If the whole should be taken away from you, there would yet remain the consolation to which we must chiefly betake ourselves, namely, to yield ourselves up entirely. It is certain, that having the Son of God, we suffer no injury in being deprived of all else: for thus highly ought we indeed to prize him.[35]

Having the Son of God, the Christian has an immeasurable inheritance:

[33] *Tracts and Letters*, 7:84.
[34] *Institutes*, I. xvii. 11, 1:225.
[35] *Tracts and Letters*, 5:18.

I pray our good Lord that he would so work in you now more powerfully than ever, to make you despise all that is in the world, and to make you breathe upwards direct to him with your whole heart, without being turned aside by anything whatsoever, making you taste what is the worth of the hope which he reserves for us in heaven.[36]

Calvin did not mean by any of this that it is wrong for the Christian to fear, since fear is a part of knowing our own weakness. He meant that we must never stop with fear, but must add to it confidence and hope in God. Indeed hope, Calvin says when commenting on Psalm 56:4, only comes out of our fear:

> Experience shows that hope truly reigns where fear occupies part of the heart. For hope does not operate in a tranquil mind, nay it is almost dormant. But it exerts its power where it uplifts a spirit worn down by cares, soothes it when troubled by grief, and supports it when it is stricken by terror.[37]

Even when writing in his final weeks, Calvin exhorts the Genevan senators to hope in God and to have sole regard to him:

> If adversity befalls you, and death surrounds you on every side, still hope in Him who even raises the dead. Nay, consider that you are then especially tried by God, that you may learn more and more to have respect to Him only.[38]

Will we follow Calvin's example? We must remember that we will suffer because we are one with the Lord Jesus Christ. As we suffer, we need to recall that, astonishing as it is, whatever the Lord orders, is the best thing for us from our Father. And we should pray that as fear occupies part of our hearts, hope will reign.

---

[36] *Tracts and Letters*, 5:18.
[37] Cited in *Portrait*, p. 44.
[38] *Life*, 1:xci.

9

IDENTITY AND LOSS ON THE EDGE
OF THE WORLD:
ANNE BRADSTREET (1612–72)

England from Henry VIII to the Civil War

The poet Anne Bradstreet (née Dudley) was born in England around 120 years after William Tyndale and just a few years before John Owen. To explain her story I will describe something of the times in which she lived and the events that had taken place in her home country.

Around 70 years before Bradstreet's birth, at the end of the 1520s, Henry VIII had decided that he wanted his marriage to Catherine of Aragon annulled. Catherine had borne him no son, and he concluded from the Old Testament that he should never have married her, since she had been married to his now-dead brother. People speak about Henry's 'divorce', but a divorce was out of the question given the church's teaching, so he hoped for an annulment. He tried different ways of getting the Pope to annul his marriage, including bribing many of the universities of Europe to encourage them to pronounce in his favour on the Old Testament question. But in the end all of his attempts failed and he had to resort to political power.

Henry's difficulty was that Catherine was able to appeal over his head to the authority of the Pope, and the Pope would never grant the annulment because Catherine was related to the powerful Holy Roman Emperor Charles V. Indeed, Charles's unpaid troops had just a little earlier sacked the city of Rome, forcing the Pope to flee and leaving him mindful of his vulnerability to imperial attack. The obvious though in many ways unthinkable solution was for Henry to remove the authority of the Pope from England so that Catherine could no longer appeal to him. An outright break from Rome was a recent Reformation phenomenon, but there was a long tradition stretching back through much of the mediaeval period of strong, even military conflict between the kings of European countries and the papacy. There was also a developed body of political thought, known as Erastianism, that maintained the supremacy of a king in his own realm. Thus in the early 1530s Henry, assisted by his advisers in church and state, passed a series of Acts of Parliament that removed the authority of the Pope from the land. First he restrained appeals outside the realm, then he made himself head of the church in England. The preamble to the Act in Restraint of Appeals sounded this ringing declaration:

> Where by divers sundry old authentic histories and chronicles it is manifestly declared and expressed that this realm of England is an empire, and so hath been accepted in the world, governed by one supreme head and king, having the dignity and royal estate of the imperial crown of the same, unto whom a body politic, compact of all sorts and degrees of people divided in terms and by names of spiritualty and temporalty, be bounden and ought to bear, next to God, a natural and humble obedience.[1]

In other words, there is one king in an empire, and he rules over everything, the church as well as the temporal affairs of the nation.

Given this removal of papal authority, Henry is often thought of as the king who made England into a Protestant country and embraced the Reformation. But this is not so. While Henry had officials such as Thomas Cranmer the Archbishop of Canterbury who were definitely Protestant, he himself was not a Protestant. This meant that when Henry died England was left, at the official level, with a version of Roman Catholicism without the Pope. It was his son Edward VI (and his protectors) who made England a properly Protestant country, and under his reign Cranmer was able to effect a real Reformation. But when Edward died aged 15, his half-sister Mary came to the throne, and she was the daughter of Catherine of Aragon. Mary had no time for the changes that had been introduced by Henry or Edward given that her mother was the woman who was

---

[1] *Documents*, ed. Bray, p. 78.

cast aside in the vanguard of those changes. Mary reversed (or attempted to reverse) the Protestant Reformation in England and executed in total just under 300 Protestant martyrs. When she died in 1558, her half-sister Elizabeth came to the throne.

Elizabeth was the daughter of Anne Boleyn who had replaced Catherine of Aragon. Her religious disposition was what we would expect: she was aware that she was the child of the break with Rome. Elizabeth introduced a religious settlement that was definitely Protestant, but it was not of the 'hotter sort' (as one pamphleteer described her opponents). That is, her church was truly committed to the final authority of the Bible and to believing that we are justified before a holy God by faith alone and not by good works. It was also clearly committed to a denial of the idea that the bread and wine in the Mass actually become the body and blood of Jesus, or that the Mass was a sacrifice for sin. But Elizabeth's church retained some vestments for the clergy, the special clothes that they wore when administering Holy Communion, and it retained the office of bishop in the church rather than following the pattern of the continental Reformed who generally speaking had removed Episcopal government. Also, Elizabeth was reluctant to allow some of the more enthusiastic activity of many of the Protestants, for example their prophesyings, preaching meetings that sometimes became centres of local revival. For Elizabeth this all looked too much like potentially destabilizing enthusiasm and needed to be restrained.

During the course of Elizabeth's reign it became clear that there were two perspectives on her church settlement. For the Queen it was a finished act, a static event. The required level of Protestantism had been attained, and there would be no further change. For many others, including many of the clergy and gentry, the reforms which she introduced were just a start, and the Reformation needed to be a dynamic process in which further change occurred. The men who supported this dynamic view came to be known as Puritans. Anne Bradstreet's family were among them.

Increasingly these divergent perspectives brought disagreement and hostility. In the 1580s a number of men who started independent congregations apart from the official church were executed or went into exile. Some of the leading advocates of further reform were imprisoned in the Tower of London. When James I came to the throne in 1603 the Puritans were very hopeful because they thought that his theology was close to their own. He met with the Puritans and considered their requests at the Hampton Court Conference in 1604, but all of them ended up being denied apart from the production of a new Bible (which would become known as the King James or Authorised Version). The initial hopes of the Puritans for progress under James were dashed. Some were content to stay where they were, but others increasingly came to feel that if they wanted a complete Reformation they would have to leave the country. Groups began to leave for Europe, and in the end for America, seeking a new home where they could implement a properly reformed church and state. In 1620 the first pilgrim ship, the *Mayflower*, sailed to America from Plymouth with exiles who had been in Leiden, seeking freedom and prosperity.

For the Puritans remaining in England, the religious situation deteriorated. Charles I and his Archbishop of Canterbury William Laud, the one whose policy led to John Owen leaving Oxford, moved away from the theology of the Reformation. They replaced the communion tables in churches with altars, suggesting the idea of the Mass again. They moved the altars from the middle of the church to the east end, again suggesting a special sacrifice removed from the people, rather than a shared meal. They even banned preaching on predestination, thus preventing ministers teaching the biblical and Augustinian message that God is sovereign in salvation and that we depend wholly on his grace. It would be hard to imagine better ways to provoke and alienate the powerful Puritans. Historian Claire Cross observes that in the way he conducted his policy 'Laud almost seemed to be deliberately planting the seeds of his own destruction'.[2]

Together with his religious innovations, Charles ruled in a tyrannical fashion, imposing spurious taxes without the consent of Parliament. In fact he did not call Parliament for the whole of the so-called personal rule from 1629–40. The dam broke when he attempted to impose bishops on the church in Scotland. The Scots rose up against him and he then had to call Parliament to raise money for the war. But Parliament itself proved to be hostile to the king. When he saw that events were turning against him, Charles withdrew from London to Nottingham and raised his standard. The English Civil War had begun.

For Bradstreet and her fellow-Puritans, the king had ranged himself against both the law of the land and the law of God. As Samuel Rutherford put it in the title of his book, *Lex Rex*: the law is king, and a king who pits himself against the law must be opposed. Those who resisted the

---

[2] *Church and People: England 1450–1660*, 2nd edn (Oxford: Blackwell, 1999), p. 163.

king nearly all did so with extreme reluctance. Many attempts were made to persuade Charles to agree and adhere to terms of peace, but he would not do so. In 1649, after a series of increasingly desperate events, he was executed, a decision that far from all the Puritans supported.

Writing in 1642, the year that the Civil War began, Bradstreet is clear that the cause of England's trouble was the 'men of might' who opposed the gospel and opened the door to Rome. For Bradstreet, the English Civil War was thus fundamentally a religious war, fought to preserve the light of the gospel. Here is how she expresses the cause of the trouble in the words of 'Old England' herself:

> Before I tell th' effect, I'll show the cause
> Which are my sins, the breach of sacred laws.
> Idolatry, supplanter of a nation,
> With foolish superstitious adoration,
> Are liked and countenanced by men of might,
> The Gospel trodden down and hath no right;
> Church offices were sold and bought for gain,
> That Pope had hope to find Rome here again.[3]

Anne Bradstreet's story

By the time Bradstreet wrote those words she was living in New England. When the Mayflower sailed in 1620, she would have been around eight years old. In the same year her father began work for the Earl of Lincoln as his steward, which gave her access to many books and a good education. She was tutored in literature, history, Greek, Latin, French, and Hebrew. When she was 16, in 1628, she married Simon Bradstreet. Simon was the son of a nonconforming minister and a graduate of Emmanuel College Cambridge, a college that had effectively been founded as a Puritan seminary. In 1630, the Bradstreets sailed with Anne's Puritan parents to America with the Massachusetts Bay Company on the ship *Arbella*.

Bradstreet had been raised in genteel fashion with an Earl's library at her disposal. She was newly married and still only around seventeen. Now she found herself on a three-month-long, cold, rough voyage to an unknown land. During the voyage several people died. Arrival on land

[3] 'A Dialogue Between Old England and New; Concerning the Present Troubles', *The Works of Anne Bradstreet* (Cambridge, MA: The Belknap Press of Harvard University Press, 1967; repr. 1981), p. 182, ll. 96-103.

hardly brought more security. In the area where they settled 200 out of 1,000 settlers died during their first winter, a period that became known as the 'starving time'. Bradstreet found herself perched precariously on the edge of the new world, a world full of promise and freedom, but also of terror and the unknown. There is much that we can learn through the poetry she wrote in that situation.

Identity and role

One of the first things that stands out in Bradstreet's poetry is the Puritan conception of the world in terms of divinely ordered identities and roles. Despite all of the uncertainties she faced, she had a clear conception of what it meant to be a godly woman. We see this in her epitaph for her mother, Dorothy Dudley, who died in 1643:

> Here lies,
> A worthy matron of unspotted life,
> A loving mother and obedient wife,
> A friendly neighbor, pitiful to poor,
> Whom oft she fed and clothed with her store;
> To servants wisely awful, but yet kind,
> And as they did, so they reward did find.
> A true instructor of her family,
> The which she ordered with dexterity.
> The public meetings ever did frequent,
> And in her closest constant hours she spent;
> Religious in all her words and ways,
> Preparing still for death, till end of days:
> Of all her children, children lived to see,
> Then dying, left a blessed memory.[4]

Here Bradstreet's mother embodies the virtues of the godly woman as the Puritans understood them. She is loving to her children, submissive to her husband, and generous to her neighbours in her community. She is clear on the ordered boundaries of society, recognizing that servants are servants yet being kind to them.

The epitaph is revealing of the simplicity and strengths of Puritan society. There was for the Puritan woman no sense of being lost, no sense

---

[4] 'An Epitaph on My Dear and Ever-Honoured Mother Mrs. Dorothy Dudley', *Works*, p. 204, ll. 6-20.

of not knowing who she was or what she was meant to be doing. To modern feminist eyes this might look like some kind of stifling constraint, but embracing the biblical definition of roles was actually liberating. It is ignorance of who we are or denial of it that brings frustration; a clearly defined role based on the created order brings security and purpose. It is no constraint to live as we were made to live. There was for the Puritans none of the massive uncertainty of identity or role that we find in our own times. They had not gleefully torn up the created order only to find themselves left with a bewildering vacuum. This is not to say that they had the definitions of the roles of men and women exactly right. Bradstreet herself is often viewed as a proto-feminist because she challenged some precise conceptions of the role of women. This is a rather ridiculous anachronism, but it is true that by being a successful poet she trespassed one established boundary, evident in the fact that her work was published under a male name. She chafes against the restraint on women writers:

> I am obnoxious to each carping tongue
> Who says my hand a needle better fits.[5]

This was not the birth of the feminist rejection of the biblical view of womanhood; rather, it was a particular disagreement with seventeenth-century expectations about the intellectual capacity of women, expectations that have no basis in Scripture. Bradstreet challenged men to consider the intellectual value of women by remembering Queen Elizabeth I:

> Now say, have women worth? or have they none?
> Or had they some, but with our Queen is't gone?
> Nay masculines, you have thus taxed us long,
> But she, though dead, will vindicate our wrong.
> Let such as say our sex is void of reason,
> Know 'tis a slander now, but once was treason.[6]

Bradstreet's critique reminds us that the answer to modern feminism is not simply to wind the clock back. All the damage that feminism has done to the family does not mean that it is wrong in every respect. I am not, therefore, arguing that the exact reproduction of the roles of the seventeenth century is desirable. Despite its weaknesses, however, the Puritan view of

---

[5] 'The Prologue', *Works*, p. 16, ll. 27-28.
[6] 'In Honour of that High and Mighty Princess Queen Elizabeth of Happy Memory', *Works*, pp. 197-8, ll. 100-05.

the identity and role of men and women was much closer to the biblical pattern than we are today.

We might contrast Bradstreet's mother with Vladimir and Estragon, the two characters in Samuel Beckett's play *Waiting for Godot*. Dorothy Dudley knew who she was and what she was meant to be doing. By contrast, Beckett's play opens with Estragon saying 'Nothing to be done'. This is ostensibly a comment on the difficulty of removing his boot, but it is taken by Vladimir to be a comment on life itself.[7] For the entire play the two characters do very little. They wait for an unidentified character who never arrives, and they seek futile ways of whiling away the time. They are aimless, pointless people, because they recognize no word from God and have no revealed identity or purpose. They are on their own. For existentialist writers like Beckett there is a certain heroism in pitching oneself into life and finding things to do. Vladimir despairs 'I can't go on!', but he does.[8] The play closes with the men saying that the next day they will commit suicide if Godot does not come, though their explorations of the possibility thus far have been half-hearted. The narrator at the end of Beckett's novel *The Unnameable* expresses the human predicament in a similar way: 'you must go on, I can't go on, I'll go on'.[9] For Beckett it matters that we keep going, but it is painfully clear that there is no metaphysical basis for our heroic perseverance. This kind of disorientation and aimlessness is not the sole preserve of playwrights and philosophers; it is the problem of our age, even if it is not drawn so starkly in the lives of most of our friends and neighbours who do not press their worldview to its bleak logical conclusions. If this is what surrounds us as Christians, and what many of us once were, then it is obviously hard for us to escape it.

The Puritans could not be more different. They knew who they were and what their roles were, because they shaped their lives and their communities from Scripture. Fundamentally, they knew who they were in Christ. It is striking when a modern man makes the same discovery through struggle. Here is the triumphant cry with which Dietrich Bonhoeffer closes a poem he wrote while he was in prison under the Nazis:

---

[7] *Waiting for Godot: A Tragicomedy in Two Acts*, 2nd edn (London: Faber and Faber, 1965; repr. 1986), Act 1, p. 9.

[8] *Godot*, Act 2, p. 91.

[9] *Three Novels: Molloy, Malone Dies, The Unnamable* (New York: Grove Press, n.d.), p. 407.

> Who am I? They mock me, these lonely questions of mine.
> Whoever I am, Thou knowest, O God, I am thine!.[10]

It is in surrender to Christ, in union with him, that we find ourselves. In him the fundamental questions of our existence are answered and we know who we are. More specifically, it is in Christ that we find the definition not just of our shared humanity, but of our differentiated roles as men, women, and children. The Lord has spoken on each of these in passages such as Ephesians 5:22-6:9 and Titus 2:1-10, passages that will reward our attention with a greater sense of who we are and who we should be.

On the edge of the world, sitting loose to it

Bradstreet records that she was not happy about her situation when she arrived in the new world: 'I found a new world and new manners, at which my heart rose', meaning rose in protest.[11] It seems to have been a couple of years before she was reconciled to her situation as the result of an illness. Her condition drove her, like Calvin, to sit loose to this world and to find her security in eternity. Reflecting in her poem *Upon a Fit of Sickness*, Bradstreet reminds us how times of deep trouble and uncertainty can have the good effect of casting us on the sovereignty of God:

> For what's this life, but care and strife
>   since first we came from womb?
> Our strength doth waste, our time doth haste,
>   and then we go to th' tomb.
> O bubble blast, how long can'st last?
>   that always art a breaking,
> No sooner blown, but dead and gone,
>   ev'n as a word that's speaking.
> O whilst I live this grace me give,

[10] 'Who am I?', in *Letters and Papers from Prison*, ed. and trans. by Reginald Fuller (London and Glasgow: Fontana Books, 1959; repr. 1963), p. 173.

[11] 'To My Dear Children', in *Works*, p. 241. The words are on a plaque at Harvard University's Bradstreet Gate, dedicated in 1997. The idea of the heart rising has been mistaken for a positive comment, but its negative sense is clear from the contrast in the next sentence of the text: 'But after I was convinced it was the way of God, I submitted to it and joined to the church at Boston.' There might be knowing irony in the use of the words, but I fear it is more likely that a misinterpretation has been enshrined in the fabric of one of the world's leading universities!

> I doing good may be,
> Then death's arrest I shall count blest,
> because it's Thy decree.[12]

In her precarious situation Bradstreet took refuge in the certain decree or plan of God, even if it meant death. In doing so she found hope not in temporal things that pass, but in eternity. In her *Contemplations* we read a reflection on the secret name given to the believer on a white stone in Revelation 2:17:

> O Time the fatal wrack of mortal things,
> That draws oblivion's curtains over kings;
> Their sumptuous monuments, men know them not,
> Their names without a record are forgot,
> Their parts, their ports, their pomp's all laid in th' dust
> Nor wit nor gold, nor buildings scape times rust;
> But he whose name is graved in the white stone
> Shall last and shine when all of these are gone.[13]

Death comes, and people are forgotten. Only our Christ-given identity will endure.

Recall her mother's epitaph:

> Religious in all her words and ways,
> Preparing still for death, till end of days.

Bradstreet praises her mother for her preparation for death. For the Puritans, this was what life was about: preparing to die. Life was always ending, time was advancing, the destroyer of mortal things. Death and eternity were coming. So the work of a responsible, serious man or woman was to prepare to die.

Here we see a way in which our material blessings can be spiritual dangers. For the Puritans, death was an ever present reality, as it is for the greater part of the human race even today. The titles of Bradstreet's poems show this: 'To the Memory of . . .', 'An Epitaph on . . .', 'In Memory of . . .', 'For Deliverance from . . .'. Of course even today death is present for everyone at some times in life. But it was ever-present for the Puritans, and all the more so for the early settlers. The Bradstreet family moved to remote frontier settings because they allowed more opportunity for Simon

---

[12] *Works*, p. 222, ll. 13-24.
[13] *Works*, pp. 213-4, ll. 226-33.

to increase his property and influence. When Anne was pregnant for the second time they hiked through the forest to build a new home in a tiny outpost called Ipswich. Twelve years after that, they helped found Andover, a settlement that was even more remote. In such places the threat of attack by native Americans was very real. A prominent family would have been particularly vulnerable to kidnap and ransom. The attackers raided and scalped settlers. Even without physical attack illness threatened death. Bradstreet was remarkably blessed in that all eight of her children survived infancy, but not all of her grandchildren did. The second half of the 1660s was a bitter time for her. In 1665 Elizabeth Bradstreet, her grand-daughter, died aged just a year and a half. In 1666 a fire destroyed her own home. On 20 June 1669 her grand-daughter Anne Bradstreet died aged three years and seven months. On September 6 her daughter-in-law Mercy Bradstreet died in her twenty-eighth year, and on 16 November her grandson Simon Bradstreet died aged a month and one day.

Bradstreet composed poems about these events that remind us poignantly of the need to sit loose to the world, to find our home and our hope in God. Here are the words she writes in memory of little Anne:

> With troubled heart and trembling hand I write,
> The heavens have changed to sorrow my delight.
> How oft with disappointment have I met,
> When I on fading things my hopes have set.
> Experience might 'fore this have made me wise,
> To value things according to their price.
> Was ever stable joy yet found below?
> Or perfect bliss without mixture of woe?
> I knew she was but as a withering flower,
> That's here today, perhaps gone in an hour;
> Like as a bubble, or the brittle glass,
> Or like a shadow turning as it was.
> More fool then I to look on that was lent
> As if mine own, when thus impermanent.
> Farewell dear child, thou ne'er shall come to me,
> But yet a while, and I shall go to thee;
> Mean time my throbbing heart's cheered up with this:
> Thou with thy Saviour art in endless bliss.[14]

---

[14] 'In Memory of My Dear Grandchild Anne Bradstreet', *Works*, p. 236.

Not without struggle, Bradstreet sat loose to the good things of this life. She enjoyed them, but she did not rest in them, knowing from hard experience their fragility. We see this perhaps most clearly in a poem written when her house burnt down in 1666:

> In silent night when rest I took
> For sorrow near I did not look
> I wakened was with thund'ring noise
> And piteous shrieks of dreadful voice.
> That fearful sound of 'Fire!' and 'Fire!'
> Let no man know is my desire.
> I, starting up, the light did spy,
> And to my God my heart did cry
> To strengthen me in my distress
> And not to leave me succorless.
> Then, coming out, beheld a space
> The flame consume my dwelling place.
> And when I could no longer look,
> I blest His name that gave and took,
> That laid my goods now in the dust.
> Yea, so it was, and so 'twas just.
> It was His own, it was not mine,
> Far be it that I should repine;
> He might of all justly bereft
> But yet sufficient for us left.
> When by the ruins oft I past
> My sorrowing eyes aside did cast,
> And here and there the places spy
> Where oft I sat and long did lie:
> Here stood that trunk, and there that chest,
> There lay that store I counted best.
> My pleasant things in ashes lie,
> And them behold no more shall I.
> Under thy roof no guest shall sit,
> Nor at thy table eat a bit.
> No pleasant tale shall e're be told,
> Nor things recounted done of old.
> No candle e're shall shine in thee,
> Nor bridegroom's voice e're heard shall be.

In silence ever shalt thou lie,
Adieu, Adieu, all's vanity.
Then straight I 'gin my heart to chide,
And did thy wealth on earth abide?
Didst fix thy hope on mold'ring dust?
The arm of flesh didst make thy trust?
Raise up thy thoughts above the sky
That dunghill mists away may fly.
Thou hast an house on high erect,
Framed by that mighty Architect,
With glory richly furnished,
Stands permanent though this be fled.
It's purchased and paid for too
By him who hath enough to do.
A price so vast as is unknown
Yet by His gift is made thine own;
There's wealth enough, I need no more,
Farewell, my pelf; farewell, my store.
The world no longer let me love,
My hope and treasure lies above.[15]

Rediscovering our past

We have lived through centuries of Christian cultural endeavour, yet we are too often unquestioning participants in the dominant non-Christian culture that surrounds us. The past is full of heroic Christians whose stories have the power to grip and inspire us in our own walk with the Lord, yet we have forgotten many of them. Anne Bradstreet is part of the vast and rich Christian culture and history that lie behind us. I commend her to you as someone whose poetry is enjoyable to read, theologically faithful, and spiritually refreshing. She will speak to you from her struggles, and she will point your thoughts 'above the sky'.

[15] 'Upon the Burning of Our House', *Works*, pp. 292-3.

10

WORKING FOR CHRIST:
JOHN LAING (1879-1978)

Why John Laing?

Whether or not you know who John Laing was depends largely on where you live and how old you are, rather than on whether or not you read church history books. This is because Laing is not known as a major figure in the history of the church. Augustine, Luther, Calvin, and Edwards you may know, but John Laing? If you do know the name it is probably because you grew up in England and saw when you were younger the single word 'LAING' written in black on a yellow sign at large building projects. Laing was not a theologian or a preacher, but a builder who inherited, ran, and grew what became a massive construction company. He is also the most recent figure considered in this book, so you might wonder how I can smuggle him into a book that is meant to be about inspiring people from church history. Let me explain the choice, and explain why Laing is worth our attention, even in place of other, more famous figures.

To start with, the twentieth century is now history and is already the subject of history books. Laing was born in 1879, which was just five years after Winston Churchill and ten years before Adolf Hitler, both of whom are certainly treated as historical figures. But why would a book like this discuss the life of a builder, even if it can justifiably be called an historical life? There are two main reasons. First, the fact that Laing was a man of business who ran a major company means that he is actually more like many of the people reading this book than Augustine or Luther were. For readers who do 'normal' jobs, Laing is an example closer to home than the great theologians or preachers of the past. Certainly every Christian today shares with the prominent figures of church history their fundamental condition of being sinners saved by grace. But there will be even more in common for many of us with a worker like Laing. Second, as I have read about Laing I have found him to be a striking example of Christian living. He was an extraordinary man, and we have a lot to learn from him because of the resolute way in which he lived his life.

Family and starting work

The Laing family is a confusing one since many of its men shared the same names and jobs. James Laing was our John Laing's great-great-grandfather. He was a stonemason. He had sons called David and James. David was a builder. He married and his son was another James. This younger James became a mason and builder, and married Ann Graham. Around 1867 they moved to Carlisle in the north-west of England, which had a growing population due to the railway and cotton spinning. There James prospered. They had among their children one named John, born in 1842. This John took over the running of the family business. He married Sarah, and they had a son who was our John, more fully John William Laing, born on 24 September, 1879. By now then Laing's choice of career was surely inevitable: he had a father, grandfather, great-grandfather, and great-great-grandfather who were all masons or builders.

Laing was a bright boy, if unusual. He won a classics prize at Carlisle Grammar School, but it made him want to leave since he feared never matching the achievement again. Leaving school aged fourteen he began work for his father. Laing's family position did not mean that he entered high up in the company. He started as an ordinary apprentice, and in later years he would be grateful for this hard experience, commenting: 'My father believed in his son having three years' practical training, so as to get a knowledge of humanity, of the British weather, and of the difficulties of actually doing work and overcoming these difficulties'.[1] The difficulties were indeed significant, and they gave Laing a deep respect

---

[1] Cited in Roy Coad, *Laing: The Biography of Sir John W. Laing, C.B.E (1879-1978)* (London: Hodder & Stoughton, 1979), p. 23. There is an earlier biography of Laing by Godfrey Harrison entitled *Life and Belief in the Experience of John W. Laing C.B.E.*, but all of my material in this chapter comes from Coad's later work.

for the working men of the building trade. We need to bear in mind that conditions then were not what they are now. The builders of 1900 make many of today's builders look effete. All the labour was manual. There were no cement mixers and no diggers. The first manually operated cranes were appearing at around that time, as were steam cranes, but more or less everything was still done by hand. If the weather prevented work, there was no pay. And at the end of a working life there was no pension. So Laing was gaining familiarity with a hard lifestyle. As he put it: 'What I am always against is people who are in an office, nicely warmed and dry, trying to tell the man who is up to the ears in mud, and drenched to the skin on a wet day, how he should do his job.'[2]

Laing was fiercely competitive in his work. He set himself to compete with the best builders he worked with, laying more bricks, cutting more stone than they could. He also studied informally, using the Mechanics' Institute, the workingmen's reading rooms, and a public library. He studied technical issues in construction and the details of financial processes. Here was a man making the very most of the opportunities before him, using every hour and devoting himself to his efforts with all his energy: 'A slack hand causes poverty, but the hand of the diligent makes rich' (*Prov.* 10:4). He finished his apprenticeship in 1897. He was then given a great responsibility, supervising the building of the first power station in the north-west of England aged just nineteen.

The growth of the Laing company

To give you an idea of Laing's success as a businessman, I will lay out some of the landmark events in the history of John Laing & Sons. The company traced its origins to a house building project completed by the younger James Laing in 1848, though it took its name from his son, the older John Laing. By the time John W. Laing was working for it, it was a local building company but not a lot more. The key to the growth of the company was the accurate costing method that Laing himself developed. He kept meticulous notes telling him the rates at which a man could work on all of the different building processes. He knew this because he had done the work himself. It meant that he could tender for work with remarkably accurate costings, knowing exactly how low he could get the price without losing money.

[2] Cited in *Laing*, p. 24.

It was the outbreak of World War I in August 1914 that led to the first major growth spurt for the company, mainly because Laing provided vital construction services for the war effort. Major work was involved in providing prefabricated timber huts and at a new factory complex at Gretna just over the Scottish border. Laing himself enlisted, but was discharged because of the importance of his work. All of this led to considerable growth in the company and in 1917 some 3-4,000 men worked for Laing. In the early 1910s turnover stood at less than £10,000, but by 1920 it had leapt to half a million pounds.[3] Laing was also a strategic thinker and he foresaw a number of pressure points within the industry and prepared for them. He anticipated, for example, the shortage of qualified bricklayers after the War. With this in mind he developed a method of system building called Easiform, which involved casting concrete walls in situ without any need for a bricklayer. Unsurprisingly, the Easiform work took off after the war.

Laing opened its London office in 1920. From 1929–39 the amount of work the company undertook quadrupled. World War II was then another period of considerable growth. Between 1939 and 1942 the amount of work doubled again, and the workforce more than tripled. Among many other projects, the company built more than twelve airfields in the three years before the war, and fifty-four more between 1939 and 1945. Laing also built the concealed RAF Bomber Command and much of the Mulberry harbour that was towed across the English Channel and used for the D-Day landings. The firm calculated that during the first four years of the war, measured by money, it was responsible for one five-hundredth of the national war effort. One of the wartime staff observed that Laing 'seemed to work like a machine in the war', adding: 'He gave everything he had to the war effort, arriving at jobs at 7:30 A.M., and he was then sixty-five years old. What a man and what a leader!'[4]

The company's role after the war was largely necessitated by the effect of the V1 rockets that Germany began launching from 14 June 1944, and the V2 rockets that followed soon after. The air-raids of the Blitz during September 1940 to May 1941 had already destroyed 85,000 houses and damaged a further one and a quarter million. In two months the new rockets damaged another million. At the height of the campaign 20,000 houses were damaged each day. Laing was heavily involved in the extensive

---

[3] With figures like these I will not attempt to translate into today's money; the growth speaks for itself whatever the modern equivalent.

[4] Cited in *Laing*, p. 154.

reconstruction effort, including the rebuilding of Coventry Cathedral. Later, the company also built much of the M1 motorway that runs from London to the north of England. By 1979 the company's turnover was 1,600 times the size it had been when Laing was in his twenties. All of this gives some idea of Lang's extraordinary achievement in the construction industry. Having sketched the outline of the company story, we will now consider John Laing the Christian.

A Christian family

Laing grew up in a Christian family. His father John had been converted when he was around twenty-five through the witness of a friend. Laing's mother's family, the Woods, had been influenced by the 1859 evangelical revival when a magazine entitled *British Evangelist* had reached their home and they were converted. The Laings were very involved in a Brethren congregation in Carlisle. The Brethren, who began in 1829, were marked by several features. They had no full-time ministers, they had a strong expectation of the end times, and they were generally abstemious, living separately from worldly activities. They were also very committed to the task of evangelism, both as individuals and as a movement. Growing up in this context, Laing dated his conversion to the age of seven.

John Laing: Christian businessman

There are many questions that we might ask of a Christian businessman like Laing: Was there anything distinctive about the company because he was a Christian? How did he treat his staff? Did he ever make tough decisions? Did he manage to maintain his integrity in the cut-throat construction industry? And what did he do with the millions that he earned? We will look first at how Laing's distinctively Christian approach to business began.

His early resolve

One of the earliest projects Laing was responsible for was the construction of surface water sewers at Barrow-in-Furness, south of the Lake District. The contract was signed in 1906, specifying the cost of the work at £10,000. The contract itself had very strict requirements and it made Laing responsible for almost everything that might go wrong. Trouble soon came. Laing had been given test results by the Corporation that indicated that the land in which they would be working was dry clay, but it transpired that it was actually running sand. Laing suspected that the bore holes for the tests had been sited deliberately away from the sand. Next, the route of the sewer had to be moved because of pressure from landowners, with the result that the new route was even harder to construct. Because of the problems caused by the unstable ground, the project got further and further behind. Also, the new route requested by the landowners damaged some local properties. The owners sued the Corporation, and the Corporation sued Laing. In the end the sewers were finished a year late and the financial dispute went to court. Laing's mother commented to friends that it would have been cheaper to move the whole family to Switzerland for a year than to let John try his hand at a civil engineering project.

Laing, still only around thirty, found himself carrying the fortunes of the family on his shoulders, with a disastrous project getting behind schedule and a legal case against them. It was in the midst of this crisis that he cast himself on the Lord. In this context of desperation he made the decisions that would shape the rest of his career. He pledged to the Lord that if he would keep him through the troubles, then he would make him a partner in the family business. Later he comments: 'The Lord has kept His part of the contract, and I wanted to assure myself that I had kept mine.'[5]

The Lord did indeed deliver the company from its troubles and as a result Laing wrote a 'programme for his life'. He sums it up like this: 'First, the centre of my life was to be God—God as seen in Jesus Christ; secondly I was going to enjoy life, and help others to enjoy it.'[6] So at this early stage Laing resolved that the centre of his life would not be the business. It would not be the latest contract. It would not even be his family. It would be the Lord. And he also resolved to be less intense and caught up in his work, more ready to enjoy the good things God had given him and to help others enjoy them, rather than be preoccupied exclusively with his work. For a man with such a future ahead of him it is a striking resolve. Did he manage to keep it?

Laing and his staff

In many ways Laing seems to have been a demanding employer. By that I mean that he was quick to fire people who failed to pull their weight. For

[5] Cited in *Laing*, p. 50.
[6] Cited in *Laing*, p. 51.

example, a story circulated in the company of Laing arriving at a site and meeting a man standing by a brazier warming himself. Laing joined the man without saying who he was. When the signal to start work was given, the man stayed where he was. Laing waited for a few minutes and then asked the man 'What is your number?'. The man told him. Laing replied: 'Then get your cards—you're fired.'[7] As a man who worked with extraordinary diligence, Laing did not tolerate those who did not.

Yet at the same time, Laing was deeply committed to his staff as people and to the idea of the company as a team, even a family. One of his staff commented: 'He knew everybody by name, all their pedigrees, their families and everything. When the firm grew bigger he had a list made out for him.'[8] And if there was a need, Laing was very generous even if it was not a crisis, though he was carefully generous. One of the staff explained how his request for a rise was met:

> The only time I ever applied for a rise in my life, before I knew where I was he had all my money allocated out. 'You're courting, aren't you? When I was your age I was courting and I used to put so much aside and give so much to my mother.' He had it all worked out. Eventually he gave me about 7s. 6d. rise.[9]

In more extreme cases of need, Laing was still careful, but he was all the more generous. On site once he met a man working a hand-operated crane who looked unwell. He asked 'You are not looking well—what is the trouble?' The man explained: 'My wife has been in bed for some time and I have had to see to the children and do all the work before starting work at seven.' Laing found out where the man lived and disappeared. Later on he returned. 'You are needed at home; take two weeks off with pay.' The man returned to his house, found that Laing had been there and discovered that the situation was indeed as he had described it, and had also left five pounds for the family. On another occasion, Laing heard that a man called Jimmy Veness who had worked for him was sick and destitute. He telegrammed another employee: 'Relieve immediate distress and report—further instructions will follow.'[10] Many such stories circulated. One Carlisle man commented 'Wherever I went, I met people who spoke

[7] Cited in *Laing*, p. 92.
[8] Cited in *Laing*, p. 91.
[9] Cited in *Laing*, p. 91.
[10] Cited in *Laing*, p. 94.

of good things John Laing had done for them.'[11]

Laing's care for his staff was also evident in more general ways. As I mentioned earlier, working conditions and terms in the building industry were atrocious at the time. If the weather was bad, workers were not paid. Nor were there paid holidays. Laing began new practices, many of them now standard, to address such issues. He introduced pay for time lost through wet weather, and he began a benevolent fund and a pension scheme for his employees. When shares were issued in the company, he made sure that employees had a significant proportion of them.

Laing and his word

It should be the case that a Christian businessman's yes is his yes. Laing took this seriously, even when it cost him money. One of his staff had been promised that his house would be built with a garage, but when the house was built there was no garage and no room left for one. Laing ordered that the building be razed to the ground and rebuilt. On another project the approach road to a factory was being concreted. Laing requested a copy of the specification for the project and found that the concrete that was being laid was a quarter of an inch thinner than the specification required. He instructed the foreman: 'We are giving the client a quarter of an inch less than he is paying for and I want you to take up all this area.'[12]

Laing and his money

We now come to the most striking part of the story, Laing and his money. After his parents died, Laing discovered that they had been giving away £750 of their £1,000 pound annual income. Laing only knew this after they died, but he had evidently already been so shaped by their pattern of living that he had himself adopted a similar approach. At the time of the crisis on the Barrow-in-Furness project Laing put in place a financial plan. This is how he described the moment and the plan:

> Following a period of solemn prayer and dedication when in Barrow, I drew upon a sheet of Furness Abbey Hotel notepaper during September 1909 showing how I proposed to dispose of my income. That says:—

[11] Cited in *Laing*, p. 92.
[12] Cited in *Laing*, pp. 139-40.

If income £400 p.a. give £50, live on £150, save £200
If income £1,000 p.a. give £200, live on £300, save £500
If income £3,000 p.a. give £1,000, live on £500, save £1,500
If income £4,000 p.a. give £1,500, live on £500, save £2,000[13]

Note how the sum to be spent on living reaches £500 and stops, while the level of giving increases. The level is never just tithing—even at its lowest proportion it is an eighth of his income, but it then rises to around a third. What about the savings though? Laing was not stockpiling to buy some luxury. The savings were not personal, they were for the company. Laing was building a capital base for the company so that if there were further disasters like Barrow it would have the reserves to survive. At the same time, Laing decided that if the saved money brought in £500 interest, then he would start living on that and no more. He would then be able to give away more than planned because the £500 from income would be replaced by £500 from interest. Half of the rest of the interest would be ploughed back into the savings, and half given away. In fact Laing far exceeded this planned giving as the business grew. In 1922, a year after the issue of shares in the company, Laing transferred 15,000 of his shares to the Stewards Company, a Brethren charity. With other share allocations counted, this left him with 23,201 out of 49,901 ordinary shares in the company. By 1922 he had already handed over more than half of the business to others.

Even when he had done this Laing continued to give from his own income. As early as 1940 he was giving away £20,000 pounds a year, many times more than he kept for himself. Apart from the Stewards Company, Laing supported different causes, although always after careful investigation and with an eye on their strategic nature. The national student ministry in the United Kingdom, then known as the Inter-Varsity Fellowship (now the Universities and Colleges Christian Fellowship), was extensively supported by Laing's money. When his oldest son approached university he became very interested in the student Christian witness. He joined the Business Advisory Committee of the IVF in 1935. Laing bought the IVF its offices in Bedford Square, and he also bought the Northgate Hall where the Oxford Inter-Collegiate Christian Union met. He funded the expansion in the number of travelling secretaries who supported the work of particular Christian Union groups. Laing did not just write cheques; he

[13] Cited in *Laing*, pp. 51-2.

would drop in to the IVF offices for an hour or two a week, opening with the same question, 'How many students and graduates have come to the Lord Jesus?'. He also played a major role in supporting London Bible College and Tyndale House, a centre for evangelical biblical research in Cambridge. Tyndale House has had a massive impact on the profile of evangelical scholarship. It is no exaggeration to say that before World War II there was hardly any evangelical theology at an academic level in Britain, whereas the situation here and globally is now transformed, with long lists of faithful commentaries on all the books of the Bible. Laing was himself not at all academic in his theology, but he saw the need for strong academic work by evangelicals that would undergird and work its way through into preaching and teaching.

Laing and his sons were generous with the company's work too. They won the contract to build the new Coventry Cathedral on the basis of a normal quotation. The architect Sir Basil Spence telephoned Maurice Laing to tell him the good news. He described what happened:

> Next day I got a letter from him saying that his firm considered it a great honour to be entrusted with this work and that at the end of the job they would give all their profit back to the Cathedral. He asked me not to publish this decision as it would detract from the spirit of the gift. I hope the Laing family will forgive me for breaking that promise now.[14]

It did not stop there. Even though he was unwell, John Laing went to the opening service at the Cathedral. Afterwards he discovered he had mistakenly put his invitation rather than his offering into the collection. Having already built the Cathedral for no profit, he wrote to the Cathedral authorities and enclosed the donation! Laing also paid for the building of many Brethren halls at cost price, and he set aside many of the houses on the estates the company built for use by missionaries home on furlough.

It is also striking to see how Laing lived. He resisted temptations to what he regarded as luxury. In one year he bought a radiogram (a combination of a radio and a record player) and he bought the best one that could be found. But at the same time he wanted to buy a new car and although he could easily have afforded to buy both, he decided to postpone purchasing the new car because two items of luxury should not be bought in the same year. When he went away on business he would pack

---

[14] Cited in *Laing*, p. 202.

sandwiches from home or eat in the canteens on the building sites. If one of the site managers put on a special meal for Laing when he came he would be rebuked for it. Laing seems also to have been suspicious of supporting luxury in others. When the 1966 Billy Graham Crusade was being planned Laing wanted to make a substantial donation. The Crusade director's phone rang. Laing said he had heard a rumour that Billy Graham would be staying at the Hilton and asked if this was true. He was assured that it was not. Then, Laing said, if Graham was definitely not staying at the Hilton, he would make a donation. There was also a pragmatic, practical side to Laing's attitude to money. He wrote to a friend in 1962: 'Everyone should have a house just big enough to serve its purpose, as to have more than that causes such a lot of work'.[15] He acted on this conviction. While living in a larger house, he had a smaller one built beside it and moved into it. A friend who was visiting while the new house was being built asked if it was for the gardener. Laing appears to have known that his attitude to money could be amusingly eccentric. One friend observed how Laing leapt up two stairs at a time with youthful vigour. Laing replied: 'Yes, and it saves the carpet!'.[16]

Despite the fact that biographers have been able to find all of these facts and figures, Laing gave confidentially. Indeed, some of the information now known was revealed against his stated wishes, though usually a long time after the event. Sometimes Laing would send money to one organization and ask them to pass it on to another so that none of the recipients would know where it had come from. We do not know how much he gave away. We do know that though he long presided over a multi-million-pound company, when he died his estate was valued at just £371 pounds. As Roy Coad puts it, 'the man who had handled millions had given them all away.'[17]

Laing and his local church

Surely, we might think, this busy man must have neglected his church responsibilities? Perhaps we secretly hope to find some glaring flaw, to salve our own consciences! On the contrary, Laing was very active in his local Brethren meeting in Carlisle and then in London. In Carlisle he built the Brethren a new building, Hebron Hall, at cost. He somehow managed to

[15] Cited in *Laing*, p. 210.
[16] Cited in *Laing*, p. 126.
[17] *Laing*, p. 215.

run a men's Bible study class at the hall. When the company opened an office in London he had three criteria for locating its base: it had to be a suitable place for the business, it had to have a country view, and it had to be a place where he could build a meeting place. He duly built Woodcroft Hall, paying for two-thirds of the cost himself. He was an elder from the start. The church grew to 300 members within a few years. He became a leader of the local Crusaders group in Mill Hill. He regularly went on the annual camps, continuing until he was seventy.

Laing the evangelist

Laing was also a bold personal evangelist. David Beattie, a friend, was asked by him 'David, if you die tonight, where will you go?' He was eventually converted.[18] At the investiture for his C.B.E., Laing was waiting with others to come before the Queen. He turned to the man beside him: 'I have been thinking what it will be like when we assemble before the throne of our Lord Jesus Christ. What shall we be thinking; and do you hope to be there?'[19] As it happened the man was a Christian. Laing was always ready to speak for Christ. In a volume of reminiscences written for Laing, one friend recalled a spontaneous opportunity for witness:

> Do you remember a walk we had, just the two of us? It was Saturday night in the market-place at Stockton-on-Tees. Time, nine o'clock—great crowds jostling and sellers of goods shouting their wares. Suddenly you said, 'What a grand place for an open-air meeting. Let's have one, Henry.' We stopped in our stride. I took your hat . . . and just a brief prayer to ask for God's help and you were telling the great crowd what the Lord Jesus meant to you. Literally hundreds of eager faces looked at the two young men standing there alone—yet not alone, for the Lord was with us. How the folk listened to your message of God's love in sending His only Son to die for sinners. On the Monday following, a man came in to my office in West Hartlepool and said, 'I saw you and your friend in Stockton market on Saturday night and listened and I want to tell you how I admire your pluck and stand for God.'[20]

This kind of behaviour was not normal then, any more than it is now.

[18] Cited in *Laing*, p. 35.
[19] Cited in *Laing*, p. 176.
[20] Cited in *Laing*, p. 58.

When we read of men standing up and preaching in the open air, it is not that everyone did that in those days. John Wesley himself captured the feeling of it when he described his decision to preach in the open air: 'I submitted to be more vile'.[21] It would be vile now, but it was also vile then.

Learning from Laing

How can we learn from John Laing? We must remember that we do not become more godly simply by considering examples from the past. The root of change is found in considering Christ and delighting in him. Laing's compulsive desire to speak to others of what Christ meant to him shows how he was captivated by his Saviour. He points us beyond himself. Then, with our eyes fixed on the grace of God, we will do well to learn from his example in terms of both its general extent, and its specific elements. By its general extent I mean the fact that his Christian commitment was a rounded one. It was not that he was zealous here but neglectful there. He was a Christian at work and at home, in public and in private, among believers and unbelievers. I think part of his challenge lies in this comprehensiveness. What is the breadth of our own commitment? But his challenge also no doubt lies in the detail. Does our own work consume us and edge out our primary commitment to the Lord Jesus Christ? Have we ever made the kind of self-conscious, deliberate resolve that Laing made at Barrow? If you have staff, how do you treat them? These are the kinds of questions that he leaves us with. We cannot address at once every challenge from Laing's example, and it would be discouraging to try. You might begin by picking one particular lesson from his rounded life and applying it prayerfully.

---

[21] Cited in Mark A. Noll, *Turning Points: Decisive Moments in the History of Christianity* (Grand Rapids, MI: Baker Academic, 2000), p. 223.

PRIMARILY FOR PASTORS AND ELDERS

11

PRIORITIES FOR THE CHURCH: JOHN CALVIN

Introduction

My intention here is to consider the breadth of John Calvin's ministry in wide-angle view to see what we can learn from the shape of his life's work. As we discovered when considering his sufferings, Calvin was an embattled man, so he had to chose his priorities carefully. What were the things of first importance to him amid all his struggles? We can find an answer to this question by looking at what he wrote and at what he did. From the long list of his works the texts written in the thick of the controversy with Rome are again particularly illuminating. From the story of his actions in and beyond Geneva we will be able to identify the focal points of his practical energies. Finally, we will examine the way in which Calvin visualized reality itself to discover the heart of his concern in the Reformation.

The urgency of reform in Calvin's writings

My material here is drawn from three texts at the heart of Calvin's defence of the Reformation. The first is one that we have already encountered, his *Reply to Sadoleto*, the Cardinal who attempted to recall Geneva to Rome in 1539. The second is his work *On the Necessity of Reforming the Church*. This was a treatise written in 1544 and addressed to the Emperor Charles V and the princes meeting for the Imperial Diet at Speier. The third we have also met before, the *Antidote* to the Council of Trent. These treatises

are interesting for two reasons: they are early, and they are overtly controversial. Their timing means that they show us Calvin's priorities in the
early days of his reforming work, at a time when he was either exiled from
Geneva or recently returned and working to establish a properly reformed
church. Their controversial character means that we hear Calvin speaking
in situations where he knew that the stakes were high. These are not the
kinds of contexts in which Calvin wasted words or misrepresented his
priorities. Indeed, each of the works exhibits a degree of leanness. The
Reply to Sadoleto was the fruit of just six days of writing. In the *Necessity*
Calvin is aware that he must not waste words because the Emperor is a
busy man, so in discussing justification he moves swiftly to focus on the
key question, the state of the human will.[1] As I mentioned in Chapter 6,
the *Antidote* reads like a brisk walk through the text of Trent, with a similarly speedy focus on the issue of original sin and free will in its treatment
of justification.[2]

Calvin's own words in these treatises show his estimation of the
seriousness of the Reformation. In the *Reply to Sadoleto* he indicates the
urgency of the question of Geneva's position by accepting the way that
the Cardinal casts the debate in the context of the day of judgement. In
the *Necessity* he argues that reform, even disruptive reform, was an una-
voidable necessity given the extremely parlous state of the church. He
uses a striking image when he explains to the Emperor that the prevailing
idolatry could not be ignored: 'What then? When we saw idolatry openly
and everywhere stalking abroad, were we to connive at it? To have done so
would have just been to rock the world in its sleep of death, that it might
not awake.'[3] Calvin sees the world dangerously lulled by Rome's idolatry, failing, drifting, fading into eternal death. Interestingly, while people
sometimes find Calvin's language too passionate, at this point he felt that
he might have been too restrained:

> I feel what nerve, what earnestness, what urgency, what ardour, the
> treatment of this subject requires. And I am well aware that persons
> will not be wanting to express their surprise, that on a subject so
> noble and splendid I should be so cold. But what could I do? I
> bend under its weight and magnitude; and I therefore see not how

[1] *The Necessity of Reforming the Church*, in *Tracts and Letters*, 1:159.
[2] *Antidote*, 3:108–109.
[3] *Necessity*, 1:188.

I can do better than set the matter before you simply, without any embellishment of words, that you may afterwards ponder and scrutinize it.

The 'fearful calamities of the Church', he explains, 'might move to pity even minds of iron'.[4]

Calvin feared Europe being lulled into the sleep of eternal death most of all, but he also envisaged severe temporal consequences if she rejected the gospel. In the *Necessity* he judges that the Holy Roman Empire was highly vulnerable, telling Charles V that 'even now, while your own eyes behold, it is half bent, and totters to its final ruin'.[5] Several times he turns to 1 Corinthians 11 and Paul's teaching on the Lord's supper. If the Corinthians were weak, ill, and even dying because they abused the supper (*1 Cor.* 11:30), then his own contemporaries should expect severe consequences for their disobedience. The specific consequence that he identifies is the threat from the Ottoman Empire, which would have been evident recently in the siege of Vienna (1529) and, as he was writing, in the struggle for control of Hungary. In a bold piece of theologico-historical analysis, Calvin argues that the threat from the Ottomans was a judgement from God. Here is how he puts it:

> We, indeed, stand amazed at our disasters, or suggest other reasons why God so afflicts us. But if we reflect how slight the error by which the Corinthians had vitiated the sacred Supper was, if contrasted with all the defilements by which, in the present day, it is sullied and polluted amongst ourselves, it is strange not to perceive that God, who so severely punished them, is justly more offended with us.[6]

Later in the same work Calvin specifically identifies the moral cause of the military threat: 'The fuel of the Turkish war is within, shut up in our bowels, and must first be removed, if we would successfully drive back the war itself.'[7] Clearly for Calvin the danger facing his age was grave in both time and eternity. It is his awareness of the urgency of the gospel cause that gives these works their terse focus and that makes them particularly useful in discerning the heart of his reformational concerns.

[4] *Necessity*, 1:231.
[5] *Necessity*, 1:233.
[6] *Necessity*, 1:197.
[7] *Necessity*, 1:233.

Doctrine and worship

In the *Necessity*, Calvin writes to the Imperial Diet about the priorities that Martin Luther had at the very beginning of the Reformation. Here he explains what Luther was doing:

> We maintain, then, that at the commencement, when God raised up Luther and others, who held forth a torch to light us into the way of salvation, and who, by their ministry, founded and reared our churches, those heads of doctrine in which the truth of our religion, those in which the pure and legitimate worship of God, and those in which the salvation of men are comprehended, were in a great measure obsolete. We maintain that the use of the sacraments was in many ways vitiated and polluted. And we maintain that the government of the Church was converted into a species of foul and insufferable tyranny.[8]

Note the way that Calvin describes the work of Luther. First of all, he 'held forth a torch to light us into the way of salvation': here is Luther bringing the gospel. Second, he 'founded and reared our churches': here is Luther reforming the corporate life of Christians. Calvin explains that Luther had to do all of this because the various 'heads of doctrine' had been obscured. He lists three specific heads here: 'the truth of our religion', 'the pure and legitimate worship of God', and 'the salvation of men'.

This is a fair description of Luther's work, but Calvin's comments elsewhere in the treatise reveal that it is just as much a summary of his own priorities for the life of the church. Lining his priorities up with Luther's was a way for Calvin to emphasise Protestant unity:

> If it be inquired, then, by what things chiefly the Christian religion has a standing existence amongst us, and maintains its truth, it will be found that the following two not only occupy the principal place, but comprehend under them all the other parts, and consequently the whole substance of Christianity, viz., a knowledge, *first*, of the mode in which God is duly worshipped; and, *secondly*, of the source from which salvation is to be obtained. When these are kept out of view, though we may glory in the name of Christians, our profession is empty and vain. After these come the Sacraments and the Government of the Church, which, as they were instituted

[8] *Necessity*, 1:125.

for the preservation of these branches of doctrine, ought not to be employed for any other purpose.[9]

Calvin specifics two things that are foremost and embrace the entire Christian religion: knowledge of the mode of worship, and knowledge of the source of salvation. These two key 'branches of doctrine' are served by the sacraments and the government of the church. There is a hierarchy here: worship and doctrine come first, with the sacraments and the government of the church serving them. The sacraments are thus dependent on the doctrine. As he puts it later on in the work, 'there is no use in the sacraments unless the thing which the sign visibly represents is explained in accordance with the Word of God'.[10] The government of the church likewise depends on the presence of the word: 'no man can claim for himself the office of bishop or pastor who does not feed his flock with the Word of the Lord'.[11]

It is clear that for Calvin doctrine has priority over the external life of the church, but he does not think that the external life of the church is a matter of indifference and can be safely ignored or left to the dictates of pragmatism. Both are necessary, as he shows when he illustrates their relationship using the analogy of the soul and body:

> I would say, that rule in the Church, the pastoral office, and all other matters of order, resemble the body, whereas the doctrine which regulates the due worship of God, and points out the ground on which the consciences of men must rest their hope of salvation, is the soul which animates the body, renders it lively and active, and, in short, makes it not to be a dead and useless carcase.[12]

Here the outward aspects of the church are the body, and doctrine is the soul. The analogy is intended to illustrate the need for attention to both doctrine and the outward life of the church, while highlighting the animating role of the former. It is not intended to denigrate the body. While doctrine has priority, the body is still essential. For many Greeks the body was a trap for the soul to be transcended. Calvin was a Hebrew: the temporary separation of body and soul in death is the result of sin, not the ideal state for human existence. Body and soul ought to be together. So

[9] *Necessity*, 1:126.
[10] *Necessity*, 1:139.
[11] *Necessity*, 1:141.
[12] *Necessity*, 1:126-27.

while he argued for the priority of the soul, he argued for the necessity of reforming both, doctrine and the church. In particular, he holds that it is the doctrine of justification that is crucial to the soul, a reminder that whatever their differences Luther and Calvin shared the conviction that this is the article by which the church stands or falls. Calvin is unequivocal: 'the safety of the Church depends as much on this doctrine as human life does on the soul'.[13]

This framework of priorities explains the way in which Beza summarizes Calvin's work following his return to Geneva in 1541. He is emphatic on Calvin's commitment to the importance of reforming the external life of the church:

> Calvin being thus restored at the urgent entreaty of his Church, proceeded to set it in order. Seeing that the city stood greatly in need of a curb, he declared, in the first place, that he could not properly fulfil his ministry, unless, along with Christian doctrine, a regular presbytery with full ecclesiastical authority were established.[14]

Here is the pairing: soul and body; Christian doctrine and an ordered church. Calvin's desire for church order was initially met by the *Ecclesiastical Ordinances* in 1541, and then in the long struggle against the Libertines as he sought to secure the integrity of the church's control of excommunication.

It is worth noting as an aside that behind Calvin's commitment to the outward forms of the church lies a deep, if posthumous, difference from Zwingli. Zwingli denied the instrumentality of external things as means of faith-building grace. In rightly opposing the mechanistic teaching of Rome that the Mass brings grace simply by being celebrated (the Latin phrase was *ex opere operato*), Zwingli over-reacted into arguing that the physical signs of bread and wine would only ever be used by God to produce an 'historical faith [*fides historica*]'.[15] They operate only on the mind, separate from faith. They function only as any human memorial functions in relation to that which it commemorates:

---

[13] *Necessity*, 1:137.

[14] *Life*, 1:xxxviii. Beza makes the same point on p. xl in terms of Calvin seeking first God's kingdom and righteousness.

[15] *An Exposition of the Faith*, in *Zwingli and Bullinger*, ed. and trans. by G. W. Bromiley (Philadelphia: Westminster Press, 1953), p. 260.

> All celebrations, monuments and statues give historical faith, that is, they remind us of some event, refreshing the memory like the feast of the passover amongst the Hebrews or the remission of debts at Athens, or it may be that they commemorate some victory like the stone at Ebenezer.[16]

The signs are used by the Lord to remind in the same way as a memorial statue. Zwingli believed that this was an important role, since the senses could distract the soul from Christ, but it did not involve any operation directly on faith itself. The role of the physical signs was thus to prevent the soul losing its focus on Christ by keeping the senses in line with faith: 'the sacraments are like bridles which serve to check the senses when they are on the point of dashing off in pursuit of their own desires, and to recall them to the obedience of the heart and of faith.'[17] That was their role and no more. By contrast, Calvin held a much higher view of the role of created, outward things. They have no power in and of themselves. They do not work automatically, *ex opere operato*, as Rome taught. Their operation is wholly dependent on the Spirit and faith. But they are used by God as instruments to strengthen our union with Christ. The Lord has pledged to give us Christ with the signs: 'when we have received the symbol of the body, let us no less surely trust that the body itself is also given to us'.[18] The external, Calvin believed, could be instrumental in the work of grace. It was this which made him so concerned about the outward life of the church. This is not to say that Zwingli lacked such concern, but it is to explain that Calvin had a more secure theological foundation for it than Zwingli.

Calvin was a man who was constantly preoccupied with the public life of the Lord's people. He was, for example, a writer of liturgies from as early as his time in Strasbourg. Throughout his ministry he paid close attention to the ongoing reform of public worship. This was also true of the Reformation as a whole. On the ground the Reformation certainly involved a change of preaching, but very often that change was preceded by an alteration in the public forms of religion. Indeed, in England the first decisive change in each of the pendulum swings of the Reformation was an Act of Uniformity prescribing new forms of public worship, and this was then followed by attempts to bring the preaching in the parishes

---

[16] *Exposition*, p. 260.
[17] *Exposition*, p. 264.
[18] *Institutes*, IV. xvii. 10, 2:1371.

into line with the new liturgy. Admittedly the outward changes to public worship had to be enforced by royal commissioners, but the formal change ran ahead of the improvement of preaching, often by several decades. In continental cities the pattern was often the same. A disputation between reformers and Roman Catholic priests would be followed by a vote. That vote would establish the city as a reformed city and would make one vital change, the abolition of the Mass in public worship. It would be another thing to see souls savingly converted through the preaching of the word.

Calvin spent time reflecting on detailed questions concerning the corporate life of the church. For example, we find him engaging in surprising reflections on baptism in his letters. Here he is writing to John Knox answering a question about admitting the children of 'idolaters and excommunicated persons' to baptism. Calvin was evidently very interested in the question since he had taken it to his colleagues. He reports that together they arrived at this unanimous opinion:

> God's promise comprehends not only the offspring of every believer in the first line of descent, but extends to thousands of generations. Whence it has happened that the interruption of piety which has prevailed in Popery has not taken away from baptism its force and efficacy. For we must look to its origin, and the very reason and nature of baptism is to be esteemed as arising from the promise of God. To us then it is by no means doubtful that an offspring descended from holy and pious ancestors, belong to the body of the church, though their fathers and grandfathers may have been apostates. . . . In the mean time we confess that it is indispensable for them to have sponsors. For nothing is more preposterous than that persons should be incorporated with Christ, of whom we have no hopes of their ever becoming his disciples.[19]

Calvin had raised this question with his colleagues and they had deliberated and worked out a careful answer. It is an answer that seeks to embrace both the promise to generations made to Abraham in the covenant of grace, and the need for the baptised child to be discipled in Christ. Knox's question is in fact a fairly obvious one to ask for any paedobaptist, but I suspect that we would struggle to find discussions of it today. Whether one agrees with it or not, Calvin's answer is indicative of his thoughtfulness concerning the life of the church and the sacraments.

[19] To John Knox, 7 November, 1559, in *Tracts and Letters*, 7:74-75.

Evaluation

The fact that Calvin did something may make us stop and think, but by itself it says nothing for the importance of doing what he did. Let me suggest three reasons why he was right to rate the external life of the church so highly. First of all, the New Testament exhibits a strong concern with corporate worship, especially in 1 Corinthians. Paul attacks idolatry, disorder, and incomprehensibility in the Corinthian gatherings, and he instructs them on how they are to conduct themselves. He even warns that their external conduct at the Lord's supper has led some of them to illness and death. Second, Calvin was right that the worship of God has an inalienable outward character. Worship is in Spirit and in truth, but it manifests itself in public. We are bodily, visible creatures. In particular, we are to praise the Lord before the rest of creation, and it is in the outward forms that we do this. Hence Paul clearly envisages an evangelistic impact for the Corinthian gatherings (*1 Cor.* 14:20-25). Third, corporate worship has a deep pedagogical function within the church. Not just what we preach but also what we say, pray, sing, and do when we gather teaches the Lord's people. To neglect it or to be indifferent to it is to invite theological ignorance and confusion. Doctrine is made visible in public worship.

Reflection

How might we learn from Calvin's priorities today? As we have seen, he found two things at the heart of true religion, 'the mode in which God is duly worshipped' and 'the source from which salvation is to be obtained'. The Reformed today are generally with Calvin on the second element. We have a right and high level of concern for preserving the truth of the doctrine of justification by faith alone. It is not unchallenged from within, but many are ready to rise to defend it. Our concern for the mode of worship is less obvious. To be an authentic Reformation Christian is to be concerned with the saving doctrine of the gospel *and* the public worship of God. The danger of neglecting worship and attending only to doctrine is that every Lord's day becomes an exercise in public self-contradiction: our doctrine says one thing and our public practice says another.

We need also to ask what it means to attend to public worship. It does not mean simply sticking to what we have always done. Dying in the ditch to defend the pattern that we grew up with against the slightest change is not reforming. In fact it is the opposite, just the kind of reactionary

traditionalism that the reformers were fighting against. Even if we conclude that it is right to follow the practice of the past we should do so only
after we have thought it through thoroughly and owned it for ourselves.
We need, in other words, an informed theological understanding of all of
the elements of public worship.

Examining our corporate worship should also help us see how we
relate to our surrounding culture. My view (and you will need to question it) is that at the moment we most often err in one of two ways here.
Sometimes we follow too closely the casual culture of our day and end
up being flippant and silly in public worship. We become so preoccupied
with outreach that we think that the primary criterion for public worship
of the living God is its accessibility to someone who does not actually
worship the living God (as we see it stated thus, does it not obviously
jar?). We think that our music can simply ape the music of our culture,
as if musical styles are entirely indifferent theologically. We think that our
preaching is best modelled on non-Christian modes of speech such as
stand-up comedy or political rhetoric. Each of these tendencies models
an aspect of corporate worship on the life of the world. We might defend
this modelling by arguing that these things are matters of indifference on
which we are therefore free to do what we wish.

But this is very hard to sustain. To think that we can safely fit biblical words to any musical style we would have to hold that the music is
itself meaningless and has no effect. Is it not obvious that musical style is
not neutral? Is there really no meaningful difference between Bach and
Blur? Can the sound of Metallica possibly have the same meaning and
effect as the sound of Mozart? I do not here argue that one is a better
model for worship than the other; my point is simply that their styles are
obviously different in significant ways. Similarly, can we really think that
comedy is the best model for preaching? Is the aim of the preacher not
fundamentally different from the aim of the comedian? Perhaps we might,
having filtered and tested it against Scripture's view of preaching, gain
the smallest insight from comedians, but they can hardly be our principal
model for communication. In sum, I ask again, can we really think that
the primary criterion for public worship of the living God is its accessibility to someone who does not worship him? Should the unbeliever
really feel comfortable standing in the midst of a group of people whose
very existence and whose very words are a condemnation of his idols? 1
Corinthians 14:20-25 is perhaps the best text for proving that we should

expect non-Christians to be present at public worship and to be affected by it, but it hardly supports making them comfortable. When they hear the Christians speaking they either think they are mad, or they fall on their faces and worship the living God. The last thing they leave thinking is 'How nice, the preacher was very funny and the music was just like the albums I listen to.'

And yet! Did you read the previous paragraph and nod vigorously, agreeing with every word against the terrible compromising worldliness of today's church? If you did, it is quite possible that you have the same problem yourself but in a more subtle form. The same temptation awaits us in two directions, not just one. For every church that is too casual in its public worship there is another that seems like it is frozen in the formalities of the 1950s. Many Reformed churches in Britain are dying because they are impenetrable for the un-churched young people of today, and because their elders and members have isolated themselves from their communities. To be brutally frank, the wagons have been circled to provide an enclave of comfortable nostalgia for an aging group of members who feel threatened by the cultural changes around them. They have embalmed a way of speaking, dressing, and behaving that was normal fifty years ago but is now found almost nowhere else. The gospel is preached, but it is hidden behind a culture that is so off-putting to people outside that they never get near enough to hear it. Younger people who do somehow join often adopt modes of dress and speech that are utterly inappropriate to them. This has the effect of isolating them from their own natural communities and disengaging them from the very people to whom they might be the most available witness for Christ. Strange as it may seem, the church that is frozen in the past like this is making exactly the same mistake as the church that has sold out to the present. Both alike are placing one particular cultural form above the Bible. They have chosen different pages of the calendar, but 2012 and 1950 are alike moments of human fashion. Allowing either to control our corporate life is subordinating the Bible to culture. Stubbornly repeating the culture of yesterday with all of its trappings is not reformation, it is stagnation, and it will lead ultimately to tragic death for churches as their members age and go to be with Christ, leaving none behind them.

I pose these questions in order to encourage more reflection on our corporate worship. Answering them would be a much harder task, and I do not mean simply to point fingers at others as if I have all the answers.

I find preparing to lead public worship much harder than preparing to preach, partly because so many of these questions are so difficult. It feels to me as if, despite their urgency, we are in our infancy of answering them, whereas the study of preaching is comparatively advanced. I expect not many pastors or elders have read a sophisticated theological analysis of the idea of musical meaning. Such works seem to exist, but they probably languish largely unread other than by specialists, whereas most preachers have studied classic texts on preaching.

Can the past help us with our questions here? It might seem unlikely. Being fashionable (or stubbornly unfashionable) was less of an issue in the past than it is today because the use of fashionability as a criterion, while not absent in the past, has grown to new proportions. Many modern phenomena such as rock music or stand-up comedy simply did not exist. But the past can help us even with our distinctively modern problems, because our reflection should not start with our contemporary situation. We ought not to think inward from our circumstances to the theology of corporate worship, but outward from the theology to our circumstances. Obviously we can never shed our context and approach the Bible uninfluenced by it, but the authority in our thinking emanates outward from the Bible, not inward from our context. This means that we can learn from ancient reflections on corporate worship, even though they come from a quite different cultural context, because they are biblical reflections. For example, Augustine lived in a time when singing was increasingly popular in churches (especially those of his enemies the Donatists), and he reflected on the practice using his understanding of the nature of worship. Consider how much we might learn from reflecting on even just this passing comment in his *Confessions*:

> I am more led to put forward the opinion (not as an irrevocable view) that the custom of singing in Church is to be approved, so that through the delights of the ear the weaker mind may rise up towards the devotion of worship. Yet when it happens to me that the music moves me more than the subject of the song, I confess myself to commit a sin deserving punishment, and then I would prefer not to have heard the singer.[20]

[20] *Confessions*, p. 208.

Calvin's priorities from his practice

We have seen something of Calvin's priorities from the evidence of his writings. If we step back and view his pastoral practice through a wide-angle lens, what do we see? We see a man engaged throughout his ministry in several main activities: preaching, teaching, writing theological books, defending the faith in person, church discipline, personal pastoral work, and correspondence. From this list only the publishing activities are arguably not universal responsibilities for pastors: every pastor must preach the word (*2 Tim.* 4:1-2), teach the people (*Eph.* 4:11; *1 Tim.* 4:11-13; *Titus* 2:1), defend the faith (*2 Tim.* 2:25), exercise discipline (*Matt.* 18:15-18), and conduct a private ministry to individuals (*Matt.* 18:15; *Phil.* 4:3; *1 Tim.* 5:1-2). Let us briefly recall each element in turn.

The statistics detailing Calvin's preaching and teaching are well-known and we saw something of them earlier when considering his burdens. He preached an average of over 170 sermons a year following his return to Geneva, alongside lecturing every third day and speaking in the *Congrégation* of ministers on Fridays.[21] His efforts to defend the faith were, as Beza puts it, Herculean:

> Little ground is there for wondering that one who was both a most powerful defender of sound doctrine, and an example of purity of life, should have been bitterly assailed. The thing to be wondered at rather is, that a single man, as if he had been a kind of Christian Hercules, should have been able to subdue so many monsters, and this by that mightiest of all clubs, the Word of God.[22]

The disciplinary work of the Consistory (Geneva's church court) was extensive: in just the first two years of operating it heard 639 cases involving 1,105 individuals.[23] The system of pastoral care in Geneva operated on an individual level through personal work, as Beza explains when he reaches 1550 in his year-by-year account of Calvin's life:

> It was determined that the ministers should at a certain season of the year, attended by an elder and a deacon, go round all the wards of the city, to instruct the people, and examine every individual briefly as to his faith. This they were to do, not only in sermons,

[21] For the statistics, see *Portrait*, p. 29.
[22] *Life*, 1:xcix.
[23] *Calvin*, p. 135.

which some neglected, and others attended, without much benefit, but also in each house and family. It is scarcely credible how great benefit ensued.[24]

Calvin's concern for individuals also shines through in his extensive correspondence, especially his letters to the persecuted Huguenots of France.

Protestant unity

There is, however, one activity that I have not mentioned, and that is Calvin's Protestant ecumenism. This may be a surprise to us. We may rightly think of Calvin as a theological warrior, opposing among others Bolsec, Gentili, Pighius, Sadoleto, and Servetus. Yet Calvin was just as much a peacemaker. He is emphatic on the importance of the unity of the church, rightly defined: 'the unity of the Church, such as Paul describes it, we protest we hold sacred, and we denounce anathema against all who in any way violate it.'[25] The qualifier here, 'as Paul describes it' is not a theoretical excuse for practical inaction, as I suspect it can be for us. For all that he believes in the invisibility of the church, Calvin does not think that unity is solely invisible. In context, the qualifier simply indicates that the unity is unity *in the truth*, not at the expense of the truth.

Calvin poured himself into attempts to achieve this unity. His peacemaking was most evident in his efforts to reach agreement on the Lord's supper with Heinrich Bullinger, Zwingli's successor at Zurich, culminating in 1549. The situation of the reformers in the 1540s was desperate.[26] In the 1520s the Emperor Charles V had been distracted from dealing with the growing Reformation by the conflict with France, the Communeros revolt in Spain, and the Ottoman threat. By contrast, from 1544 he was increasingly free to turn his attention to the now still more pressing Protestant problem. Francis I of France had surrendered to Charles in the Peace of Crépy (18 September 1544), and by the end of 1547 both Francis and Henry VIII of England were dead. Charles had agreed a five-year peace with Sultan Suliman I in June 1547. It was also clearer that there could now be no compromise with the Protestants since the failure of the Colloquy of Ratisbon (1541) and the start of the Council of Trent

[24] *Life*, 1:lv.

[25] *Necessity*, 1:214.

[26] The following description of the background to the *Consensus* is based on *Calvin*, c. 10.

(1545). It was not long before the Emperor and the Protestant Schmal-kaldic League entered military conflict. Charles gained a series of victories. On 21 March 1547 the city of Strasbourg surrendered and the Burger-meister did obeisance to him. As a result the reformer Martin Bucer fled secretly to England. On 21 April Charles won against the Protestants at Mühlberg and took the Elector of Saxony prisoner. Just two months after that the Protestant leader Philip of Hesse surrendered. As Bruce Gordon puts it, 'The game was over: the Lutheran church had been crushed and the Reformation had failed. It now fell to those who were left to continue, and this made unity among the Swiss churches all the more imperative'.[27]

Calvin wrote letters and travelled extensively in search of this unity. Most significantly, he visited Bullinger at Zurich in June 1548. As Gordon explains, 'Around the table in Bullinger's house weighty matters, above all the sacraments, were discussed in Latin, and for both men the scales began to drop and mutual suspicions dissipate.'[28] The result in May 1549 was the *Consensus Tigurinus*, a series of twenty-four agreed articles on the Lord's supper. Gordon thinks that Calvin 'essentially allowed Bullinger to dictate the terms', and it was not long before he felt the need to add two more articles. Even after this stretching effort the *Consensus* never succeeded as a general Swiss agreement because the key powers such as Berne and Basel did not sign up to it.[29] In that sense, Calvin's attempt failed. But attempt he did. Whereas Luther refused even to consider Zwingli a brother in the Lord after the Marburg Colloquy of 1529, during the 1540s Calvin clearly rejected this aggressive approach. In a letter to Bullinger after one of Luther's stinging attacks he urges him not to reply in kind. He reminds him that they all owed a great deal to Luther who had 'devoted his whole energy to overthrow the reign of Antichrist'. But he then goes on to reject Luther's belligerence:

> Would that he had rather studied to curb this restless, uneasy tem-perament which is so apt to boil over in every direction. I wish, moreover, that he had always bestowed the fruits of that vehe-mence of natural temperament upon the enemies of the truth, and that he had not flashed his lightning sometimes also upon the serv-ants of the Lord.[30]

[27] *Calvin*, p. 176.
[28] *Calvin*, p. 172.
[29] *Calvin*, p. 179.
[30] Calvin to Bullinger, 25th November, 1544, in *Tracts and Letters*, 4:433.

This is a striking depiction of Luther. He appears as a mix of greatness and volatility, bravery against true enemies and a lack of judgement in opposing men who were really his friends.

Was Calvin right to be so concerned with Protestant unity? We need to remember that it is very serious to oppose someone who should be treated as a brother. If I identify one of Christ's sheep as an enemy and oppose him then I am opposing someone for whom Christ shed his blood. I am treating as an enemy someone loved by the Lord Jesus. Calvin's properly Protestant ecumenism is instructive for us. We have circumstances that are urgent, like those that impelled Calvin. While we may not face a military threat from Roman Catholic powers, we are in many senses as beleaguered as the Swiss were in the sixteenth century, if not more so. This is true both at the wider cultural level and also, for many, at the level of our own small churches. The urgency of unity is surely all the more pressing. Like Calvin, we must never think that this mandates uniting where the truth must divide us, for example in the broad ecumenical movement. But it does mandate fraternal relations with other Bible-believing Protestants. Surely it is obvious that if we have a theological issue with a fellow Bible-believing Protestant we should sit down with him and talk like Calvin did with Bullinger, rather than condemn him from afar? Too often we go in guns blazing like Luther against Zwingli, sometimes falling short even of Luther's willingness to go to Marburg to meet face-to-face, preferring instead to judge from far afield having read a few pages of someone's weblog.

Might we find here a specific application to the issue of Anglican evangelical and Nonconformist relations in Britain (and no doubt to parallel situations in other countries)? The suspicion of many Nonconformists toward Anglicans is understandable given the historic persecution of Nonconformity and the compromise of some evangelicals in the Church of England. Anglican evangelicalism that favours unity with liberals and anglo-catholics is gravely mistaken. On this count I have some serious concerns about even the broadly conservative Global Anglican Futures Conference (GAFCON) and its fruit, which seems to be far too ready to ally with anglo-catholicism in the struggle against liberalism. We see an example of this in the first article of its *Jerusalem Declaration*: 'We rejoice in the gospel of God through which we have been saved by grace through faith in Jesus Christ by the power of the Holy Spirit'.[31] Where are the vital

---

[31] The *Declaration* is reproduced in *Being Faithful: The Shape of Historic*

adverbs of the Reformation? The Bible and the reformers teach not salvation by grace through faith, but salvation by grace *alone* through faith *alone*. It is theologically extremely dangerous to think that my enemy's enemy is my best friend, which is what I suspect happened here. Nevertheless, there are today also many Anglican evangelicals who hold to a genuine Reformed theology that are prepared to take a stand and to maintain clear boundaries. If we compare Nonconformist evangelicals and these Anglican evangelicals, then we find that they hold the same doctrine of revelation, the same doctrine of God, the same doctrine of sin, the same doctrine of the person and work of Christ, the same soteriology, and in many cases the same eschatology. On some important questions within ecclesiology and sacramentology they disagree (episcopacy, separation, establishment, perhaps baptism). These disagreements matter and must not be ignored, but they are not the kind of disagreements that should lead us to behave like Luther toward Zwingli. Calvin knew that he disagreed with Luther and Melanchthon, and he thought that the issues they disagreed on mattered. But still he made every effort to live at peace with them and to maintain bonds of fellowship. We need to realize that, for all our disagreement on important issues, we are united on the saving doctrines. All that is important is not saving. If we cannot recognize the difference between the important and the saving, then we are doomed to endless enervating division. I may disagree with someone on an important question, but he remains my brother. Some kind of close, supportive friendship between Nonconformist evangelicals and Anglican evangelicals is surely appropriate. Recall, for example, the friendship that Calvin extended in his letters to the leaders of the Church of England in his own time. Calvin was not an episcopalian and he thought the Church of England insufficiently reformed in its rites, but he knew that the men leading it were godly, Bible-believing men, and so he related warmly to them. In return, many of them acknowledged the theological and ecclesial brilliance of Calvin and looked to him as a leader of the Reformation. From 1579 the statutes at Oxford even required all students to study the *Institutes*.

There are promising signs of this kind of friendship today. Perhaps

---

Anglicanism Today, ed. by Nicholas Okoh, Vinay Samuel, and Chris Sugden (London: The Latimer Trust, 2009), p. 6. The omission is compounded rather than corrected in the *Commentary* provided by the GAFCON Theological Resource Group, pp. 28–9. It is highly unlikely that this is just a mistake, and it would be just as worrying if it were.

the remaining difficulty we face at the moment is less overt hostility than distance and ignorance. For all of us this issue arises at an individual level: with whom do I cultivate friendship in my locality? It arises at a group level: to whom is our fraternal open? Will we be involved with local evangelical partnerships? It arises at a congregational level: with whom will we cooperate in some endeavour? And for those in connectional churches such as presbyterians, it arises at the denominational level too: which other denominations will we recognize? Whose ordination will we accept? These are some of the questions with which Calvin's example leaves us.

The centre of Calvin's vision of reality

We have considered Calvin's ministerial priorities as evidenced by his writings and his practice. We turn lastly to examine the way in which he visualizes the world to discover the heart of his concern in the Reformation. Part of the reason that Calvin's writing has lasted and has had such an influence is the vividness with which he writes. You may recall some of his famous illustrations. The natural man is lost in a labyrinth and Scripture is the thread that he follows to find his way. Scripture functions like a pair of spectacles to bring our naturally blurred sight into focus.[32] In the *Antidote* Calvin explains how justification and sanctification are distinct but inseparable using a favourite image: 'The light of the sun, though never unaccompanied with heat, is not to be considered heat.'[33]

Calvin was a master of visual imagery, but it is a mistake to think that he was just using it to illustrate a point with similes and mere metaphors. It is misleading to speak of 'mere metaphors' from the pen of any author. Classing a description as a metaphor does not mean that it is somehow less true or does not refer to reality. It simply explains *how* it refers to reality. For example, if I go to the dentist with a gnawing pain in my tooth, I will not be too pleased if he tells me 'Don't worry, "gnawing" is only a metaphor.'[34] It is a metaphor, and it hurts! Nor are metaphors simply flowery devices that can be replaced with literal language without any loss. If I say that the Queen is the head of the body politic, I say more than I do if I just describe her as our 'ruler'. I evoke the image of the body; I identify her with the planning, deliberative mind; I give to her authority to command,

[32] See, for example, *Institutes*, I. vi. 3, 1:73; I. vi. 1, 1:70.

[33] *Antidote*, 3:116.

[34] On the nature and function of metaphors, see Janet Martin Soskice, *Metaphor and Religious Language* (Oxford: Clarendon Press, 1985).

and I also open the possibility of disease in a body that does not function properly, or a body that will not respond to the mind's instructions. Metaphors are expansive evocations. Take the metaphor of Scripture as a thread through the labyrinth. The image evokes the sense of being lost, of delight in finding the thread, of the need to cling to it, of our dependence on it. By using visual imagery Calvin thus opens up worlds of meaning.

This should be enough to stop us speaking dismissively of metaphors, but with one of Calvin's pervasive visual images we find that there is more going on than even the evocative richness of metaphor. In his work on the Acts of the Apostles, Matthew Sleeman argues that we should attend to the 'salvation geography' of Luke's book and the ways in which he re-conceives space around the ascended Lord Jesus: 'Christ's ascension generates a radical theological restructuring of space'.[35] My claim here is that the same kind of reading can usefully be applied to Calvin's work. When Calvin speaks of union with Christ he radically re-conceives the space of the world, locating all things in relation to the physical body of Jesus. Every Christian theologian grasps that each person stands in some kind of relationship to Christ, but Calvin speaks specifically and concretely of our relation to Christ's physical body. This is one of the less-known features of his christology that emerges strongly in his doctrine of the Lord's supper. Calvin is emphatic that we are united to the actual, physical, flesh and blood of Jesus, not of course by the elements in the supper changing, but by the work of the Holy Spirit. For Calvin we are not simply indwelt by the Spirit:

> I am not satisfied with those persons who, recognizing that we have some communion with Christ, when they would show what it is, make us partakers of the Spirit only, omitting mention of flesh and blood. As though all these things were said in vain: that his flesh is truly food, that his blood is truly drink [John 6:55]; that none have life except those who eat his flesh and drink his blood [John 6:53]; and other passages pertaining to the same thing![36]

Rather, Calvin explains, the Spirit unites us to the body of Jesus so that we receive life from it: 'the flesh of Christ is like a rich and inexhaustible fountain that pours into us the life springing forth from the Godhead into

---

[35] '"Under Heaven": The Formative Place of Heaven Within the Salvation-Geography of Acts', paper presented to the Society of Biblical Literature Conference, Philadelphia, PA, 2005.

[36] *Institutes*; IV. xvii. 7, 2:1366–67.

itself'.[37] Calvin is clear that it is not the flesh in and of itself that is life-giving: 'the flesh of Christ does not of itself have a power so great as to quicken us, for in its first condition it was subject to mortality; and now, endowed with immortality, it does not live through itself.'[38] Here we see Calvin's Chalcedonian christology at work. The life-giving power comes from the union of the humanity of Christ with the eternal Son who is himself life:

> He teaches not only that he is life since he is the eternal Word of God, who came down from heaven to us, but also that by coming down he poured that power upon the flesh which he took in order that from it participation in life might flow unto us.[39]

By the Spirit we receive eternal life from the divine Word through his human nature, in particular through his flesh and blood. This is a real spiritual union with his physical body. The body has a definite location, at the right hand of God, and is the actual vessel for eternal life coming to the believer by the Spirit.

For Calvin, it is not just the believer who is related in some way to the physical body of Jesus. Here is how he challenges Rome:

> Let our opponents, then, in the first instance, draw near to Christ, and then let them convict us of schism, in daring to dissent from them in doctrine. But, since I have made it plain, that Christ is banished from their society, and the doctrine of his gospel exterminated, their charge against us simply amounts to this, that we adhere to Christ in preference to them.[40]

Rome is far from Christ and needs to draw near to him. Her relation is the opposite to that of the believer, since she has driven Christ out, or at least she has attempted to do so. The attempt to get away from Christ is actually futile, because, try as we might, we can never rid ourselves of the way we are made. In an important passage, Calvin describes how even fallen man is inalienably religious despite his most strenuous efforts not to be:

> The very Majesty of God extorts this much from us, that we are unable to withdraw entirely from his service. Therefore, as we

---

[37] *Institutes*, IV. xvii. 9, 2:1369.

[38] *Institutes*, IV. xvii. 9, 2:1369.

[39] *Institutes*, IV. xvii. 8, 2:1368.

[40] *Necessity*, 1:215.

cannot evade the necessity of worshipping him, our only remaining course is to seek out indirect substitutes that we may not be obliged to come directly into his presence; or rather, by means of external ceremonies, like specious masks, we hide the inward malice of the heart, and, in order that we may not be forced to give it to him, interpose bodily observances, like a wall of partition.[41]

Here is the religious but God-hating man. He attempts desperately to hide from God by replacing him with substitutes, seeking to conceal his heart behind the masks of ceremony. These bodily observances serve as a defensive wall to keep the body of Christ at bay.

Calvin finds Rome guilty of more than just being far from Christ. When he explains what is wrong with Rome's teaching about the intercession of the saints, he describes it as an attempt to fight with Christ, to wrestle from him his dignity in order to give it to others. Rome physically assaults Jesus: 'Are we, then, to be silent when the peculiar dignity of Christ, the dignity which cost him such a price, is wrested from him with the greatest contumely, and distributed among the saints, as if it were lawful spoil?'.[42] Similarly, Calvin depicts Rome trying to steal from God his glory in order to hand it out to the saints: 'In word, indeed, they concede to God the glory of all that is good, but, in reality, they rob him of the half, or more than the half, by partitioning his perfections among the saints'.[43]

Calvin's descriptions of what false teaching does to the body of Christ can be unsettling. For example, in the *Antidote* he explains that a Roman Catholic bishop 'hesitates not to strip Christ in order that he may deck his Pope with the spoils'.[44] He speaks often of ripping Christ apart. To separate faith from a changed life would be to 'rend the gospel, and divide Christ himself'.[45] Calvin describes Christ being physically assaulted by the range of Rome's false teaching:

> In all these things, have we not just as many execrable blasphemies as we have words, blasphemies by which the glory of Christ is rent, and torn to shreds? For, being in a great measure despoiled of his honour, he retains the name, while he wants the power. Here,

[41] *Necessity*, 1:154.
[42] *Necessity*, 1:191.
[43] *Necessity*, 1:129.
[44] *Antidote*, 3:51.
[45] *Antidote*, 3:116.

too, no doubt, we might have been silent, though we saw the Son, on whom the Father hath bestowed all authority, and power, and glory, and in whom alone he bids us glory, so classified with his servants, that he had scarcely any pre-eminence above them. When we saw his benefits thus in oblivion—when we saw his virtue destroyed by the ingratitude of men—when we saw the price of his blood held in no estimation, and the fruits of his death almost annihilated—when, in fine, we saw him so deformed by false and profane opinions, that he had more resemblance to an unsubstantial phantom than to himself, did it behove us to bear it calmly and silently? O accursed patience, if, when the honour of God is impaired, not to say prostrated, we are so slightly affected, that we can wink and pass on![46]

This is a horrifying picture. It is of course a picture that we know from the cross: Jesus was indeed marred 'beyond human semblance' (*Isa.* 52:14). What is shocking is that Calvin applies the description to the risen and reigning Jesus now, when he is ascended and enthroned far beyond harm. Calvin understood that while Christ is enthroned, he is also joined to his people, so that when they suffer he somehow suffers too. Hence, Christ asked Saul on the road to Damascus: 'Saul, Saul, why are you persecuting me?' (*Acts* 9:4).

We can see from these examples how powerful Calvin's way of visualizing reality is. He has re-conceived life in terms of our relation to the spatial and physical body of Jesus. When Calvin sees someone, he sees them in union with Christ or he sees them running from him. In the worst cases he sees them attacking him and harming him. This vision of reality is the fruit of a mind soaked in Scripture, especially a mind so filled with Christ that he sees all people in relation to him. All things stand around him as the centre of reality. This is more than a physical illustration of spiritual reality. People's eternal destiny is for Calvin determined by their actual relation to the physical body of Jesus. This is a biblical conviction, even if it is unfamiliar to us. We may, for example, shy away from preaching the physical afflictions of Jesus for fear of downplaying his spiritual suffering, but Isaiah tells us that we are healed by his *stripes* (*Isa.* 53:5), Peter that Christ bore our sins in his *body* on the tree (*1 Pet.* 2:24), and Paul that God condemned sin in the *flesh* (*Rom.* 8:3). The Lord Jesus himself said that unless we eat of

---

[46] *Necessity*, 1:192-93.

his *flesh* and drink his *blood* we have no life in us (*John* 6:53). Every human being does indeed stand in some relation to the bodily crucified, bodily risen, and bodily ascended Lord Jesus.

In these recurring depictions of human closeness to Christ or violent distance from him we find the heart of Calvin's concern in the midst of the Reformation. Not the chummy 'best mates with Jesus' of some contemporary spirituality, but the question of where we stand in relation to the very body of Jesus Christ, the question of our sharing or not sharing in the saving work that he accomplished in that body. This is the word of life that lay at the heart of Calvin's Reformation ministry, his concern for 'saving doctrine'. This was the focus of Calvin's agenda. The split with Rome was all about being near to or far from the body of Jesus. There was a tragic irony here, since Rome taught that her priests held in their hands and gave to the people the very flesh of Jesus to chew, thus claiming the closest contact with the physical body of Jesus. But by that very kind of false ceremony she was in fact far from him. As Calvin puts it at the start of Book III of the *Institutes*, all that Christ possesses 'is nothing to us until we grow into one body with him'. This we do not by taking the substance of his body in our mouths, but only 'by faith' and 'the secret energy of the Spirit'.[47] Calvin's longing was to see people restored to this true saving closeness to Christ. May this be our longing as we seek the ongoing reformation of doctrine and worship.

[47] *Institutes*, III. i. 1, 1:537.

12

PREACHING THE GOD-MAN: CHALCEDON REVISITED

A Different Angle on Chalcedon

In Chapter 2 we explored the Christological controversy that culminated with the Council of Chalcedon in 451 A.D. My aim there was to set out a biblical account of the doctrine of the incarnation. I wish now to revisit that material with a different aim: to help preachers faithfully to proclaim the God-Man. How do you speak about the Lord Jesus, both explicitly and by implication? For example, reflect for a moment on whether or not you have ever referred to Mary as 'the mother of God' in your preaching. Have you ever preached that God suffered and died on the cross? Have you ever taught that the blood of Jesus is sufficient to save because it is the blood of God himself? My aim in this chapter is to think through how we should preach and teach the incarnation by revisiting the biblical position of Chalcedon. The argument for these conclusions is found in Chapter 2. so here I will simply restate and then presume them:

1. Jesus Christ is fully God.
2. He is fully man.
3. There is one person Jesus Christ.
4. There is a communication of properties in the one person Jesus, such that Mary is the mother of God.

Preaching the God-man

What do these conclusions mean for our preaching and teaching? Essentially, they require of us great care in how we speak of Jesus Christ, the God-man. My intention here is not to induce paranoia in you as you preach, since your liberty as a preacher matters. Even the most note-bound preacher must surely sometimes find himself diverging from his script, and when he does so he does not want to be constantly looking over his shoulder. But liberty in preaching does not mean speaking however we wish. When we pray for a preacher to have liberty we pray for him to be unrestrained in preaching the word of God with clarity and boldness, not for him to teach a slipshod christology! A modicum of proper paranoia is no bad thing. We need to remember that how we speak about Jesus teaches the congregation who he is. It is not just the stated points in our sermons that teach but our whole way of referring to him. This extends beyond our preaching to include public prayer and sung worship, as well as personal conversation.

Might we not expect that speaking rightly of God will require effort and care? It hardly comes naturally to us to speak rightly of him, at least not to the old nature. We might perhaps say that it is natural to the new nature to speak rightly of God, but that would not mean that it comes automatically and without thought. Even the renewed mind of the regenerate believer needs to be taught the word of God, since conversion does not render it suddenly innate in a perfected Christian. This suggests that there should be a phase during which a young preacher finds himself having to make conscious, deliberate decisions to use christologically careful forms of words. But that phase will not last long; soon the biblical and Chalcedonian modes of expression will become second-nature to the new nature.

Preach the divinity of Christ

We turn now to consider some specific ways in which we should preach Christ the God-man in the light of the Chalcedonian definition. The key is to maintain a diversity of description that reflects the different elements of the biblical doctrine of the incarnation expressed in the definition. We need first to preach the fullness of Christ's divinity. This means that we must not deny to Jesus Christ any of God's attributes. There must be no suggestion of a kenotic christology in which the Son loses his divinity.

There must be no denials of his timelessness, immateriality, immutability, impassibility, or any other divine attribute.

Perhaps a word is needed here on immutability and impassibility (the teaching that God does not change or suffer). The film *Enemy at the Gates* depicts the activity of the Russian sniper Vassili Zaitsev during the battle of Stalingrad in 1943. At one point, Zaitsev describes how he lies still and hidden, waiting for his enemy to pass by: 'I am a stone. I do not move.' Many people seem to think that the doctrines of divine immutability and impassibility imply a kind of Vassili Zaitsev god, a god who is utterly static and stone-like, lacking any passionate involvement with the world. The mistake is made of taking the term *apatheia*, used by the Greek church fathers of God, and thinking that it implies all that 'apathy' implies in contemporary English. This is a crude and inaccurate reading of the classical doctrines of immutability and impassibility. Paul Gavrilyuk gives a much more careful and accurate account in a recent study in which he shows that 'for the Fathers, divine impassibility was fully compatible with God's providential care for the world, with direct divine involvement in history, and with praiseworthy emotionally coloured characteristics, such as love and compassion'.[1] The intent of the doctrine was not to render God lifeless, but to show that the God of the Bible is different from the capricious, raging gods of the heathens. God is always the same not because he has no life, but because he has total possession of his whole life in eternity, with none of it left behind and none of it yet to come. This is why the Christian philosopher Boethius (c. 480–c. 524) spoke of God's eternity not as lifelessness but as 'the whole, simultaneous and perfect possession of boundless life'.[2] Note how even in this classic definition of eternity Boethius uses a temporal term ('simultaneous') to describe God's existence beyond time. This is what God himself does when he reveals himself to us in thoroughly human words.

Equally, there must in our language about the death of Jesus be no idea of the Trinity being ruptured, because this is a denial of the divinity of God. It can be striking to preach of God's own triune life being ruptured at the cross as the Father and Son were torn apart, but it is utterly

---

[1] *The Suffering of the Impassible God: The Dialectics of Patristic Thought* (Oxford: Oxford University Press, 2006), p. 16.

[2] *The Consolation of Philosophy*, trans. by S. J. Tester, in *Boethius*, The Loeb Classical Library, 74 (Cambridge, MA: Harvard University Press; London: William Heinemann, 1973; repr. 1978), v. 6, p. 423.

wrong. First, it is wrong because the need for atonement applies to Christ in his humanity, not to Christ as God (as Jonathan Edwards reminded us in Chapter 4). The perfect substitute needed to share flesh and blood to atone (*Heb.* 2:14), not to die as God. Second, it is wrong because the Father loved the Son as the Son died on the cross, and love is the very fabric of the union of the persons. This was especially so because the cross was the Son's supreme act of obedience to the Father, in which the Father delighted: 'I do as the Father has commanded me, so that the world may know that I love the Father' (*John* 14:31). This is why Paul speaks of the cross as a 'fragrant offering' to the Father (*Eph.* 5:2). Why would the Father be sundered from the Son in the midst of the Son's greatest act of obedience and love to him? Third, the very idea of the Trinity being ruptured is nonsensical, unless we take a sub-trinitarian view of God. God's triune life is not something that could be ruptured without God ceasing to be God. The idea that God's triune life could be ruptured implies that the trinitarian existence is something additional to his being that could be set aside for a time. It implies an insufficiently trinitarian view of God that reduces his triunity to an optional and dispensable extra. In our preaching we must, therefore, be clear that, according to his divine nature, Jesus Christ possessed all of the attributes of God within the eternally perfect trinitarian relationships even as he died.

This raises the question of the cry of dereliction uttered by Jesus on the cross: 'My God, my God, why have you forsaken me?' (*Mark* 15:34, quoting *Psa.* 22:1). If this text does not mean that the Father and the Son were divided as Christ died, what does it mean? We saw in Chapter 2 that the biblical christology of Chalcedon sometimes requires the clarification that strictly speaking the one person Jesus Christ does something 'according to his manhood'. This must be the answer here. Just as Mary was the mother of God in his human existence, so the eternal Son was cut off from his Father in his human existence. The dissolution of the Trinity would not only have been impossible, it would also have been irrelevant for the atonement, whereas the forsakenness of the eternal Son *as a man* was the fulfilment of what the law of God required. We may, therefore, say that the Son was forsaken by the Father, but when we explain what that means we need to be clear that he was forsaken in his human nature.

It is tempting to think that the clear proclamation of the divinity of Christ will detract from the proclamation of his humanity. In fact, the opposite is the case: preaching the full divinity of Christ increases the wonder of his full humanity. Our preaching of his sufferings, for example, is all the more underlined by preaching his divinity. If we were to preach that a mere man suffered, or that the eternal Son divested of his divinity suffered, then we would actually reduce the wonder of his suffering. What wonder if a man suffers, or a being less than God? It is when we preach the full divinity of Christ and his suffering that the wonder of the incarnation of God is revealed. The higher he is, the further down he stoops when he descends to take on servant form and to die on the cross: when we magnify his divine exaltation we magnify the wonder of his humiliation.

Preach the humanity of Christ

We must also preach the fullness of Christ's humanity. This means preaching his birth, his growth in wisdom, his human sympathy, his tears, his sweat, his suffering, and his death. Christ died a thoroughly human death as he bore the punishment deserved by his people. As we saw when considering Jonathan Edwards on the atonement in Chapter 4, there were some differences between his death and the death awaiting sinners. Christ did not despair as the lost will despair without hope, since he suffered for the joy set before him (*Heb.* 12:2). Nor did Christ know the personal hatred of the Father for him as himself, since he had committed no sins, and all the more because his death was an act of obedience that pleased his Father. Rather, the wrath that he bore was imputative, arising from the sin laid upon him. Nevertheless, Christ's death was a fully human death.

In his human life Jesus also experienced the limits of humanity. When preaching on the Olivet discourse, we should preach that the humanity of Christ meant that he actually did not know the time of his return: 'concerning that day and hour no one knows, not even the angels of heaven, nor the Son, but the Father only' (*Matt.* 24:36). This was the ignorance of the Son according to his human nature. This may unsettle us, but it is really no harder than the idea that Christ was born or grew or died: each of these, just as much as ignorance, is a limit wholly alien to God as God. As Calvin puts it, 'if Christ, as man, did not know the last day, that does not any more derogate from his Divine nature than to have been mortal'.[3]

---

[3] *Commentaries*, 17:154.

Preach the unity of Christ

We must preach that there was and is one Lord Jesus Christ. We can and no doubt do preach this by speaking of him as a single acting subject. Every time we say that Jesus did something, we speak of one Jesus. It is highly unlikely that we intend this only in the limited Nestorian sense of an *appearance* of oneness: we are not that philosophically sophisticated! But if we are trying to be mindful of the two natures of Christ we can easily fall into speaking about 'the man Jesus' in a way that suggests the independent activity of his human nature. We might, for example, preach that 'the divine Jesus knew when he would return but the human Jesus did not'. Note the structure of the sentence and its implication: 'the divine Jesus . . . the human Jesus'. We have preached two Jesuses, even if we did not intend it. Rather, we should, in explaining the ignorance of Christ, distinguish the *one* Jesus *as* God and *as* man. Natures do not act and are not acted on. Jesus Christ the one Son acts in his two natures.

Putting it positively, preaching the unity of Christ means preaching the communication of the properties of the two natures in the one person. We can do this by preaching that Mary was the mother of God. In contexts where Roman Catholic devotion to Mary is an issue, this must obviously be done with due qualifications. In particular, we should be clear that the doctrine of the *Theotokos* is properly taught not because of what it says about Mary, but because of what it says about the divinity and unity of Jesus: it exalts him, not her. It certainly does not require that she was herself immaculately conceived without original sin. Nor does it mandate praying to her. As well as preaching the *Theotokos*, we should preach that the same Son who became man existed before Abraham (*John* 8:58), and that the Son died on the cross, purchasing the church with his own blood (*Acts* 20:28). This clearly excludes the possibility that the separate man Jesus died or that there were two Jesuses.

Alongside emphasising the unity of the person and the communication of attributes, I do think that sometimes we should make explicit that the one Son was acting according to only one nature. We need to do this to be clear that the two natures were preserved intact in the union. If we only ever preach that 'The eternal Son died', then someone will soon conclude that God literally died as God. Or if we only ever say that 'Mary was the mother of God', then someone will soon conclude that God was literally born as God. We should, therefore, sometimes add the clarifications: 'The eternal Son died according to his human nature'; 'The eternal

Son was born as a man'. The risk of doing this is that we separate the natures, but if we express ourselves carefully this ought not to happen. If we are clear that it is the one person, the single acting subject, the eternal Son, who acts in his natures, then the danger of teaching a divided Christ is avoided.

Let the text lead

This is not all intended to suggest that we artificially plan our preaching to make this range of christological points. We might decide to preach a deliberately chosen series on Chalcedonian christology, and that might be a good thing to do amid a wider expository ministry. But the more important and pervasive application is that as we prepare and preach we should be alert to the biblical christology, and should explicitly draw it out where it is textually appropriate. We should be looking for the details in the text that lend themselves to bringing out one of these emphases. If, for example, we were preaching Colossians 1, we might make the point that Paul speaks of the same person, the same acting subject, when he describes the pre-existence of Christ and his death. He writes both 'For by him all things were created . . . he is before all things' *and* 'through him to recon-cile to himself all things . . . by the blood of his cross' (verses 16, 17, and 20). Paul's way of writing shows the unity of Christ, and it shows that one and the same person is divine and human. In other words, the point is that we should be christologically alert preachers, looking for opportunities to teach some of the principal elements of the Bible's christology in our preaching. It is in doing this that we preach the authentic God-man, our glorious Lord Jesus, as he is and as he has shown himself to be.

13

PREACHING THE WORD:
MARTIN LUTHER (1483-1546)

Luther the preacher

It is easy to miss Luther the preacher. I was asked to speak on the topic in 2004, by which time I had been studying the Reformation for sixteen years. But until I started to prepare specifically for that talk I had barely encountered Luther the preacher. I knew of some of his famous sermons such as those on his return to Wittenberg in which he urged restraint on the radicals like Karlstadt. But generally I knew less of Luther the preacher and more of Luther the dutiful monk, Luther the anguished sinner seeking grace, Luther the Bible teacher discovering the gospel, Luther the rebel against Rome standing before the imperial Diet at Worms, Luther the fugitive translating the New Testament into German in the Wartburg, and Luther the theologian pulling the cloth off the table to challenge Zwingli at Marburg. The neglect might simply be mine, but the few authors who write about Luther the preacher normally begin by saying that no one writes about Luther the preacher. In 1983, just before the 500th anniversary of Luther's birth, Fred Meuser gave a challenge: look at all the programmes and publications for the celebratory events and 'if you can point out one, even one, that features a single lecture or program on Luther the preacher, you will be my guest for dinner at a restaurant of your choice.'[1] I do not

---

[1] *Luther the Preacher* (Minneapolis: Augsburg Publishing House, 1983), pp. 9-10. Most of the general information about Luther's preaching in the following

know whether anyone dined with Meuser, but he evidently thought it unlikely!

The neglect of Luther the preacher is in a sense not surprising, because the story of the Luther we do know is so mesmerising. Indeed, in a sense we are right not to think of Luther the preacher, if by preacher we mean 'minister', because Luther was never a minister. He was professor of biblical studies at Wittenberg University, and Wittenberg had its own pastor, Johannes Bugenhagen. Nevertheless, Luther was a preacher on a phenomenal scale. The statistics are mind-numbing. He preached about 4,000 sermons in all, mainly in the town church at Wittenberg. Given that he preached between 1512 and 1547, with a gap of about two years, this means that he preached on average around 120 sermons a year, or one sermon every three days. He preached so many sermons because in Wittenberg there were three sermons on a Sunday and a sermon every day during the rest of the week. So even with a pastor at Wittenberg there was plenty of scope for Luther to preach. Sometimes he preached significantly more than the average number. In 1528, for example, he preached 200 times. It is amusing to recall that when Johann von Staupitz started Luther preaching in 1512 he did so to busy his mind with something other than despair.

As well as preaching, Luther was engaged in a mighty struggle with Rome, he reformed the church in much of Germany, he wrote huge volumes of theological treatises, he engaged in fiery theological disputes face to face and in writing, and he had a wife and six children. Preachers often find that the task of preaching lays heavy upon them, but few add to it the cause of a national reformation and fear for their lives. Perhaps these facts about Luther will only serve to crush rather than to encourage us. The last thing I want to do in a book seeking to provide help is to exalt the extraordinary. As I said at the start of this book: God has gifted each of us differently in different situations and expects different things of us. It is wrong to dream of being a reformer like Luther or to measure yourself against the particular shape of his ministry. It is our sinful nature that wants to be someone else. The desire might arise from a lack of contentment with our own situation, or perhaps from a desire to be known like our heroes. We should indeed want to share Luther's godly qualities, but in our own specific context with the particular tasks and gifts that God has given us, and, if he wills it, in utter obscurity.

---

pages comes from this informative book.

Luther's weakness

We may well find more encouragement in another side of the story about which we hear still less, Luther's weakness. In using Luther, God used a man who like so many of us was capable of being crushed by the discouragements of his ministry. Certainly he preached and preached. Indeed, he esteemed the role of preacher, saying: 'If I could today become king or emperor, I would not give up my office as preacher.'[2] But despite that conviction, Luther did give up preaching. This man, so greatly used by God, stopped preaching. Interestingly, he stopped not when things appear to us to have been toughest for him, but after he had made much progress. In 1530, with a few exceptions, he did not preach at Wittenberg from January until the Autumn.[3] At that stage politically and militarily his situation was still far from secure, but he was in a much better position than when he left the Imperial Diet of Worms in 1521 afraid for his life. Luther seems to have found the challenges of a secure ministry more difficult than the uncertainties of a pioneering work. He gave up because he found the longer-term challenge harder than the immediate crisis, the slow attrition of ministering to an unresponsive congregation more discouraging than the enmity of all Rome. Strong opposition can spark strong resistance, a rising to the moment. In Luther's case it was the slow siege that brought down the city, not the attempt to storm the walls.

It was the stubbornness of the ordinary people that discouraged Luther. He was so disheartened by the spiritual state of the people of Wittenberg that in 1529 he warned them with these characteristically blunt words: 'I am sorry I ever freed you from the tyrants and papists. You ungrateful beasts, you are not worthy of the Gospel. If you do not improve, I will stop preaching rather than cast pearls before swine.'[4] Preaching to them was, he said, worse than preaching to crazed animals: 'I would rather preach to mad dogs, for my preaching shows no effect among you, and it only makes me weary'.[5] There was more to the difficulty than just the people's ingratitude. Luther felt the oppressive work of the world and the devil in the way his preaching was received: preaching was, in his experience, a hardship. Recall his positive comment that he would rather be a

---

[2] Cited in *Preacher*, p. 39.

[3] See *Preacher*, p. 28 for the details.

[4] Cited in *Preacher*, p. 29.

[5] Cited in Patrick Ferry, 'Martin Luther on Preaching', *Concordia Theological Quarterly*, 54.4 (1990), p. 277.

preacher than a king, and then compare these words: 'I would rather be stretched on a wheel or carry stones than preach one sermon.'[6] In 1530 he wrote to the clergy in Augsburg:

> No message would be more pleasing to my ears than the one deposing me from the office of preaching. I suppose I am so tired of it because of the great ingratitude of the people, but much more because of the intolerable hardships which the devil and the world mete out to me.[7]

Luther's experience speaks to preachers today. For many it is not the overtly embattled times when it is most tempting to give up, but the quieter times of little fruit. All seems relatively calm, but we are not getting anywhere. Things are not dramatically bad, but they are discouragingly slow, and it is the slowness which eats away at us. Here, I hope, is an encouragement: God used this man mightily, a man who abandoned preaching just because of that kind of attrition. God used a man who clearly struggled as we do and even gave up for a time because he was so discouraged. Luther is no super-human exception to the biblical principle that God's strength is made perfect in our weakness (*2 Cor.* 12:9).

The necessity of preaching

Let us look more closely at Luther's understanding of preaching, and first at his convictions concerning its vital necessity. Luther believed that preaching is necessary because it is commanded by God: he preached because he was told to preach. In the statement quoted above, where he speaks about wishing to be deposed as a preacher, he adds this answer to his own desire: 'There is a man whose name is Jesus Christ. He says no. Him I justly follow as one who has deserved more of me.' Jesus Christ says no. Luther believed in the office of preaching. For all of his affirmation of the priesthood of all believers, he knew that God calls certain people to preach, that he commands them to preach. Are you struggling to preach? Is preaching slipping down your agenda? Are the sermons getting the fag end of your time? Hear what Luther heard: 'There is a man whose name is Jesus Christ. He says no.'

Luther also believed in the necessity of preaching because he saw that the sermon is the most extraordinary, indispensable event for the people of

---

[6] Cited in 'Luther on Preaching', pp. 276-7.
[7] Cited in *Preacher*, p. 33.

God. It is the voice of God speaking. To the modern mind this is of course an outrage, and the identification of the preacher with God troubles even some preachers themselves. Here is Rowan Williams reflecting the sense of danger:

> Those who claim to speak in the name of God will always be dangerously (exhilaratingly) close to the claim that in their speech, their active presence, the absent God who is never an existent among others is actually present: a claim of stupendous importance in legitimating any bid for power.[8]

No doubt in a qualified sense such warnings have their place: speaking the word of God can be displaced by speaking my own words as the words of God to make myself powerful. Even when we preach what is true we can do so in order to dominate our hearers or manipulate them. But the warnings of danger can become a way of neutralizing the preached word by subjecting it to universal post-modern suspicion. How markedly different was Luther's reaction to the idea of speaking for God: 'The pastor must be sure that God speaks through his mouth. Otherwise it is time for him to be quiet'. Or again: 'whoever cannot boast like that about his sermon should leave preaching alone, for he surely denies and blasphemes God'.[9]

There is a fascinating contrast here with the Roman Catholicism from which Luther broke away. For Rome, Christ's presence was in the sacrament of the Mass. Luther's teaching reconceived the presence of Christ with his people. Unlike Calvin, Luther held that Christ is indeed really present in the bread and wine, but even he subordinated the sacramental presence to the verbal presence. For Luther the sacrament is a visible word, making the word the governing category. Here we can see why Luther took up preaching again: he believed that without it Christ is absent from the church. The sermon is the way in which Christ comes to his people. In particular, it is the way that he finds his elect:

> For one should not quit simply because so few are changed for the better in hearing the preaching of the gospel. But do what Christ did: He rescued the elect and left the rest behind. This is what the apostles did also. It will not be better for you.[10]

---

[8] *Lost Icons* (Edinburgh: T&T Clark, 2000), p. 162.
[9] Cited in *Preacher*, p. 12.
[10] Cited in 'Luther on Preaching', p. 277.

The Lord has his people, and preaching is his appointed means for reaching them. The results are the Lord's business, not ours, and he knows what he is doing. So keep preaching. Keep preaching so that Christ finds his chosen people.

The form of preaching

Luther also had much to say about the form of sermons. He was convinced that a preacher needed to be clear and simple. Here again he had his eye on Rome. As I mentioned in Chapter 1, the mediaeval church kept the people distant from the heart of the service. At Mass they would normally just look at the elevated host rather than consume it, often through a screen that separated them from the priest. Even the words of the Mass would be spoken in a language they could not understand, and often inaudible anyway. Against such an exclusive priestly view Luther was eager to engage the common man in the heart of the service in terms that he could understand. First and foremost that meant in a language he could understand, but it also meant keeping the content intelligible:

> A preacher should bare his breast and give the simple folk milk, for every day a new need of first principles arises. One should be diligent with the catechism and serve out only milk, leaving the strong wine of high thoughts for private discussion with the wise. In my sermons I do not think of Bugenhagen, Jonas and Melanchthon, for they know as much as I do, so I preach not to them but to my little Lena and Hans and Elsa. It would be a foolish gardener who would attend to one flower to the neglect of the great majority.[11]

Notice the reasoning here. The preacher must keep it simple, so that the people thrive. There is a link from the form of the sermon back to its purpose: given that it is intended to feed a baby at the breast, put it in terms he can understand. Given that it is intended to nurture the mass of flowers, address it to them. Without the preached word, babies starve, flowers wither, and souls die. Luther is unequivocal: Christ is our life. If Christ is not accessible in our midst, people will perish.

The other contextual feature exerting an influence here was Renaissance humanism. The humanists had rediscovered the art of classical

---

[11] Martin Luther, *Conversations with Luther: Selections from the Recently Published Sources of the Table Talk*, ed. and trans. by Preserved Smith and Herbert Percival Gallinger (New Canaan, CT: Keats Publishing, 1979), pp. 192-3.

rhetoric, and for them form and style were everything. Luther, who had a scholastic rather than a humanist training, self-consciously resisted this view. As he said, 'simple speech is the best and truest eloquence'.[12] This meant that Luther had no time for flowery renaissance preaching. Indeed, he did not even think that he could produce it himself: 'I can never compose a sermon by the rules of rhetoric' (readers of his brilliant theological works may be excused a little scepticism on this point!).[13] Luther was intolerant of preachers who used the original languages of the Bible in their sermons. He complained about Zwingli: 'How do I hate people who lug in so many languages as Zwingli does; he spoke Greek and Hebrew in the pulpit at Marburg!'[14] Luther went so far as refusing to acknowledge Zwingli as a Christian brother, so we may think that he is being unduly harsh on him here, especially since Marburg was not Zwingli's normal setting for preaching. But the point is clear: do not preach flowery sermons. In advocating simplicity like this, Luther was not advocating being simplistic. For example, while he was clear that a preacher should not use Hebrew or Greek in the pulpit, he was also clear that before he enters the pulpit he should have been pouring over the original languages. On that note, we turn from considering what he said about the nature and form of a sermon to what he said about its preparation.

Sermon preparation

Luther did not like sermons by those who could not read Hebrew and Greek, because he thought that ignorance of the languages fostered superficiality. Preaching by 'simple preachers without a knowledge of the languages', he said, is 'flat and tame'. This may be uncomfortable for some today, but it is what Luther said. Here are his words: 'One cannot preach the word of God if one does not master the languages. History illumines God's work and God's word, [but] the languages are the scabbards in which the sword of the Spirit is sheathed.'[15] Why did Luther make this strong claim? He said it because he believed that God deliberately reveals himself to us in a book. Books are written in words, and words are written in languages. It is the fact that the revelation of God is found in the words of the Bible that objectifies it, that gives it stability and constancy: 'The

[12] *Conversations*, p. 195.
[13] *Conversations*, p. 192.
[14] *Conversations*, p. 249.
[15] Cited in *Preacher*, pp. 42-3.

apostles themselves considered it necessary to put the New Testament into Greek and to bind it fast to that language, doubtless in order to preserve it for us safe and sound as in a sacred ark.'[16] On the basis of this reasoning about the original languages, Luther could say some quite extreme things:

> It is a sin and shame not to know our own book or to under-
> stand the speech and words of our God; it is a still greater sin and
> loss that we do not study languages, especially in these days when
> God is offering and giving us men and books and every facility
> and inducement to this study, and desires his Bible to be an open
> book.[17]

In other words, you may think it bad that you do not know your Bible better than you do, but Luther says that it is a more serious problem, even a sin, if you cannot read the original languages. Note the plural; Luther did not just mean Greek. For Luther, to deny the languages centre-stage is to deny the word of God's character as word. Luther looked back over history and saw that mediaeval neglect of the languages brought darkness and death, while attention to them brought light: 'No sooner did men cease to cultivate the languages than Christendom declined, even until it fell under the undisputed dominion of the pope. But no sooner was this torch relighted, than this papal owl fled with a shriek'.[18] Languages, in other words, were an instrument for the Reformation.

We are seeing here a hint of how serious Luther was about theological education. He was, we recall, a professor of the Bible in a university, albeit at a time when universities were rather different from what they are now. The reformers were serious about theological institutions where the word of God stands supreme. Having experienced it first-hand, I have little sympathy with much of what passes for 'theology' in many universities today. But it is undeniable that the reformers would have been horrified by the idea that someone could pastor a church without serious theological study first. We pride ourselves on being their heirs, but on this point much of our evangelical culture, at least in Britain, is increasingly un-Reformed. The reformers set up theological institutions to teach ministers, largely to teach them biblical languages. The Puritans did the same, reforming

---

[16] Cited in *The Legacy of Sovereign Joy: God's Triumphant Grace in the Lives of Augustine, Luther, and Calvin* (Wheaton, IL: Crossway Books, 2000), p. 82.

[17] Cited in *Preacher*, p. 43.

[18] Cited in *Legacy*, p. 97.

colleges such as Christ Church, Oxford and starting others such as Emmanuel College, Cambridge. The New England divines and revival leaders did it too, founding what would later become famous American universities such as Harvard, Princeton, and Yale. By contrast, the growing trend in the United Kingdom at the moment is to try to keep a potential pastor in his home congregation to teach him there. There are good reasons for this. It is a real weakness that some seminary faculties have very few lecturers with any significant experience as pastors. There is also a real danger that a man at seminary disappears into the library for three or four years and falls increasingly more in love with his books and less in love with the Lord's people. These risks are not, however, arguments against theological seminaries, but arguments against particular kinds of theological seminary. The problem with a pastor thinking that he can do the work of an entire seminary is the sheer difficulty of doing the task well. There are some ministers who could train their apprentices in biblical languages, but very few. There are also not many who could provide a broad training in church history and systematic theology. I do not mean this as a criticism of them: it would be unreasonable to expect any pastor to be a one-man seminary. But this is in effect what the model of in-house training requires. Perhaps a network of churches might have the capacity to draw together pastors with the requisite skills, but they would then have formed in effect a seminary.

Pastors who have no Hebrew and Greek or only rusty remnants can react in different ways to Luther's strong injunction to study them. We can fear that we are inadequate, and so react by denying the need to study the languages. If we are tempted to follow this path then we should recall Luther's substantive theological argument, that the verbal character of revelation entails its existence in particular languages. If we are serious about the revelation and if it is verbal, then how can we not be serious about the words? It is obviously vital to remember other parts of the revelatory process: the events behind the Bible, and the illuminatory work of the Holy Spirit today. It is also true that the words of the Bible do not trap the revelation, as if it is lost when translated into other languages. But God has given the revelation in these particular words of Hebrew and Greek (and some Aramaic). They are the primary and abiding form of objective revelation today. We cannot therefore dismiss the call to know the languages.

We are, however, where we are. Especially in Britain, theological education has not exactly been flourishing on a large scale, and many pastors have had no formal training at all. Many in ministry have little linguistic competence, and many have lost what they once had. Clearly we cannot and should not suddenly abandon our pastoral charges, but neither should we deny the problem. Would it not be much better to take small steps, where we are, to begin to address our linguistic inadequacy? Might we not dust off the grammars and give them half an hour a day? And in particular would it not be better to resolve to do all that we can to make sure that the next generation of ministers has what so many of us lack? Should we not encourage serious, full-time preparation for ministry?

With the languages in place, we must make sure that our preaching remains clear for the people. Luther is an excellent example of holding together an emphasis on linguistic competence for the pastor with a rejection of its display in the pulpit. It is very tempting for those of us who preach to show off. It is very easy to shore up the authority of our proclamations by quoting a little Hebrew or Greek in a display of apparent erudition. Luther warns us that a pastor sins if he does not know the languages, but he also tells us that he should not 'lug' them into his preaching. Neither emphasis must erase the other: the simple form of the sermon is not an excuse for superficial preparation, but the deep preparation does not mandate complex presentation.

Luther on Psalm 69: Christological typology

These are some aspects of Luther's thinking about preparing to preach. Turning to his preaching itself, perhaps the most outstanding feature for us to note is the way that he preached Christ from all the Scriptures. We see this clearly already in an early lecture he gave on Psalm 69. Technically, we are not looking here at a sermon but at the work behind a sermon. Nonetheless, we meet Luther a long way down the road toward preaching, which explains why much of it sounds so sermonic. The vast majority of Luther's sermons were on the Gospels, an interesting fact for those who think that Protestants only read Paul, but the greater part of his lecturing was on Old Testament passages such as this. The lecture makes an interesting case-study because although it was given between 1513 and 1515, we see a lot of Reformation theology already in place. The exact date of Luther's theological breakthrough is disputed, but it is evidently underway here.

Here are verses 1-5 of the Psalm:

[1] Save me, O God!
   For the waters have come up to my neck.

²I sink in deep mire,
 where there is no foothold;
I have come into deep waters,
 and the flood sweeps over me.
³I am weary with my crying out;
 my throat is parched.
My eyes grow dim
 with waiting for my God.
⁴More in number than the hairs of my head
 are those who hate me without cause;
mighty are those who would destroy me,
 those who attack me with lies.
What I did not steal
 must I now restore?
⁵O God, you know my folly;
 the wrongs I have done are not hidden from you.

Luther teaches that this is a Psalm about the passion of Christ: 'This psalm speaks literally about the suffering of the Lord in His own person.'[19] We might defend this Christocentric reading by pointing out that the apostles applied verse 9 to Jesus, for example in John 2:17 and Romans 15:3, but Luther did not feel the need to do that. He held that this Psalm is about Christ because the whole Bible is about Christ. We do not need a specific indicator of a New Testament fulfilment to find Christ in the Old Testament. Even the words of verse 5 are Christ's words: 'O God, you know my folly'. Luther intends no blasphemy here when he finds these words on the lips of Christ. Rather, he maintains that Christ speaks them as our substitute, as the one who has taken our sins upon himself. Luther explains that the Jews thought that Jesus was cursed for his own sins, but they were wrong:

> They do not know My offenses, but You know them. That is, they do not understand how they are Mine, for I have made the sins of others Mine. Nor did they understand that that curse could not swallow up the whole person, but since God was not able to bring Him under any curse, only His flesh was swallowed up. Therefore

[19] *First Lectures on the Psalms*, ed. by Hilton C. Oswald, in *Luther's Works*, ed. by J. Pelikan and H. T. Lehmann, 55 vols (Saint Louis, MO: Concordia Publishing House, 1974), 10:351.

He is at the same time cursed and blessed, at the same time alive and dead, at the same time grieving and rejoicing, so that He might absorb all evils in Himself and bestow all blessings from Himself.[20]

In other words, Christ could not say verse 5 in his own person because he was not a sinner, but he could say it in the place of sinners as their substitute. It was as the substitute that he bore the curse on sin and absorbed all evils. Hence in verse 1 the water that comes up to the Psalmist's neck is our sin and its punishment: 'the *waters* are the very punishments and sufferings of Christ, but at the same time they are our iniquities'.[21] Again in verse 2: 'In the same way the *mire of the deep* (v. 2) is His punishment for our lust of the flesh, as the waters are the lust of the eyes.'[22] The lecture format does not stop Luther putting this in simple and vivid terms: 'Therefore Christ was stuck in our mud'.[23] The Psalm even speaks of Christ being in hell for us. When in verse 15 Jesus asks that the pit would not close on him, he is speaking about entering hell for sinners and not remaining shut in there:

He entered into hell, which opened its mouth, but it could not close its mouth on Him and hold Him. But the way out was entirely open to Him. The mouth of death received Him by the same death, but it could not shut Him up.[24]

Jesus Christ was swallowed by death, but he burst its bonds asunder. Even Psalm 51, on this logic, could be read as uttered by Christ. Luther was a Christ-centred reader, in ways that most of us today have not dared to be. It is noteworthy that even this early he preaches the doctrine of penal substitutionary atonement plainly and boldly, even shockingly. He takes a verse which is a confession of sin and reads it as uttered by Christ the penal substitute for sinners. This exhibits a striking and thoroughgoing commitment to penal substitution at an early stage in Luther's thinking.

Today this exegesis of Psalm 69 might be viewed even among Bible-believing Christians as exegesis that has run out of control. But there is control here. First, there is the basic control that the Psalms have a definite subject, Christ. To this conviction Luther adds a further rule in his

[20] *Psalms*, 10:364-65.
[21] *Psalms*, 10:354.
[22] *Psalms*, 10:354-55.
[23] *Psalms*, 10:355.
[24] *Psalms*, 10:363-64.

prefatory comments, one that had long been used to control readings that went beyond the literal sense: 'In the Scriptures, therefore, no allegory, tropology, or anagogy is valid, unless the same truth is expressly stated historically elsewhere. Otherwise Scripture would become a mockery.'[25] Thus, given that elsewhere the Bible plainly teaches penal substitutionary atonement, we may legitimately find it in the description of the suffering of Christ in Psalm 69.

Luther's approach is a challenge to much of our contemporary conservative biblical interpretation with its restrictive emphasis on the historical sense of Scripture at the expense of more traditional typological readings. The rejection or reduction of Christological typology has resulted from the influence of modern biblical criticism. In the nineteenth century liberal anti-supernaturalists rejected the possibility of typology because it required a high level of divine involvement in the writing of the Bible. Only the Holy Spirit could set up and fulfil the rich range of types that had previously been found in books of the Bible from so many authors across such a wide span of history. If he did not author every word of the Bible, then the connections could not be there. We have rightly accepted the insight of grammatico-historical exegesis that the meaning of the words in their original context is vital for determining their sense. The context of Bible words is not, however, limited to the time at which they were given. They have their full context in the canon of Scripture because the whole canon was authored by the same Spirit. The meaning of the words is not restricted to senses known by the human authors, but is part of the meaning of Scripture as a whole, the *sensus plenior*. This wider context shows us what the Holy Spirit intended the word to signify. We have so emphasised the human author as to lose almost any place for a more typological reading such as we find in Luther. He believed that the Holy Spirit could make remarkable links between the different parts of Scripture. This is not exegesis out of control. It is rather a right openness to the canonical significance of words all authored by the same Holy Spirit.

Luther on Psalm 69: The application to Christ's people

Lastly, we note that Luther's attention to Christ did not mean that he neglected to apply the text to Christ's people. Here are his opening words again, this time in full: 'This psalm speaks literally about the suffering

---

[25] *Psalms*, 10:4. Cf. Thomas Aquinas, *Summa Theologica*, 1a. 1. 10.

of the Lord in His own person. At the same time all the sufferings and weaknesses of the church are also told here.' Luther justifies this double interpretation with a wonderful theological argument which shows why almost any text about Jesus is a text about his people. He explains it in his comments on Psalm 4:1:

> As all His saints flow from Him [Christ] like rivers, so Scripture, being similarly constituted and thus representing Him with His saints, speaks of Him in the sense of the first source. Then it distributes the same sense to the rivers (that is, individual explanations), speaking the same words concerning the saints by way of participation. For if they participate with Him in grace and inherit all things from Him, then also the words of Scripture which speak of Christ participate with Him in a similar way and inherit the same words of praise and description from Him and with Him and in Him, 'who is blessed.'[26]

This is an argument from our union with Christ: because we are united to Christ, what is said of him is said of us. What is true of the source, Christ, is true of the river, his people. What Scripture says about him it also says, by participation, about us. This means that just as Christ suffered, so we must suffer. Like Calvin, Luther is repeatedly clear that a Christian ought to suffer. This is one of the dominant themes of his work, and he put it in very strong terms. For example, after saying that Christ entered hell, he goes on:

> So also the saints go into death, into the mouth of the deep, but they will not be shut up in it, because they will rise from the dead, and the pit of hell or purgatory cannot swallow them up and shut them up like the ungodly.[27]

We are united with Christ in going down into hell. The hell that we enter is obviously not the literal hell of the damned. It is rather the hell-like experience that Luther describes using the Latin *tentatio* and the German *Anfechtung*. This is the inner torment, the trial and affliction of the Christian: 'Thus all the prayers of the Psalms which are uttered in the person of Christ as being in hell, are also uttered in the person of the saints, as

---

[26] *Psalms*, 10:52. The words quoted are used by Paul in Romans 1:25 and 2 Corinthians 11:31.

[27] *Psalms*, 10:364. The reference to Purgatory reflects the early date of the lectures in Luther's theological development.

descending to hell in their mind and heart.'[28] Such suffering of discipline on earth, Luther held, is vital for our spiritual health. In his explanation of the Psalm he repeatedly insists that the comfortable Christian is in grave danger: 'The greatest temptation of all is to have no temptation. And the supreme misfortune is to have no misfortune.'[29] Or again: 'He who is secure is least secure, and he who is fearful and terrified is blessed, because he will be least afraid.'[30] We have such a need for suffering that we must create our own if none comes to us from outside: 'So let us be our own tyrants, tormentors, heretics, stirring up such attitudes as keep after us and urge us on to better things, lest we be destroyed through peace and security.'[31] What happens to Christ in our place on the cross must happen to us in our own inner mortification, even if it is not happening in external assault. This is the argument of Paul in Romans 6: because Christ has died and we are united to him, we must die by mortifying our sinful nature. The Christian, Luther says, must be daily suffering crucifixion. This is a sustained emphasis in his theology. The Christian life is life united to Christ in his death. A Psalm about suffering is a Psalm about Christ and his cross, and it is a Psalm about Christ's people and their mortification.

Even at this early stage of his career, Luther's preaching exhibits several strengths that we can emulate. It is consistently focused on the Lord Jesus Christ. It takes us to his cross. It comforts us with the good news of his substitutionary suffering, and it challenges us to suffer with him. Let us pray that our preaching would, in these ways, be like his.

---

[28] *Psalms*, 10:372.
[29] *Psalms*, 10:356.
[30] *Psalms*, 10:377.
[31] *Psalms*, 10:373.

14

FEASTING WITH THE LORD: NICHOLAS RIDLEY (c. 1500-55)

Ridley and the Mass

Having considered preaching in the company of Martin Luther, we turn now to consider the Lord's supper with another reformer, Nicholas Ridley. Ridley was one of the reforming bishops of the Church of England under King Edward VI. He was executed by Mary I on 16 October 1555 for his refusal to embrace Rome. The account of his burning in John Foxe's *Acts and Monuments* is, like many of Foxe's accounts, a moving one. Ridley and Hugh Latimer died together, Latimer exhorting Ridley to play the man, saying they would light a candle that would never go out. The fire took slowly, burning around the lower half of Ridley's body and leaving him conscious for a long time. Like Polycarp and other martyrs so many centuries before in the early church, Ridley saw clearly the choice that he faced, a choice between a brief fire that burns but for a moment, and the fire of hell that burns forever. As he himself puts it in a farewell letter to fellow-sufferers that he wrote while he was in prison:

> What though our troubles here be painful for the time, and the sting of death bitter and unpleasant? yet we know that they shall not last in comparison of eternity, no not the twinkling of an eye; and that they, patiently taken in Christ's cause, shall procure and get us unmeasureable heaps of heavenly glory, unto the which

these temporal pains of death and troubles compared, are not to be esteemed, but to be rejoiced upon.[1]

Nicholas Ridley died because he refused the Roman Catholic Mass. When he was burnt, it was for rejecting the doctrine that the body and blood of Christ are substantially present in place of the bread and wine, and for denying that the Mass is an atoning sacrifice. This is an important fact which must not be overlooked or belittled. The English reformers did not somehow miss the central point of the Reformation when they took their stand over this issue. They did not die on the wrong hill, failing to notice that justification by faith alone was the key point of contention. First, it is evident from the work of recent Roman Catholic historians that the Mass was the main event in the experience of the late mediaeval congregation. Eamon Duffy explains that the central fact of religious life in the church before the Reformation was the liturgy, and 'the Mass lay at the heart of the liturgy'.[2] It was the Mass which was the focus of all hope in the church, both for the individual, and for the body. For many the Mass *was* the church. The centrality of the Mass was also taught at the Council of Trent:

> [Christ] wished that this sacrament should be received as the spiritual food of souls, whereby they may be nourished and strengthened, living by the life of Him who said: *He that eateth me, the same also shall live by me*, and as an antidote whereby we may be freed from daily faults and be preserved from mortal sins.[3]

Those receiving the sacrament are kept alive by it. Later, in the 22nd session, Trent states the propitiatory effect of the Mass:

> If we, contrite and penitent, with sincere heart and upright faith, with fear and reverence, draw nigh to God, *we obtain mercy and find grace in seasonable aid*. For, appeased by this sacrifice, the Lord grants the grace and gift of penitence and pardons even the gravest crimes and sins.[4]

[1] Letter 33, *The Works of Nicholas Ridley*, ed. by Henry Christmas (Cambridge: Cambridge University Press, 1843), p. 421.

[2] *The Stripping of the Altars: Traditional Religion in England 1400-1580* (New Haven: Yale University Press, 1992), p. 91.

[3] *Canons and Decrees of the Council of Trent*, trans. by H. J. Schroeder (Rockford, IL: Tan Books and Publishers, 1978), 13th session, c. 2, p. 74. The quotation in italics is from John 6:57.

[4] 22nd session, c. 2, *Canons and Decrees*, p 146. The quotation in italics is from

Not that the people took communion often. Duffy tells us that for most people the Mass was 'something to be seen, not to be consumed'.[5] The Mass was the central spectacle which the people watched as they worshipped the supposedly transubstantiated elements. Given the centrality of the Mass to late mediaeval piety, it made excellent sense for the reformers to focus their attention on it and to take their stand against it. It was the central act in the life of the system they were attacking.

Second, the Lord's supper formed a nodal point within all the theologies of the sixteenth century. The theology of the Lord's supper connected together a number of the vital branches of Christian doctrine, as it still does. The reformers knew that the question of the presence of Christ in the supper is closely tied to the question of the relation between his two natures. In short, how you understand the sacrament reveals how you understand the person of Christ himself. Ridley says as much in a letter he wrote to those suffering: 'For it is not any ceremony for the which we contend; but it toucheth the very substance of our whole religion, yea, even Christ himself'.[6] A Christ substantially present in the Mass could not at the same time be located in a truly human fashion in just one place at the right hand of the Father. The implication of the doctrine of the Mass is that Christ is not properly human. The natural properties of his human body cannot be preserved if his flesh and blood are present substantially on earth after his ascension. By contrast, we saw in Chapter 2 that the Council of Chalcedon teaches that the divinity and humanity of Christ are united 'without the distinction of natures being taken away by such union, but rather the peculiar property of each nature being preserved and being united in one Person and subsistence'.[7] Further, the Mass was connected to the doctrine of justification. The reformers knew that Rome taught that the Mass brings life, so they faced a challenge to the Bible's doctrine of justification by faith alone. No doctrine is an island, and the Mass was no exception. Thus it made good sense for the reformers to focus on this issue as a nodal point for so many others.

The Mass was also a *visible* nodal point because it was a tangible act. Christian theology can be a knotty business, and it can be hard to dissect its nuances rightly. For the English reformers, focusing their attack on the Mass made the Reformation a visible reality for the people. By reforming

---

Hebrews 4:16.

[5] *Altars*, p. 95.

[6] Letter 7, *Works*, p. 344.

[7] *Ecumenical Councils*, p. 265.

the Mass into the Lord's supper, and by making this a centre-piece of the Reformation, they could induce English parishioners to see with their own eyes that the church had changed. Conversely, Rome could use the refusal of the Mass as a simple test for the reformers. It would be easy for an inquiry into the details of someone's theology to spin off into confusion. Even on the comparatively straightforward question of Christ's presence in the sacrament, the representatives of Rome sometime struggled to identify what they regarded as the errors of the reformers. While Ridley was being held he was asked by the Bishop of Lincoln, John White, to clarify his views on the Mass, and on what he had taught about it at Oxford during April–July 1554. He was presented with three articles summarizing his views. The first denied that the true and natural body of Christ is 'really present' in the sacrament.[8] Ridley was then pressed to affirm or deny the article, but he refused to do so. He explained that the article is true if taken in one sense, false if taken in another. The words used by Rome to describe Christ's presence, *vere et realiter*, 'indeed and really', can be read two ways, one of which he accepted, the other of which he denied. Ridley refused to give a simple affirmative or negative reply because the statement is equivocal. He reminded the Bishop of a basic lesson in philosophy: in the case of equivocation 'except distinction be given, no direct answer can be made; for it is one of Aristotle's fallacies, containing two questions under one, the which cannot be satisfied with one answer'.[9] Ridley then affirmed his belief in the spiritual presence of Christ's body:

> Both you and I agree herein, that in the sacrament is the very true and natural body and blood of Christ, even that which was born of the Virgin Mary, which ascended into heaven, which sitteth on the right hand of God the Father, which shall come from thence to judge the quick and the dead; only we differ *in modo*, in the way and manner of being: we confess all one thing to be in the sacrament, and dissent in the manner of being there. I, being fully by God's word thereunto persuaded, confess Christ's natural body to be in the sacrament indeed by spirit and grace, because that whosoever receiveth worthily that bread and wine, receiveth effectuously Christ's body, and drinketh his blood (that is, he is made effectually partaker of his passion); and you make a grosser kind of being,

[8] 'The Order and Manner of the Examination of Dr Ridley', in *Works*, p. 271.
[9] 'Examination', in *Works*, pp. 273-4.

enclosing a natural, a lively, and a moving body, under the shape or form of bread and wine. Now, this difference considered, to the question thus I answer, that in the sacrament of the altar is the natural body and blood of Christ *vere et realiter*, indeed and really, for spiritually, by grace and efficacy; for so every worthy receiver receiveth the very true body of Christ.[10]

The next day the Bishop summarized the proceedings and reported that the notaries had been unable to take a 'determinate' answer down from Ridley on the first article.[11] In the end, however, Ridley was found guilty of 'denying the true and natural body of Christ, and his natural blood to be in the sacrament of the altar.'[12] Amid the theological subtleties along the way, the refusal to participate in the Mass was a clear and tangible starting and finishing point for convicting someone of 'heresy'. Conversely, acceptance of it was a sign of victory for the Marian authorities. It is no surprise, therefore, that we see Thomas Cranmer, weakened by prolonged harassment, going to Mass at Christ Church Cathedral in Oxford, and after his fifth and catastrophic recantation (5 February 1556) asking for sacramental absolution and hearing a Mass celebrated especially for him. Here was an obvious point on which to attack the reformers, since it promised clarity.

Ridley's virtues

As we saw with John Calvin on justification, we should be interested not only in what a man believed, but also in how he held his beliefs. Ridley's virtues were revealed long before his death. He was a man of discipline. This is evident in the way that he ordered his household around the word of God. He trained its members in the Scriptures, handing out New Testaments and having his family memorize portions, especially Paul's overview of biblical history in Acts 13. Foxe comments that 'nothing but virtue and godliness reigned in his house'.[13]

Ridley was a man who cared for others, even for the relatives of his opponents. Foxe details how he treated the mother of his predecessor as Bishop of London, Edmund Bonner. When Bonner was deprived of his

[10] 'Examination', in *Works*, p. 274.
[11] 'Examination', in *Works*, p. 278.
[12] 'Examination', in *Works*, p. 286.
[13] Cited in *Works*, p. viii.

bishopric in 1550 and replaced by Ridley, the new Bishop had Bonner's mother living next-door to his manor in Fulham. Ridley invited Mrs Bonner to dinner and supper (as they called them), along with Bonner's sister. 'Mother Bonner', as he called her, always sat at the end of the table. Even if members of the royal council were present, Ridley would say to them 'By your lordships' favour, this place of right and custom is for my mother Bonner'.[14]

Ridley was a man who dealt plainly and boldly with others. During the reign of Edward VI he visited Princess Mary at Hunsden, near his own house at Hadham in Hertfordshire. Foxe records that after an earlier exchange of pleasantries Ridley saw her again and offered to preach for her:

> After the dinner was done, the bishop being called for by the said lady Mary, resorted again to her Grace, between whom this communication was: first the bishop beginneth in manner as followeth. 'Madam, I came not only to do my duty to see your Grace, but also to offer myself to preach before you on Sunday next, if it will please you to hear me.'
>
> At this her countenance changed, and after silence for a space, she answered thus: 'My Lord, as for this last matter, I pray you make the answer to it yourself.'
>
> *Ridley.*—'Madam; considering mine office and calling, I am bound to make your Grace this offer to preach before you.'
>
> *Mary.*—'Well, I pray you, make the answer, as I have said, to this matter yourself, for you know the answer well enough; but if there be no remedy, but I must make you answer, this shall be your answer, the door of the parish church adjoining shall be open for you, if you come, and ye may preach if you list, but neither I nor any of mine shall hear you.'
>
> *Ridley.*—'Madam, I trust you will not refuse God's word.'
>
> *Mary.*—'I cannot tell what ye call God's word—that is not God's word now, that was God's word in my father's days.'
>
> *Ridley.*—'God's word is one at all times, but hath been better understood and practised in some ages than in other.'
>
> *Mary.*—'You durst not for your ears have avouched that for God's word in my father's days that now you do; and as for your new books, I thank God, I never read any of them, I never did nor

---

[14] Cited in *Works*, p. viii.

ever will do.'

And after many bitter words against the form of religion then established, and against the government of the realm, and the laws made in the young years of her brother, which she said she was not bound to obey till her brother came to perfect age, and then she said she would obey them; she asked the bishop whether he were one of the council? He answered, 'No.' 'You might well enough,' said she, 'as the council goeth now-a-days.' And so she concluded with these words: 'My lord, for your gentleness to come and see me I thank you, but for your offering to preach before me, I thank you never a whit.'

Then the said bishop was brought by Sir Thomas Wharton to the place where they had dined, and was desired to drink.

Foxe records what happened next, and a statement of regret from Ridley; that is not what we might expect. His regret was not for having gone to Mary in the first place, but for having stayed:

And after he had drunk, he paused awhile, looking very sadly, and suddenly brake out into these words,—'Surely I have done amiss.' 'Why so?' quoth Sir Thomas Wharton. 'For I have drunk,' said he, 'in that place where God's word offered hath been refused, whereas if I had remembered my duty, I ought to have departed immediately, and to have shaken off the dust of my shoes for a testimony against this house.' These words were by the said bishop spoken with such a vehemency, that some of the hearers afterward confessed their hair to stand upright on their heads. This done, the bishop departed, and so returned to his house.[15]

Ridley's virtues are seen most clearly in the events leading up to his execution. Here we see his resolve. On the last day of September 1555 he refused to acknowledge the Pope. Before the commission at Oxford in the Divinity School he removed his cap for the Bishop of Lincoln as a representative of a Cardinal of royal blood (Reginald Pole), but when the Bishop stated that the Cardinal was the representative of the Pope, Ridley put his cap back on. It was removed by the Beadle. Ridley was able to maintain his resolve because he looked to the Lord for strength. He explains in a letter to Latimer his own weakness and trust in God:

For surely, except the Lord assist me with his gracious aid, in the

---

[15] The account is cited in *Works*, pp. x–xi, n. 1.

time of his service I know I shall play but the part of a white-livered knight. But truly my trust is in him, that in mine infirmity he shall try himself strong, and that he can make the coward in his cause to fight like a man.[16]

Ridley exhibited in his suffering the virtues of a true theologian: he believed that theology mattered, and he lived out what he believed to the very end. His martyrdom was a detailed theological business. He died for articulating with some nuance a theological position and refusing to move from it. He was not merely an academic who studied the subject; he lived and died for his theological convictions. Of his theological ability there can be no doubt. It is hard to read Ridley's works and agree with Alister McGrath that the English Reformation was characterized by 'theological mediocrity'.[17] The editor of Ridley's works comments that he had 'a mind of the very highest order, both as to power and acuteness'.[18] Even his Roman persecutors granted the ability of Ridley. The Bishop of Gloucester famously sought to expose the weakness of the Reformation project in his words against Ridley on 1 October 1555:

> For what a weak and feeble stay in religion is this, I pray you? Latimer leaneth to Cranmer, Cranmer to Ridley, and Ridley to the singularity of his own wit: so that if you overthrew the singularity of Ridley's wit, then must needs the religion of Cranmer and Latimer fall also.[19]

Ridley denied the picture of everything resting on him, though it is certainly true that Cranmer was heavily influenced by him in his own view of the Lord's supper. In particular, Ridley was noted for his 'immense patristic learning'.[20] He learned his own view of the Lord's supper in part at least from reading the early mediaeval 'heretic' Ratramnus of Corbie (d. 868), who was one of several mediaevals who anticipated aspects of Reformed theology. All of this knowledge Ridley deployed in his theological teaching and writing, and he stood by it in his death.

In the events of his execution we see again Ridley's concern for

---

[16] 'A Second Conference between Ridley and Latimer', in *Works*, p. 117.
[17] *Iustitia Dei: A History of the Christian Doctrine of Justification*, 3rd edn (Cambridge: Cambridge University Press, 2005), p. 258.
[18] *Works*, p. xii.
[19] 'Examination', in *Works*, p. 283.
[20] *Works*, p. xii.

others, especially for the poor. The Apostle Paul tells us that when he went to Jerusalem and met Peter, James, and John, they affirmed his ministry to the Gentiles, asking only that he and Barnabas and Titus 'remember the poor' (*Gal.* 2:10). This Ridley did. During his life his preaching, like that of Latimer, had an emphasis on the 'commonwealth'. Edward VI himself noted the impact that Ridley's preaching had on him in his endeavours for the poor. At the time of his death it was the plight of the poor that weighed on Ridley's mind: 'There is nothing in all the world that troubleth my conscience, I praise God, this only excepted'.[21] He had given leases to 'divers poor men', including his widowed sister, which were now being set aside by his successor. He wrote to Queen Mary asking her to provide for these poor tenants, and in his final hours he took pains to make sure that the Queen received the letter. Just after he had been degraded (that is, after the symbols of his ministry had been removed from him as they had been from Tyndale), he read the letter to the man who had degraded him, Bishop Brookes, asking him to forward the request to the Queen. Then, at the very scene of his death, Ridley explained the problem to Lord Williams and told him that his brother had a copy of the letter.

Ridley against transubstantiation

Having explored the significance of the Mass and some of the ways in which Ridley's life and death show us his character, we will spend the rest of this chapter looking more closely at his critique of the Roman Catholic doctrine of transubstantiation and his own positive doctrine of the Lord's supper. The critique is found in *A Treatise Against the Error of Transubstantiation*, written during Ridley's imprisonment in 1555. J. C. Ryle comments that 'Among the many goodly volumes published by the Parker Society, not a few, I suspect, sleep quietly on library shelves, unopened and uncut'.[22] We can at least make sure that this is not true of Ridley.

The work has several marked characteristics. First of all, we find that Ridley is careful. Like the mediaeval scholastics before him and the Reformed scholastics after him, Ridley begins by stating what the issue is not, before homing in on what it is. All are agreed, he explains, that those who receive the Lord's supper are either blessed or cursed by it: 'whosoever receiveth this holy sacrament thus ordained in remembrance of Christ, he receiveth therewith either death or life. In this, I trust, we do all

---

[21] 'Examination', in *Works*, p. 297.
[22] *Five English Reformers* (London: The Banner of Truth Trust, 1961), p. 124.

agree.'[23] This particular power of the supper was not the question. Rather, he goes on, there are five points of contention:

> Whether there be any transubstantiation of the bread, or no? Any corporal and carnal presence of Christ's substance, or no? Whether adoration, only due unto God, is to be done unto the sacrament, or no? And whether Christ's body be there offered in deed unto the heavenly Father by the priest, or no? Or whether the evil man receiveth the natural body of Christ, or no?[24]

Ridley then explains that all of these five issues actually depend on the single question of the mode of Christ's presence in the supper: 'all five aforesaid points do chiefly hang upon this one question, which is, What is the matter of the sacrament, whether it is the natural substance of bread, or the natural substance of Christ's own body?'[25] The first two of the five questions (concerning transubstantiation and the corporal presence of Christ) ask this very thing. The third (concerning adoration), fourth (concerning the offering of Christ's body) and the fifth (concerning evil receiving) all depend on the substance of the body being present. Ridley thus effectively identifies and narrows the set of pertinent issues in his critique. We see him here as a precise thinker, much like Calvin. He was not one to engage with straw men or imagined enemies.

Second, we find that Ridley offers a critique of transubstantiation which is based on close exegesis of the biblical evidence. He begins by detailing the accounts of the Lord's supper in the synoptic Gospels and 1 Corinthians, and he notes the differences between them. At various points his argument rests on specific features of the four narratives. For example, he opposes one variety of the Roman view, the claim that the bread was changed as Christ took it and blessed it so that he actually broke his body, not the bread. To refute this, Ridley works through the biblical accounts of the Supper and points out how often Scripture plainly describes the breaking of *bread*. He concludes:

> St Paul, which setteth forth the most fully in his writings both the doctrine and the right use of the Lord's supper, and the sacramental eating and drinking of Christ's body and blood, calleth it five times, 'bread,' 'bread,' 'bread,' 'bread,' 'bread.'[26]

[23] *A Brief Declaration of the Lord's Supper*, in *Works*, p. 8.
[24] *Brief Declaration*, in *Works*, p. 11.
[25] *Brief Declaration*, in *Works*, p. 11.
[26] *Brief Declaration*, in *Works*, pp. 16-17.

Similarly, he points out how Christ speaks of drinking the fruit of the vine again in the kingdom, showing that this is what he drank when he drank in the upper room. Ridley is also capable of using details to turn Roman Catholic arguments back against themselves. For example, he points out that in 1 Corinthians Jesus is described as saying 'This cup is the New Testament' (11:25). If Rome holds that the word 'is' in the statement 'This is my body' necessarily denotes a change of substance into the body of Christ, then, he infers, the verb must have the same meaning here. Paul's words thus 'turn the substance of the cup into the substance of the New Testament'.[27] If Rome denies that Christ meant to describe a change of substance in the cup, Ridley agrees and applies the same reasoning to the statement 'This is my body'. He anticipates that they will say that 'cup' is a metonymy, a figure of speech where a word for one thing is used for another with which it is closely associated (like referring to 'the Crown' when we mean the Queen or 'The White House' when we mean the President). Hence, they might say, 'cup' stands for wine, and so the change is in the wine not the cup itself. But, Ridley points out, if they say that, then they have granted that Christ used one figure of speech in the institution of the supper, and the way is open for saying that he used two: 'This is my body' may then also be figurative.

Third, Ridley uses his prodigious patristic learning to good effect. We can illustrate this by looking at how he continues the same argument about the cup. Having shown that 'This is my body' may be figurative, Ridley asks how we may discern a figure of speech in Scripture. For help he turns to Augustine and the guidance he gives in his work *On Christian Doctrine*. Augustine argues that whenever Scripture appears to enjoin what is ungodly, or to forbid what is good, it must speak figuratively. He himself gives the words of John 6:53 as an example: 'Except ye eat the flesh of the Son of Man, and drink his blood, ye cannot have life in you.' This verse seems to command what is wicked, eating the flesh of a man. Hence, Augustine concludes, 'it is figurative'.[28] The second half of Ridley's work consists of an account of patristic views of the Lord's supper in which he argues, from primary evidence, that the church fathers understood the truth as the reformers now teach it. He focuses his attention on Origen, Chrysostom, and Theodoret from the Greek writers, and Tertullian, Augustine, and Gelasius from the Latin. As he goes through the patristic material he attacks the sophistical character of much of the

[27] *Brief Declaration*, in *Works*, p. 20.
[28] *Brief Declaration*, in *Works*, p. 21, citing *On Christian Doctrine*, iii. 16.

Roman Catholic reading of the fathers. For example, he quotes Theodoret of Cyrus explaining that, in referring to bread and wine as his body and blood, Christ 'was not changing the nature itself'. Theodoret affirms that the sacraments, 'after the sanctification, do not go out of their own nature'. Ridley describes the Roman reply to this evidence:

> At these words the Papists do startle; and, to say the truth, these words be so plain, so full, and so clear, that they cannot tell what to say: but yet they will not cease to go about to play the cuttles, and to cast their colours over them, that the truth, which is so plainly told, should not have place.[29]

Hence he depicts Rome as a cuttlefish, confounded by the evidence and resorting to casting ink over it to hide the truth.

Fourth, Ridley was not a hasty theologian, particularly in that he avoided over-reacting against the Roman Catholic position and throwing out the biblical teaching with it. In the face of a corruption of the Lord's supper which emphasised the substantial presence of Christ and which gave the Mass a sacrificial function, it would have been very easy to react into the opposite extreme, taking the Supper as a mere memorial with no power. The temptation to this kind of theological ricochet is great for Christians who are rightly outraged by some abuse of theology or practice. The mainstream reformers of the sixteenth century were remarkable for their ability not to take this path. On countless issues, we find that they did not just run as far as they could from Rome for the sake of it. Sometimes they stuck too close, as with Martin Luther's doctrine of the Lord's supper in which he maintained the idea of Christ's real presence according to both natures. But often they trod carefully, for example in not abandoning infant baptism because it had been abused, and, in the case of the Calvinists, in maintaining the idea of Christ's presence in the Supper and its powerful effects.

This is what Ridley did. We have already heard him speaking before his trial of his belief that 'the sacrament is the very true and natural body of Christ' which makes the one who receives rightly an 'effectual partaker of his passion'.[30] He says the same thing in the *Treatise*. His position is almost exactly that of Calvin explored in Chapter 11. The presupposition here is that Christ's human nature, by virtue of its union to the eternal Son of God, has in it divine life:

[29] *Brief Declaration*, in *Works*, p. 36.
[30] 'Examination', in *Works*, p. 274.

The same natural substance of the very body and blood of Christ, because it is united in the divine nature in Christ, the second Person of the Trinity, therefore it hath not only life in itself, but is also able to give, and doth give life unto so many as be, or shall be partakers thereof.[31]

In other words, the human flesh of Jesus is life-giving. We need then to ask how we receive life from his flesh in the Supper. Here is where the crucial distinction from the Roman view comes in: we do not receive it by eating the substance of the flesh. The life-giving body of Christ remains in heaven and the life comes to us by grace with the word and the sacraments. Ridley compares this with the beams of the sun:

Even as, for example, we say the same sun, which, in substance, never removeth his place out of the heavens, is yet present here by his beams, light, and natural influence, where it shineth upon the earth. For God's word and his sacraments be, as it were, the beams of Christ, which is *Sol justitiae*, the Sun of righteousness.[32]

This is a beautiful image: Christ, like the sun, powerfully shines his goodness on his people, communicating life from himself to them as they hear his word and eat his supper. The Supper is, as Paul puts it, our fellowship with Christ's body and blood (*1 Cor.* 10:16), which are themselves life-giving (*John* 6:54). Ridley rightly held on to the power and dignity of the Supper despite the way Rome had corrupted it.

Ridley's work exhibits excellent theological qualities: precision in forming the question, close exegesis of Scripture, awareness and use of the tradition, and avoidance of hasty over-reaction. All of these qualities produced the Reformed theology that he then lived out as a true theologian, even to the point of death. It will be by imitating Ridley as a theologian, as well as his discipline, concern for others, plain dealing, resolve, and trust in God, that ministers of the gospel will keep the flame alight into the future.

[31] *Brief Declaration*, in *Works*, p. 13.
[32] *Brief Declaration*, in *Works*, p. 13.

EPILOGUE

15

MAKING THE CASE FOR
CHRISTIAN HISTORY

No neutral ground

The blood of the martyrs testifies to the hostility of the world toward Christ and his people. Attacks on the church by persecutors like Nero and Mao show that history itself is a realm of conflict. But is history in the sense of the *activity of telling history* an arena of conflict? This will be our field of exploration in this chapter as a conclusion to the history-telling that I have been attempting. It may look like a rarefied question at first glance, of concern only to historians themselves. But I hope to show that the answer to it is actually important for all Christians, because the telling of history is an arena of conflict that we ignore at our peril.

How do you react to the idea at first glance? It is tempting to think that history is 'just history'. There is good history and there is bad history. Good history is history which gets all the true facts in the right order. Bad history is history which is fabricated or mistaken in some way. Surely history is just history, an essentially neutral attempt to repeat the facts? As soon as we think this we have forgotten our theology. There are two theological reasons why we must hold that telling the story of the past is itself an arena of conflict.

First, there is the extent of human depravity. All of the activities of Adamic humanity are fallen. There is no area of our lives where the flesh has not taken its toll. The biblical, Augustinian, and Reformed doctrine of total depravity tells us that every aspect of our being is depraved. If every aspect of our being is depraved, then every human activity is depraved. It follows necessarily: every part of us, therefore everything we do. In some areas of our lives, in some activities, this depravity is very obvious. But there are other areas where it has a less obvious effect. What about the telling of history? If we think that we can have spiritually neutral history, then we have forgotten that we are a race in rebellion, and that our rebellion affects all of our activities. As Cain wanders in the land of Nod east of Eden, what does he tell his son Enoch about Uncle Abel? Does he explain about his own sin? Or does he complain of his lot? As the Pharaohs recount the escape of the Hebrews, how do they describe the events? As Caiaphas tells his tale, does he speak the truth about the Son of God whose death he deemed expedient? These figures were all historians. As soon as someone speaks of the past, he is an historian. Even if the Pharaohs scrupulously did not speak of this moment in their past, that would be as much an attempt to tell history by omission. Moreover, these figures were spiritually hostile historians, and there is no reason why the unregenerate mind will be different now. The history of the world as told by the world today will be as unreliable as it has always been. We see this in notorious examples such as the Jesus Seminar or the pro-Gnostic literature that stands behind the novels of Dan Brown. Non-Christian history is hostile history that springs from the fallen human heart.

The same is true for every human intellectual activity. The Reformed theologian Cornelius Van Til applies this analysis even to the seemingly naked truths of mathematics:

> Now the fact that two times two are four does not mean the same thing to you as a believer and to someone else as an unbeliever. When you think of two times two as four you connect this fact with numerical law. And when you connect this fact with numerical law you must connect numerical law with all law. The question you face then is whether law exists in its own right or is an expression of the will and nature of God. Thus the fact that two times two are four enables you to implicate yourself more deeply into the nature and will of God. On the other hand when an unbeliever says that two times two are four he will also be led to connect this fact with the whole idea of law but will regard this law as independent of God. Thus the fact that two times two are four enables him to get farther away from God.[1]

[1] *Essays on Christian Education* (Phillipsburg, New Jersey: Presbyterian and

This may be hardest to accept with mathematics, since it looks like the purest, most neutral of disciplines. It is perhaps at the level of the philosophy of mathematics that the conflict becomes clearest, when we ask 'Do numbers exist?' or 'Why are the laws of mathematics constant?'

The conflict is more immediately obvious with history. Think, for example, of the Tudor kings and queens of England. The fact that Henry VIII wanted to annul his marriage to Catherine of Aragon and in so doing opened the door to Protestantism in England is, to a Christian, obviously a fact only rightly understood in reference to the progress of the kingdom of Jesus Christ. The discovery of America is likewise a fact rightly interpreted as important because of its role in the spread of the life-saving gospel around the globe. As we look ahead, will we not see that the global dominance of China will make sense only as part of this same story? It is no coincidence that the gospel came to an empire in Rome, from there to what would later be European empires, from there to the American empire (using the term without intending a political point), from these countries to China, and from China . . .? Surely we can discern God's hand here. As Pascal comments: 'How fine it is to see, with the eyes of faith, Darius and Cyrus, Alexander, the Romans, Pompey and Herod working, without knowing it, for the glory of the Gospel!'[2]

The telling of history is Christian telling, or it is hostile telling. Van Til's point is that no 'fact' exists in isolation. Even the most boring historians do not hermetically seal facts in little capsules and hand them over in a vacuum. They come as part of a wider, running explanation of the history within which those facts exist. If no such explanation is apparent, if they do seem to come in hermetically sealed capsules, then that in itself means they come with an interpretation implied. The delivery of isolated facts would say in effect that each fact can be treated in isolation from any other considerations at all. History would be meaningless, and the overarching Lordship of Christ would make no difference to the details. Van Til puts this very strongly: 'it is a satanic falsehood to say that a fact is a fact for everybody alike'.[3] Facts come in the context of stories of the world, and that means that the natural mind will produce history hostile to Christ and his people.

Reformed, 1979), p. 190.

   [2] *Pensées*, in *Pascal*, trans. by W. F. Trotter, Great Books of the Western World, XXXIII (Chicago: Encyclopaedia Britannica, 1952), No. 701, p. 302.

   [3] *Essays*, p. 199.

The second reason why we should expect hostile history is that *all* people are historians, including all unbelievers. It is not just a few academic historians off in the dark corners of the British Library or the Library of Congress who are doing history which is hostile to the gospel. All unbelievers tell an anti-Christ history. Many today *behave* as if they think that history is simply irrelevant. As we saw with Mark Steyn at the start of this book, we even use the word 'history' to mean 'irrelevance'. Parts of our culture seem to be allergic to the past, to be afflicted with a kind of neophilia. But this is impossible to maintain. No culture can live long without an articulated history. In telling history we define our world, and we locate ourselves at a particular point in it. History is fundamental to our sense of who we are. For this reason history is an inalienable human activity. Even those postmodernists who see no point in doing history do history—they cannot stop themselves. They maintain, as Jean-François Lyotard puts it, 'incredulity toward metanarratives', big stories of the world, but then they tell them anyway.[4]

The reason that all people have histories is that all people are in fact religious people. We read in Ecclesiastes that God 'has put eternity into man's heart' (*Eccles.* 3:11). Human beings have an innate desire to worship, and therefore worship either Christ or an idol. Everyone is religious, and insofar as everyone is religious he is to some extent an historian. To maintain a religion is to tell the story of the world, where it came from, how it got here, and where it is going. There are obvious examples. Think of the materialist who worships this world or our human ability to fathom it: there is a religious person, and there too is an historian. His project generates a particular story of the world that denies its creation by a transcendent creator God, and that rewrites all subsequent history to exclude any divine action. Think of the existentialist who believes that life is meaningless, but who tries to live with passion and nobility. There is a religious person, worshipping his pointless cause, and there too is an historian. The existentialist project relies on history having no purpose and on a vision of heroic individuals pitting themselves against a meaningless universe. Take away the history, and the worldview will crumble. Being an historian is part of being a religious creature, even if the religion is man-made. Here then are two reasons why we must expect hostile history: because human

---

[4] *The Postmodern Condition: A Report on Knowledge*, trans. by Geoff Bennington and Brian Massumi (Manchester: Manchester University Press, 1984; repr. 2004), p. xxiv.

beings who narrate history are fallen, and because all human beings, being religious, narrate history.

Reasons for redeeming history

Necessarily, then, we face the challenge of hostile history-telling. How should we respond to it? My conviction is that as Christians we must engage in Christian counter-history, thus redeeming history-telling itself. First, the Bible itself commits us to being historical because it describes the history of the world and our place in it. Telling history is a fundamental Christian activity because it is what the Bible does. Studying the Bible is being inculcated into a history, *the* history, the authoritative, defining history of the world. In doing theology biblically we are already engaged in being historians. Scripture does not tell the story of an abstracted a-historical Christ, but of 'Jesus Christ, the son of David, the son of Abraham' (*Matt.* 1:1).

Does this argument secure solely the importance of the history recorded by the Bible, of the years from Adam to the early church? That would be a strange conclusion to reach, because the historical scope of Scripture itself extends beyond the apostolic era. Scripture speaks about all later history. I do not mean that we should all become students of Saddam Hussein's project to rebuild Babylon, as if it were the literal fulfilment of biblical prophecy, or that we should keep logging on to check the latest reading of the 'Rapture Index'.[5] This is not what I mean by saying that Scripture tells us how we should view post-biblical history, but Scripture does have a pan-historical reach. Think, for example, of the visions in Daniel of the kingdoms, of the stone that grows into a mountain that fills the earth (*Dan.* 2). Think of the parables of the growing seed and the mustard seed that becomes a great plant that shelters the birds (*Mark* 4:26-32). Think of the yeast in the lump, leavening the whole (*Matt.* 13:33). Think even of the Great Commission, of the discipling of all nations commanded and empowered by the Jesus who has all authority in heaven and on earth (*Matt.* 28:18-20). All of these are biblical depictions of *post*-biblical history. If we are telling the story of the mediaeval period, then we are not telling the story of a period about which the Bible is silent. In broad terms, how we view the last 2,000 years is determined by Scripture itself.

[5] You can find this 'prophetic speedometer of end-time activity' at http://www.raptureready.com/rap2.html. As I write it stands at 158, against a record high of 182. Is it a spoof? Who can tell?

This argument does not mandate any particular interpretation of a single historical event. There can be great difficulties in 'reading' providence, especially with more recent history. Nevertheless, all our history-telling must be located explicitly within the broad biblical framework.

Second, we must engage in Christian counter-history because the Lord Jesus Christ claims *total* lordship over the earth. The Christian religion must become a universal religion because Jesus is the universal Lord. Jesus has a right to lordship as the creator, the one by whom all things were made: 'all things were created through him and for him' (*Col.* 1:16). He has a right to lordship as the risen one: 'He is the beginning, the firstborn from the dead, that in everything he might be preeminent' (*Col.* 1:18). This shows why his right to lordship is utterly exhaustive. There is no nook of the creation that he did not make, no cranny over which his sceptre is not extended. All that is, he owns; all that is, he rules. This means that history, the fundamental human task of telling the story of our world, is subject to his claims. So our history will either be obedient, Christ-serving history, or else it will be history in the death-throes of a tragic and futile rebellion.

Third, we must engage in Christian counter-history because if we do not then we will pick up a non-Christian history by default. If we neglect telling history from a distinctively Christian viewpoint, someone else's history will fill the vacuum that we have created. We will acquire, probably without noticing it, a narrative from a scroll found in a temple library, a library which resources the worship of a false god. We must be engaged in a battle over history, because if we are not then we will have bought into a Christ-hating history without knowing it.

Turning the tide of history-telling

How should we start? Our first act as we begin to form a counter-history must be an act of self-scrutiny. In being taught history by non-Christians, as most of us probably were, we have been taught history which is hostile to Christ. It is no reply to say that Christ was not even mentioned when we studied the Tudors or World War I at school, since that is precisely the point. To omit to mention the Lord whose kingdom is unfolding is to deny him. We need each to look to ourselves to see what kind of history we have absorbed, and to bring it into submission to Christ. Then we can go on re-forming our historical understanding.

This is a considerable task. I do not mean to burden you; that is my last intention. We can waste a lot of time wishing we knew more about this or that and feeling bad that we do not. Instead of measuring our-selves against some mythical standard of full historical literacy, it would be better to advance by increments, making small, steady progress. This might mean a limited reading programme. It might mean studying an overview of church history or the history of the world written from a Christian perspective. For parents and others who minister to children and young people it will involve teaching them to understand the history of the world as God describes it in his word. For preachers it may involve using historical examples in preaching so that congregations become alert to history. Even if you have never read a volume of Christian history before, you are already on the road by making it this far in this book.

Hopeful history

Our spirit as we seek to understand history through the gospel should be one of supreme optimism and confidence. The very idea of history is metaphysically coherent in Christ alone. The effort to produce non-Christian history is like the priests of Baal striving to get an answer from their god at Mount Carmel. They can arrange the meat. They can dance and dance and dance. They can even cut themselves and bleed. But Baal sleeps. In terms of coherence, the fire will not kindle for non-Christian history. We know from Scripture that the creation is sustained by Christ: 'He is before all things, and in him all things hold together' (*Col.* 1:17). Paul is clear: things cohere in Christ. They are connected in him. Apart from Christ the universe would unravel and spin out into billions of unconnected parts, becoming an abyss of confusion; in fact it would not exist at all. If all things can only hold together in Christ, then our thoughts can only hold together in him. If everything coheres in him, then so too must our reasoning, our intellectual activity. The fact that all things cohere in and only in Christ has all-embracing consequences for every intellectual discipline. Put starkly, no non-Christian can think consistently and coherently. Apart from the Christ in whom all things cohere, our very thoughts dissolve. The Christian historian should be supremely optimistic and confident because it is only the gospel that provides a foundation for all knowledge. The Lord Jesus Christ will win, because outside of him, there is, finally, nothing.

The self-contradictory success of non-Christian history

Now perhaps you think I have gone a bit over the top. In particular, you may be thinking that what I have just said does not ring true, because non-Christians manifestly *can* think coherently. Indeed, when it comes to history books, they often write the best and most successful ones. This is true. There is an ocean of non-Christian historical work that is rewarding to study and is in many respects better than the rare volumes of serious history written today by Christians. The point of Van Til's analysis is not to disprove the immediate fact or quality of non-Christian thought, it is to question its consistency and ultimate viability. The upper parts of the edifice may appear secure and well-furnished, but there are deep cracks in the foundations. Non-Christian thought is successful *despite* itself. It can cohere only because of the coherence of all things in Christ, yet it denies that same Christ. By denying the very one in whom it coheres it is ultimately self-destructive. It rejects the one and only foundation on which it might stand. Van Til puts it like this, describing the non-Christian's attempt to teach:

> The fact that he can and does teach is intelligible only because that which he assumes not to be true is actually true. He teaches, therefore, but he teaches by accident. He is able to teach because his own principle is not true and because the principle of Christianity is true.[6]

The more a non-Christian teacher teaches and the better the history he writes, the more acute the tension between the fact of his work and its internal impossibility. The more beautiful the building is, the more alarming its lack of foundation. If a shed is falling we may not worry; when Venice is sinking, we do. Brilliant non-Christian historical work desperately needs a firm foundation in Christ.

It is important to note that emphasis on the antithesis of belief and unbelief, and on the triumph of Christian thought, does not mandate a pietistic withdrawal from engagement with non-Christian history-telling. Scripture teaches the antithesis of Christ and Satan, but it also teaches common grace. By God's grace, non-Christian thought is temporarily protected from its incoherence. The non-Christian, in self-contradiction, does believe things that are true and can do things very well, in some

---

[6] *Essays*, p. 89.

limited senses better than the Christian. The restraining hand of God's grace explains why non-Christians, whose belief system is ultimately incoherent and without metaphysical foundation, can write such brilliant books. The Christian can rightly use the fruits of common grace as they are found in the world. Indeed, he takes what is good from non-Christian writing and relocates it within the metaphysically coherent and grounded Christian faith. The Egyptians press on the Hebrews their treasure as they leave Egypt (*Exod.* 12:35, 36), and the kings of the earth finally bring in their glory to the New Jerusalem (*Rev.* 21:24). Van Til has a memorable picture of what happens to the positive fruits of non-Christian culture:

> Though men do not recognize the truth about the world they can, in spite of themselves, produce much culture. They cannot help but do so. They are like the rebellious sailor who tries to burn up the ship because he hated the captain. This sailor, instead of being thrown into the brig, is made to employ his gifts, whatever they may be, so that the ship may go forward to the harbour. When the ship arrives at its destination all the fruits of this sailor's labor will be preserved, but they will be given to others and he himself will be lost. What he has accomplished constructively will enter into the new heavens and the new earth for their adornment.[7]

The humble possession of God's view of history

Many deny that we can have a God's-eye view of the world. The claim is thought to be arrogant and to tend necessarily toward abuse. It is right that we must guard against simply baptizing our own view and claiming that it is God's. We need to be highly suspicious of ourselves. But God has spoken. If we know the mind of God rightly, our knowledge will not lead to arrogance or abuse, but to gentleness. Moreover, given that God has revealed his view of history, it is no humility to refuse to hear that revelation. If he has revealed his mind then it is humble to bow before it, not to pretend that we cannot know it. It is in rejecting it that we exalt ourselves. God calls us to have his view, and not our own, to possess humbly and gently his reading of history, for it is this view that he has revealed to us. May we all in our different ways be humble historians, telling the story of our world to the glory of God. Happy history!

---

[7] *Essays*, p. 16.

BIBLIOGRAPHY

Aquinas, Thomas, *Summa Theologica*, trans. by Fathers of the English Dominican Province, 5 vols (Westminster, MD: Christian Classics, 1948; repr. 1981).

Augustine, *Augustine: Anti-Pelagian Writings*, ed. by Benjamin B. Warfield, trans. by Peter Holmes and Robert Ernest Wallis, Nicene and Post-Nicene Fathers: First Series, 5 (New York: Christian Literature Publishing Company, 1887; repr. Peabody, MA: Hendrickson, 1994).

Augustine, Saint, *Confessions*, trans. by Henry Chadwick (Oxford: Oxford University Press, 1992).

Augustine, St, *The City of God*, ed. by John O'Meara, trans. by Henry Bettenson (London: Penguin Books, 1984).

Beckett, Samuel, *Waiting for Godot: A Tragicomedy in Two Acts*, 2nd edn (London: Faber and Faber, 1965; repr. 1986).

———, *Three Novels: Molloy, Malone Dies, The Unnamable* (New York: Grove Press, n.d.).

Being Faithful: The Shape of Historic Anglicanism Today, ed. by Nicholas Okoh, Vinay Samuel and Chris Sugden (London: The Latimer Trust, 2009).

Beza, Théodore, *The Life of Calvin*, ed. and trans. by Henry Beveridge, in *Selected Works of John Calvin: Tracts and Letters*, ed. Henry Beveridge and Jules Bonnet, 7 vols (Edinburgh: Calvin Translation Society, 1851; repr. Grand Rapids, MI: Baker Book House, 1983), I.

Bock, Darrell L., *Luke*, 2 vols (Grand Rapids, MI: Baker Books, 1994; repr. 2002).

Boethius, *The Consolation of Philosophy*, trans. by S. J. Tester, in *Boethius*, The Loeb Classical Library, 74 (Cambridge, MA: Harvard University Press; London: William Heinemann, 1973; repr. 1978).

Boettner, Loraine, *The Reformed Doctrine of Predestination* (Phillipsburg, New Jersey: Presbyterian and Reformed, 1932).

Bonhoeffer, Dietrich, *Letters and Papers from Prison*, ed. and trans. by Reginald Fuller (London and Glasgow: Fontana Books, 1959; repr. 1963).

Bouwsma, William J., *John Calvin: A Sixteenth Century Portrait* (Oxford: Oxford University Press, 1988; repr. 1989).

Boyd, Gregory A., *God of the Possible: A Biblical Introduction to the Open View of God* (Grand Rapids, MI: Baker Books, 2000).

The Works of Anne Bradstreet (Cambridge, MA: The Belknap Press of Harvard University Press, 1967; repr. 1981).

Calvin, John, *Canons and Decrees of the Council of Trent, with the Antidote*, in *John Calvin: Tracts and Letters*, ed. and trans. Henry Beveridge, 7 vols (Edinburgh: Calvin Translation Society, 1851; repr. Edinburgh: Banner of Truth, 2009), III.

———, *The Necessity of Reforming the Church*, in *John Calvin: Tracts and Letters*, ed. and trans. Henry Beveridge and Jules Bonnet, 7 vols (Edinburgh: Calvin Translation Society, 1851; repr. Edinburgh: Banner of Truth, 2009), I.

———, *Reply by Calvin to Cardinal Sadolet's Letter*, in *John Calvin: Tracts and Letters*, ed. and trans. Henry Beveridge and Jules Bonnet, 7 vols (Edinburgh: Calvin Translation Society, 1851; repr. Edinburgh: Banner of Truth, 2009), I.

———, *Institutes of the Christian Religion*, ed. by John T. McNeill, trans. by Ford Lewis Battles, 2 vols, The Library of Christian Classics, 20-21 (Philadelphia: The Westminster Press, 1960).

———, *John Calvin: Tracts and Letters*, ed. by Henry Beveridge and Jules Bonnet (Edinburgh: Banner of Truth, 2009).

———, *Commentary on the Book of Psalms*, trans. by James Anderson, in *Calvin's Commentaries*, 22 vols (Grand Rapids, MI: Baker Book House, 1993), IV.

———, *Commentaries on the Epistle of Paul the Apostle to the Romans*, ed. and trans. by John Owen, in *Calvin's Commentaries*, 22 vols (Edinburgh: Calvin Translation Society, n.d.; repr. Grand Rapids, MI: Baker Book House, 1993), XIX.

Canons and Decrees of the Council of Trent, trans. by H. J. Schroeder (Rockford, IL: Tan Books and Publishers, 1978).

Chamberlain, Ava, 'Self-Deception as a Theological Problem in

Jonathan Edwards's "Treatise Concerning Religious Affections"', *Church History*, 63 (1994), 541-556.

Coad, Roy, *Laing: The Biography of Sir John W. Laing, C.B.E (1879-1978)* (London: Hodder & Stoughton, 1979).

Cottret, Bernard, *Calvin: A Biography*, trans. by M. Wallace McDonald (Grand Rapids, MI: William B. Eerdmans; Edinburgh: T&T Clark, 2000).

Cross, Claire, *Church and People: England 1450-1660*, 2nd edn (Oxford: Blackwell, 1999).

Cyril of Alexandria, *On the Unity of Christ*, ed. and trans. by John Anthony McGuckin (Crestwood, NY: St Vladimir's Seminary Press, 1995).

Daniell, David, *William Tyndale: A Biography* (New Haven: Yale University Press, 1994).

Documents of the English Reformation, ed. by Gerald Bray (Cambridge: James Clarke, 1994).

Duffy, Eamon, *The Stripping of the Altars: Traditional Religion in England 1400-1580* (New Haven: Yale University Press, 1992).

Edwards, Jonathan, *Religious Affections*, ed. by John E. Smith, in *The Works of Jonathan Edwards* (New Haven: Yale University Press, 1959), II.

———, *Original Sin*, ed. by Clyde A. Holbrook, in *The Works of Jonathan Edwards* (New Haven: Yale University Press, 1970; repr. 1997), III.

———, *A History of the Work of Redemption*, ed. by John F. Wilson, in *The Works of Jonathan Edwards* (New Haven: Yale University Press, 1989), IX.

———, *Letters and Personal Writings*, ed. by George S. Claghorn, in *The Works of Jonathan Edwards* (New Haven: Yale University Press, 1998), XVI.

———, *The "Miscellanies": 833-1152*, ed. by Amy Plantinga Pauw, in *The Works of Jonathan Edwards* (New Haven and London: Yale University Press, 2002), XX.

———, *Works of Jonathan Edwards* 2 vols, ed. Edward Hickman (1834; repr. Edinburgh: Banner of Truth, 2009).

Eusebius of Caesarea, *The Proof of the Gospel*, ed. and trans. by W. J. Ferrar, 2 vols (London: SPCK; New York: Macmillan, 1920).

Ferry, Patrick, 'Martin Luther on Preaching', *Concordia Theological Quarterly*, 54.4 (1990), 265-280.

The Future of the European Past, ed. by Hilton Kramer and Roger Kimball (Chicago: Ivan R. Dee, 1997).

Gavrilyuk, Paul L., *The Suffering of the Impassible God: The Dialectics of Patristic Thought* (Oxford: Oxford University Press, 2006).

Gordon, Bruce, *Calvin* (New Haven: Yale University Press, 2009).

Helm, Paul, 'Edwards on True Religion', *Helm's Deep* <http://paul-helmsdeep.blogspot.com/2011/04/edwards-on-true-religion.html#links > [accessed 29 June 2011].

Holbrook, Clyde A., 'Jonathan Edwards and His Detractors', *Theology Today*, 10 (1953), 384-396.

Luther, Martin, *First Lectures on the Psalms*, ed. by Hilton C. Oswald, in *Luther's Works*, ed. J. Pelikan and H. T. Lehmann, 55 vols (Saint Louis, MO: Concordia Publishing House, 1974), X.

——, *Conversations with Luther: Selections from the Recently Published Sources of the Table Talk*, ed. and trans. by Preserved Smith and Herbert Percival Gallinger (New Canaan, CT: Keats Publishing, 1979).

Lyotard, Jean-François, *The Postmodern Condition: A Report on Knowledge*, trans. by Geoff Bennington and Brian Massumi (Manchester: Manchester University Press, 1984; repr. 2004).

Marsden, George M., *Jonathan Edwards: A Life* (New Haven: Yale University Press, 2003).

Martin, Hugh, *The Atonement: In Its Relations to the Covenant, the Priesthood, the Intercession of Our Lord* (Greenville, SC: Reformed Academic Press, n.d.).

McGrath, Alister, *Iustitia Dei: A History of the Christian Doctrine of Justification*, 3rd edn (Cambridge: Cambridge University Press, 2005).

McGuckin, John A., *St. Cyril of Alexandria and the Christological Controversy: Its History, Theology, and Texts* (Crestwood, NY: St Vladimir's Seminary Press, 2004).

Meuser, Fred W., *Luther the Preacher* (Minneapolis: Augsburg Publishing House, 1983).

Miller, Perry, *Jonathan Edwards* (New York: Meridian Books, 1959).

Murray, Iain H., *Jonathan Edwards: A New Biography* (Edinburgh: Banner of Truth, 1987; repr. 1988).

Nestorius, *The Bazaar of Heracleides*, ed. and trans. by G. R. Driver and Leonard Hodgson (Oxford: Clarendon Press, 1925).

Noll, Mark A., *Turning Points: Decisive Moments in the History of Christianity* (Grand Rapids, MI: Baker Academic, 2000).

O'Donnell, James J., *Augustine: A New Biography* (New York: HarperCollins, 2006).

Owen, John, *The Nature, Power, Deceit, and Prevalency of the Remainders of Indwelling Sin in Believers*, in *The Works of John Owen*, ed. William H. Goold, 16 vols (Edinburgh: Banner of Truth, 1965; repr. 1995), VI.

———, ΦΡΟΝΗΜΑ ΤΟΥ ΠΝΕΥΜΑΤΟΣ: *Or, the Grace and Duty of Being Spiritually Minded*, in *The Works of John Owen*, ed. William H. Goold, 16 vols (Edinburgh: Banner of Truth, 1965; repr. 1994), VII.

———, *The Death of Death in the Death of Christ*, in *The Works of John Owen*, ed. William H. Goold, 16 vols (Edinburgh: Banner of Truth, 1965-68; repr. 1993), X.

———, *A Discourse Concerning the Holy Spirit*, in *The Works of John Owen*, ed. William H. Goold, 16 vols (Edinburgh: Banner of Truth, 1965-68; repr. 1995), III-IV.

———, *A Dissertation on Divine Justice*, in *The Works of John Owen*, ed. William H. Goold, 16 vols (Edinburgh: Banner of Truth, 1965-68; repr. 1993), X.

———, *Of the Death of Christ, and of Justification*, in *The Works of John Owen*, ed. William H. Goold, 16 vols (Edinburgh: Banner of Truth, 1965-68; repr. 1991), XII.

———, ΧΡΙΣΤΟΛΟΓΙΑ: *Or, A Declaration of the Glorious Mystery of the Person of Christ - God and Man*, in *The Works of John Owen*, ed. William H. Goold, 16 vols (Edinburgh: Banner of Truth, 1965-68; repr. 1993), I.

Pascal, Blaise, *Pensées*, in *Pascal*, trans. by W. F. Trotter, Great Books of the Western World, XXXIII (Chicago: Encyclopaedia Britannica, 1952).

Piper, John, *The Legacy of Sovereign Joy: God's Triumphant Grace in the Lives of Augustine, Luther, and Calvin* (Wheaton, IL: Crossway Books, 2000).

Reformed Confessions of the 16th Century, ed. by Arthur C. Cochrane (London: SCM Press, 1966).

Ridley, Nicholas, *The Works of Nicholas Ridley*, ed. by Henry Christmas (Cambridge: Cambridge University Press, 1843).

Ryle, J. C., *Five English Reformers* (London: The Banner of Truth Trust, 1961).

Sadoleto, Jacopo, *Sadolet's Letter to the Senate and People of Geneva*, ed. and trans. by Henry Beveridge and Jules Bonnet, in *John Calvin: Tracts and Letters*, 7 vols (Edinburgh: Calvin Translation Society, 1851; repr. Edinburgh: Banner of Truth, 2009), I.

Scrivener, Emma, *A New Name: Grace and Healing for Anorexia* (Nottingham: Inter-Varsity Press, 2012).

The Seven Ecumenical Councils, ed. by Henry R. Percival, Nicene and Post-Nicene Fathers: Second Series, 14 (New York: Charles Scribner's Sons, 1900; repr. Peabody, MA: Hendrickson, 1994).

Sisman, Adam, *Hugh Trevor-Roper: The Biography* (London: Weidenfeld & Nicolson, 2010).

Sleeman, Matthew, '"Under Heaven": The Formative Place of Heaven Within the Salvation-Geography of Acts', paper presented to the Society of Biblical Literature Conference, Philadelphia, PA, 2005.

Soskice, Janet Martin, *Metaphor and Religious Language* (Oxford: Clarendon Press, 1985).

Thomson, Andrew, *Life of Dr Owen*, in *The Works of John Owen*, ed. William H. Goold, 16 vols (Edinburgh: Banner of Truth, 1965; repr. 1993), I.

Turretin, Francis, *Institutes of Elenctic Theology*, ed. by James T. Dennison, trans. by George Musgrave Giger, 3 vols (Phillipsburg, NJ: P&R Publishing, 1992-97).

Twain, Mark, *Mark Twain's Letters*, ed. by Albert Bigelow Paine, 2 vols (New York: Harper & Brothers, 1917).

Tyndale, William, *The Works of William Tyndale*, ed. by Henry Walter, 2 vols (Cambridge: Cambridge University Press, 1848; repr. Edinburgh: Banner of Truth, 2010).

Van Til, Cornelius, *Essays on Christian Education* (Phillipsburg, New Jersey: Presbyterian and Reformed, 1979).

Walton, Brad, *Jonathan Edwards, 'Religious Affections' and the Puritan Analysis of True Piety, Spiritual Sensation and Heart Religion*, Studies in American Religion, 74 (Lewiston, NY: Edwin Mellen, 2002).

Warfield, Benjamin Breckinridge, *Studies in Tertullian and Augustine*, in *The Works of Benjamin B. Warfield*, ed. Ethelbert D. Warfield, William Park Strong and Caspar Wistar Hodge, 10 vols (Oxford: Oxford University Press, 1930; repr. Grand Rapids, MI: Baker Book House, 1991), IV.

Weinandy, Thomas G., *Does God Change? The Word's Becoming in the Incarnation*, Studies in Historical Theology, 4 (Still River, MA: St. Bede's Publications, 1985).

Werrell, Ralph S., *The Theology of William Tyndale* (Cambridge: James Clarke, 2006).

Westminster Confession of Faith (Edinburgh: Banner of Truth, 2012).

William Tyndale's New Testament (Ware: Wordsworth Editions, 2002).

Williams, Rowan, *Lost Icons* (Edinburgh: T&T Clark, 2000).

Wright, N. T., 'New Perspectives on Paul', in *Justification in Perspective: Historical Developments and Contemporary Challenges*, ed. by Bruce L. McCormack (Grand Rapids, MI: Baker Academic; Edinburgh: Rutherford House, 2006), pp. 243-64.

Zwingli, Ulrich, *An Exposition of the Faith*, in *Zwingli and Bullinger*, ed. and trans. by G. W. Bromiley (Philadelphia: Westminster Press, 1953).

OTHER BANNER OF TRUTH PUBLICATIONS

Puritan Books

'Ministers never write or preach so well as when under the cross: the Spirit of Christ and of glory then rests upon them. It was this, no doubt, that made the Puritans such burning and shining lights. Though dead, by their writings they yet speak; a peculiar unction attends them to this very hour; and for these thirty years past I have remarked that the more true and vital religion has revived, the more the good old Puritanical writings have been called for.' GEORGE WHITEFIELD.

'Doctrine with them meant something, and we pray "God give the church in this respect a new race of Puritans."' ARCHIBALD G. BROWN.

★ ★ ★ ★ ★

Since the 17th century the effect of Puritan books has been felt at every period of evangelical recovery and missionary advance. At times forgotten, they have been repeatedly recovered, to speak with fresh power and to challenge superficial and lukewarm Christianity.

JOHN OWEN, the 16 volumes of his *Works* can be bought individually or as a set. For many preachers they have become the companions of a lifetime.

Owen on Hebrews is the only major Owen title not included in the above *Works*. It constitutes 7 volumes of outstanding exposition, illuminating not only the Epistle to the Hebrews but the whole Bible.

Works of JOHN FLAVEL, 6 vols. Flavel remains permanently among the Puritan authors who lead in instruction and readability. Two centuries after his death, one of his books was the means of the conversion of Archibald Alexander, first professor of Princeton Theological Seminary.

Works of RICHARD SIBBES, 7 vols. Once read, Sibbes is unforgettable. He was a favourite of Martyn Lloyd-Jones. Archibald G. Brown told his hearers, 'It is old Master Sibbes, one of the sweetest of the Puritans, who well observes that the desires of the heart are the best proofs of saintship.'

THOMAS WATSON is the author who has often been the means of leading later generations to renewed interest in the Puritans. Spurgeon reprinted Watson's *Body of Divinity* in his own day, and Billy Graham used Watson on *The Ten Commandments* when preaching in London in 1955. Banner publishes most of Watson's works and they are popular with all age groups.

Works of THOMAS BROOKS, 6 vols. For value he is not behind Flavel, Sibbes and Watson. For any who suppose Puritans are dull reading there is no better antidote than the engaging pages of Brooks.

Works of STEPHEN CHARNOCK, 5 vols, including his great work on 'The Attributes of God'. It is Charnock's doctrinal depth that has been his main appeal to gospel ministers, including in recent times, John MacArthur. Not light reading, he always rewards serious students.

A number of other Puritans are published by the Trust including, THOMAS MANTON, JOHN BUNYAN, GEORGE SWINNOCK, and DAVID CLARKSON. For those only making a start on this reading we recommend the Puritan Paperback series, which includes some of the best of the main authors.

★ ★ ★ ★ ★

Books Relating to Revival

There have been many distinct periods of revival in the English-speaking world, and there are publications covering several of these periods.

J. H. MERLE D'AUBIGNÉ, *Reformation in England*. It is often forgotten that at the heart of the Reformation was an amazing spiritual revival. It was so understood by d'Aubigné and no one has written better on it in that light. This is history written with the 'excitement' that such events ought to inspire. Few volumes are more abidingly relevant.

J. C. Ryle, *Christian Leaders of the Eighteenth Century*. This is a key book for awakening interest in what happens in true revival. It is handled masterfully in a series of biographical sketches of leading men, Whitefield, Wesley, and others.

Joseph Tracy on the *Great Awakening* is second to none in its definitive treatment of the 'Revival of Religion in New England in 1740', one of the most important and remarkable eras in the history of the Christian church in modern times.

Arnold Dallimore, *George Whitefield, the Life and Times of the Great Evangelist of the 18th-Century Revival*. This is a 2-volume, in-depth account of the leader in times of awakening on both sides of the Atlantic. 'Justice has at last been done to the greatest preacher that England has ever produced' (D. Martyn Lloyd-Jones.)

W. M. Baker, *Making Many Glad: the Life of Daniel Baker*. Baker was an evangelist of the mid-19th century, who saw both powerful revivals and steady patient ministry. An easily read introduction to the work of God in parts of the United States.

Edward Morgan, *Life of John Elias*. This is one of the best of Banner's biographies of preachers, dealing with the revival period in North Wales in the 19th century, and including Elias's important letters and observations. He was one of the first to recognise the danger of 'revivalism', *i.e.,* excitement worked up and dangerously misleading for individuals.

Jonathan Edwards, *Thoughts on the Revival in New England*. Edwards is in the front rank as a discriminating author on revival. Himself a leader in the work of the Holy Spirit in the early 1740s, he found that work threatened from two sides, from those led away by emotionalism and critics who stood aloof and questioned whether there was any proven work of God taking place. His examination of what happened, and his defence of what was biblical, remains a standard text book for the whole subject. This work is also to be found in the expansive 2-volume *Works of Jonathan Edwards*.

W. B. SPRAGUE, *Lectures on Revivals*. The insight of a preacher and teacher who lived during the Second Great Awakening. 'The outstanding classic on this vital and urgently important matter' (D. Martyn Lloyd-Jones). 'A most valuable book. I love the good sense of Dr Sprague' (Charles Simeon).

JOHN WEIR, *The Ulster Awakening* is a book that was written in 1860 to defend the Ulster Awakening against the attacks of a sceptical press. Its author, an Irish Presbyterian minister, skilfully weaves correspondence from the leading figures of the revival into a truly fascinating, eye-witness account of the soul-stirring events of 1859, when the Spirit of God was poured out in great abundance upon the churches and people of Ulster, one of Ireland's four ancient provinces.

IAIN H. MURRAY, *Pentecost Today? The Biblical Basis for Understanding Revival*. 'If you only ever read one book on revival—and all serious Christians should read at least one—read this one. Drawing on a wealth of pastoral wisdom, an almost unrivalled grasp of the history of God's people in these islands and a thorough working knowledge of the Puritans, Iain Murray is well placed to give a definitive statement of the biblical basis for revival. The fanatic and the sceptic and all shades between will be challenged and helped by the clear presentation found here.' GRACE MAGAZINE

IAIN H. MURRAY, *Revival And Revivalism*. Marrying careful historical research to popular and relevant presentation, this book traces the spiritually epoch-making events of the eighteenth and nineteenth centuries through the eyes of those who lived at their centre. Fundamental to the book's thesis is a rejection of the frequent identification of 'revival' with 'revivalism'. The author demonstrates that a common understanding of the New Testament idea of revival was prevalent in most denominations throughout the period 1750-1858. Revivalism, on the other hand, is different both in its origin and in its tendencies. Its ethos is man-centred and its methods too close to the manipulative to require a supernatural explanation. Iain Murray argues that an inability to recognize this distinction has led many to ignore the new and different teaching on evangelism and revival which began to be popularized in the 1820s. While the case against that teaching was argued almost universally by the leaders of the Second Great Awakening their testimony was submerged beneath propaganda which promised a 'new era' if only the churches would abandon the older ways. Today, when that propaganda is largely discredited, there is a great need to rediscover the earlier understanding of revival possessed by those who most intimately experienced it. *Revival and Revivalism* will do much to aid this rediscovery. Powerfully presented, it contains a message of major importance for contemporary Christians.

★ ★ ★ ★ ★

Iain H. Murray, *The Life of Martyn Lloyd-Jones (1899–1981)*, paperback, 496pp. This book is a re-cast, condensed and, in parts, re-written version of the author's two volumes *D. Martyn Lloyd-Jones: The First Forty Years* (1982) and *The Fight of Faith* (1990). Since those dates, the life of Dr Lloyd-Jones has been the subject of comment and assessment in many publications and these have been taken into account. The main purpose of this further biography, however, is to put Dr Lloyd-Jones' life before another generation in more accessible form. The big story is all here.

When Lloyd-Jones left medicine, he intended only to be an evangelist in a mission hall in South Wales. No one was more surprised than he in being called to a ministry which would eventually affect churches across the world. How this happened is here explained, but the theme is the person described by F. F. Bruce: 'a thoroughly humble man. He was a man of prayer, a powerful evangelist, an expository preacher of rare quality, in the fullest sense a servant of the Word of God.'

Behind that theme a greater one emerges. In Martyn Lloyd-Jones's own words: 'My whole life experiences are proof of the sovereignty of God and his direct interference in the lives of men. I cannot help believing what I believe. I would be a madman to believe anything else—the guiding hand of God! It is an astonishment to me.'

'*The most powerful and persuasive voice in Britain*'—John R. W. Stott

'*The greatest man I have ever known*'—J. I. Packer

'*No preacher had greater influence on me*'—John MacArthur

The Banner of Truth Trust originated in 1957 in London. The founders believed that much of the best literature of historic Christianity had been allowed to fall into oblivion and that, under God, its recovery could well lead not only to a strengthening of the church today but to true revival.

Inter-denominational in vision, this publishing work is now international, and our lists include a number of contemporary authors along with classics from the past. The translation of these books into many languages is encouraged.

A monthly magazine, *The Banner of Truth,* is also published and further information about this and all our other publications can be found on our website, or by contacting either of the offices below.

THE BANNER OF TRUTH TRUST

3 Murrayfield Road, PO Box 621, Carlisle,
Edinburgh, EH12 6EL Pennsylvania 17013,
UK USA

www.banneroftruth.co.uk